THE STORYTELLER: BOOK ONE

KEZ WICKHAM ST GEORGE

 Published by MMH Press, 2023
Copyright © 2023 Kez Wickham St George

All rights reserved. No part of this book may be used or reproduced by any means, graphic, electronic, or mechanical, including photocopying, recording, taping or by any information storage retrieval system without the written permission of the copyright owner except in the case of brief quotations embodied in critical articles and reviews.

This is a work of fiction. Names, characters, businesses, places, events and incidents are either the products of the author/s' imagination or used in a fictitious manner. Any resemblance to actual persons, living or dead, or actual events is purely coincidental.

Because of the dynamic nature of the Internet, any web addresses or links contained in this book may have changed since publication and may no longer be valid. The views expressed in this work are solely those of the authors and do not necessarily reflect the views of the publisher and the publisher hereby disclaims any responsibility for them.

Cover Design: Dylan Ingram
Interior Design: Chelsea Wilcox

National Library of Australia
Cataloguing-in-Publication data:
Jigsaw/Kez Wickham St George

ISBN: 978-0-6451483-2-9 (paperback)

DEDICATION

To those who believe in me as a storyteller, my family friends.
To those who said, 'Yes YOU Can' – thank you.
To the team at MMH Press – thank you.
To all the storytellers no matter the genre, age, religion or ethnicity, I embrace you all.
You are the ones who will inspire others to be adventurous, to tell their stories to discover the magic of the imagination; to carry on with the fables stories of our ancestors that connect us all as one. To my own ancestors – I am part of you as you are of me. Sadly, I only know a small part of your story, so I leave behind a little of mine, in the hope that my family will one day read it.
To my husband, Lou – your faith in me as a storyteller has never wavered.
Thank you.

Kez

MY MISSION

To promote the ripple effect as an amazing tool to help our young people realise their potential as powerful leaders in their own right. How do we do this? By becoming honest, kind leaders ourselves. My belief is that holding out a hand to guide, teach, support, to being a caring, considerate, authentic guide in another's life, has more kudos than any medal or award. Most of all, it is an honour that another entrusts us to mentor, share wisdom, to guide others in this world to assist them to share their stories through storytelling

Thank you.

Kez

FOREWORD

Two creative women sit opposite one another excited to share their next venture. I am one of those women, Kez Wickham St George is the other. Coffee and conversations between us happen every few months and we always end up discussing new projects. Inspiring one another is easy as we share the same enthusiasm and passion for storytelling. And Kez is a master at this craft. My story encompasses the roles of screen writer, playwright, award-winning poet, visual artist and film producer. That is how coffee dates between Kez and myself became more frequent. I never imagined working on a professional level with an international bestselling author. Opportunity. Instinct. Trust. I was honoured to be gifted these three things and in turn write and produce *The Cry of Morrow* short film. Kez Wickham St George is a passionate, nurturing author, mentor and friend. I have been fortunate to read her previous bestselling books and am sure readers of *Jigsaw* will agree, Kez has written another bestseller with this latest novel. As the chapters of the main character's life unfolds with each page, it is easy to see how a person's inner strength can carry them through adversity. Let the story of *Jigsaw,* inspire you to reach your full potential and find your place of connection. For myself, the coffee and new ideas are brewing as I look from the pen to the lens and wonder, is this the story is next for the big screen?

Sally Newman – Creative Director Lyrical Infusion:
Finalist: WA Made Film Festival 2021, 2022, 2023. Selected Film: UK Lift Off Festival 2023. State Finalist: Australian Slam Poetry 2021. Rotary Shine On Award Recipient 2017. Best Community Event Finalist WA Fringe World Festival 2019

PROLOGUE

'What! Me, your ghostwriter, why?'
'Because you will make my story shine,' was the reply. How could I refuse?

My Aunt's once authoritive clear writing, now a scribble of words, at times hard to read but nevertheless mesmerising. As I read page after page every night of my family history, often reading into the early hours of the morning, I found there was one major lesson in the papers entrusted to me *We are here to learn to be the best version of ourselves.* This book had haunted my Aunt Cassie for many years, now it was in my care. The smile on her face as I gave her the published version a year later was more than money can buy. Today, her book *Jigsaw* sits on my desk, the photograph of her on the sleeve of the book has captured her joy. I hope I have done her story the justice it deserves. If there was any quote suited to this book it would be, in the words of Maya Angelou: 'I've learned that people will forget what you said, people will forget what you did, but people will never forget how you made them feel.'

So first let me set the scene for you:

Three sharp raps on the back door was always accompanied by a

Jigsaw

familiar stench the same question muttered from toothless mouths, 'Got soup for an old Anzac?' Hot veggie soup with a chunk of dark homemade bread, plus a mug of murky brown tea that simmered endlessly on the kitchen stove, along with a basin of warm soapy water offered to wash the faces and hands of the constant stream of worn out old men with red rimmed eyes, haunted with sadness or terror from a war they did not understand. I would watch from behind my Dad's legs as he helped the old solders onto the stoop in the backyard, their palsied dirt-grimed hands holding out chipped tin mugs, while tears leaked down their faces, as they gratefully appreciated my folks' community spirit.

I was born in the 1940s. My folks were in their forties, in those days it was considered too old to have a baby. I had two older sisters: a foster sister Lois and a blood sister Cilleen. My Dad had turned forty-one when he was demobbed from the ANZAC medical team in the New Zealand army. He came home with severe liver damage and chronic jaundice, the man I grew up with was an alcoholic and suffered severe PTSD. I knew a different man that my two older sisters had known.

The Second World War may have ended, but the consequences of devastation and war-torn spirit did not. It was the great depression New Zealand was faced with, the harshest of financial climates. We were a poor family of Irish, English, Maori and Jewish heritage, if we wanted anything we made it or bartered for it, especially when we gathered with our extended family to share our meagre fortunes of food and clothing. It was imperative to learn to survive, thrive with what we had. But we were also blessed to share our empathy with our own stories. I know that's where I developed my strong beliefs of sharing. Money was scarce, Dad always allowing the returned solders, with no one nowhere to call home, to camp on our front lawn. He would administer his meagre medical knowledge, while Mum fed the unfortunate that the war had produced. It was a familiar sight to see, not only our front yard, our neighbours,

Kez Wickham St George

also offering refuge for the night in any space available. I was brought up in a time when life was a lot simpler than today. We shared willingly. We lived at a slower pace. It was a time when a chat and a cuppa took the place of loneliness.

Storytelling became food, a medicinal balm for lost hearts.

It was a time to dream of what was, what is and what might be.

'May you all have enough.'

CHAPTER 1

I was told my mother cried with disappointment when I was born, when 'it's a girl' was announced. Dad promptly got drunk with his brothers who commiserated with him. The story 'you were such a disappointment to our family' was told to me repeatedly. As I grew up, its effect on me was unpleasant, to say the least. I was a misfit, a jigsaw piece that didn't fit in; the black sheep. My presence in their lives was not welcomed. Mum looked after me, there's no doubt about that, but she preferred pretty, cute, like my two older sisters, which I was not. I was plain looking with a deep olive complexion, mousy brown hair, a round body with a lazy eye (as it was called then). I was also clumsy. To add to this picture, once I had lost my baby teeth, the two front teeth were what was known as buck teeth (protruding), they crossed over each other.

Mum's niche was dressmaking. It was known if you hired Mrs Wickham then you had employed the very best of Wellington's society dressmakers. She was always busy with appointments or requests for formal society events, especially weddings.

We lived in a housing commission home, but ironically we were called 'middle class'. In those days it was a compliment to those like us who sat teetering on the breadline week after week. Yet, in the eyes of our society, you had only made it socially if there was a son born into the family, if you owned a car, or had bought a house. When the government rented us a home, my father cried 'why buy?' My mum's dreams of being a proud home owner were dashed, as they had achieved none of those requirements to be considered upper-class, so in a small two-bedroom government-owned brick house with a quarter-acre plot, she ran a popular dressmaking business, raised not only three girls, but many foster children plus extended family.

Once I could dress and feed myself, Mum was over mothering me, eager to get on with her socialising lifestyle. If she was not dressmaking, she would be attending high teas with all sorts of socialites, mainly from the theatre or radio. Mum enjoyed entertaining some of her 'well to do' clients with an afternoon soiree. Being born into a ready-made family, with two older sisters, both in their teens. Lois, whom I adored, was the eldest and a foster child. Mum's charitable offer of bringing up another woman's child was retold in so many ways. Then there was my blood sister Cilleen, who was bipolar (as it is recognised now). I was terrified of Cilleen as I never knew when she was in one of her abusive moods.

It was Lois who alerted my folks to the fact that Cilleen was abusing me. I remember being terrified of this strange moody girl, who whispered death threats or cruelly pinched me. Fear would filter into every part of my little body, so I always did as she demanded.

I truly feared the days when Mum would usher me out of the house to 'go play with your sister,' while Lois, being the eldest, was Mum's helper. There was nowhere to hide. What does a three-year-old do when confronted with such hatred? I knew, even at such a young age, that this sort of behaviour was wrong. When Lois saw blood streaming down my legs she raced in to tell my folks. They were both shocked. No doctor

Jigsaw

was called as it would have brought shame to the family. Mum bathed me, treating the inner thigh abrasions herself. They spoke to Cilleen in private when she began to scream that I was a liar. I overheard Dad say, 'Enough, behave or I will have you removed from this house,' the beatings stopped, but the slapping or sly pinching, name-calling hatred towards me did not.

Both my sisters were referred to as 'beauties of the family,' but there was always a slight pause when Mum introduced me. 'This is our youngest,' she would say as I hid behind her dress. Mum was always busy being president or treasurer of several different societies. If I needed her attention, she would gently push me away saying, 'go play, dear.' With no one else to turn to for affection or attention, I became my Dad's shadow.

The Wickham garden was full of citrus trees, one plum tree, berry bushes, a large veggie patch including four beehives. In the corner of this busy productive backyard, was Dad's little tool shed where he would show me how to build all sorts of things. I helped him to make a little stool for my fourth birthday. When I was five years old, he taught me to prime the gas burner to make him his beloved cuppa, with three large teaspoons of sugar. Then I would reach into his hidey-hole behind the bench, find his stash of whisky adding a good slug of it into his tea.

I learnt how to sharpen knives and axes. At six, I was a dab hand, chopping kindling for the house fire. In this tiny shed, I knew what I could play with or what was off limits. Mum and Lois either ignored me or worked around me. Cilleen was the one to hide from, which I did, often, locking myself in the shed, hiding under the workbench. I would hear her trying to open the shed's door or the window, softly calling my name, 'Cassie, come and play.'

Saturday morning was when both sisters prepared for the Naenae street dance club. All day their heads would bristle with tight curlers when the hair was released, bouncing curls of blonde or brunette hair fell onto pale powdered shoulders. Make-up was applied liberally, eyelashes were coated in thick black mascara. I loved to watch them as they added perfume and jewellery to their wrists, throats and ears, twirling in front of the mirror showing off their dance dresses. As long as the two girls were together, I was safe. I was also the one who would answer the doorbell as their beaus arrived. By that time, Dad would be in the kitchen, where I would lead these young men to join him for a drink. 'I like to meet the boys taking my girls out,' he would say. I could not wait until I would be able to do the same.

Most Saturday nights at the Wickham house was party night, where I would take my aunty's coats placing them in the hall cupboard. I was the one who wound up the record player so the women could dance. The best time of all was before anyone arrived, Dad would waltz me around the room, too little for his big strides I would stand on his feet, with his strong arms around me, I felt safe, happy I was dancing with my Dad.

I was very proud of my responsibilities. Dad would give me a light shandy in a small glass, my dinner would be a piece of hot crayfish with salty fried chips, more often than not I would fall asleep on cushions I had pushed under the table, out of the way of the drunk, clomping feet.

Mum wore many hats, she would often be invited to host dinners for the well-off or well-known, her skills in 'celebration formality' were known city wide. However, if it fell on a Saturday night, Dad would visit with his family, my sisters out dancing, if Mum couldn't find a sitter, I would be deposited with the kitchen staff at the event. I thought she looked beautiful, a tall lady in a long black frock, a black beaded bolero jacket, curly auburn hair, her make up impeccable. She would meet, greet, then seat the guests. Once dinner was over, the wine was flowing, the entertainment had arrived, with all the guests mingling nicely, we would leave. At five years old I had no idea I was listening to or peeking at the royalty of New Zealand theatre, Cabaret or the Prime minister

Jigsaw

of New Zealand, Sir Walter Nash or his cabinet. Through these society dinners, Mum became close friends with the head mistress of the city's top boarding school, becoming deeply involved with their society high teas or garden teas, everything went like clockwork when Mrs Wickham hosted any soiree.

Also in the summer, the family would often meet at a place called the Taita River. A large bonfire was built, while eels plus pots of Koura (small fresh water crayfish) were caught and cooked for our dinner. Fresh damper bread was made, the smell of an open fire with delicious food cooking is still etched in my memory. My young cousins and I were allowed to splash in the shallows, while the older cousins would swim in the deeper water. To me this was heaven; family, food and fun.

Growing up, I loved Sunday's, as it was my Sunday School day. Mum woke me early to make sure I was there on time. She would give me two pennies; one penny went into the charity donations, while the other was saved for a bag of sweets on the way home. I always attended on my own, as my family were much too tired from the previous night of partying.

I loved Sunday School, the stories told to me about angels. The kind Nuns, especially sister Mary Kay, would pat my head every Sunday saying with a sigh, 'on your Todd again then?' I had no idea what she meant or who this Todd was, but I would nod and quickly find my seat. That was life, until one Sunday I was called into the senior Nun's office. Mother Theresa Mary asked me to explain the red welts on my body. I had been warned by Cilleen, 'not to tell anyone or I would cop it again,' so I said I had fallen over. My parent's received a visit from the two nuns and when they left with their black gowns billowing behind them in the fresh Wellington wind I overheard Sister Mary Kay muttering, 'this child of God deserves more.'

From that point on, my folks decided Catholicism was not for our family. I would now attend Mum's Church of England Sunday School.

She came with me, just the once, to introduce me, then it was up to me. I loved knowing that Jesus and the angels loved me, no matter what I looked like. Apparently, he even liked 'cross-eyed fatties,' a name they had called me at kindergarten. When Mum learned of this, she was shocked, removing me from the kindergarten, not telling me why, just saying 'we don't put up with such rudeness, and we don't associate with low lives.'

I enjoyed the stories at Sunday School, often receiving presents from the teachers; little cards with pictures of the disciples on them. I would run my fingers over the intricate borders of the artwork, wishing I was clever like that, the deep richness of the colours, hypnotic. Dawdling home, no one questioned my lateness, Mum would be sewing, my sisters busy with the weekly ironing. A plate of sandwiches waiting for me, so I would trot behind Dad, telling him about my morning as he planted his seedlings, mowed the lawn or collected honey from the hives. He never commented or asked how I was. My adult relations often looked at me with sadness, as my cousins refused to include me in their games. I was too clumsy, always falling over, with scratches, cuts and bruises. I was the one who ruined their games; I was never fast enough or smart enough, so I would find a corner, a book or pencil and paper, much simpler than asking to be included.

Then came the day when Dad asked me to help him build a swing in the old plum tree in the backyard. This swing was all mine, I was in seventh heaven. Here I could swing high, daydream that one day I would fly. However, to 'earn' the swing, I was to learn the Catechism of the Catholic Church. Not to be left out, Mum decided I was to be baptised in the Church of England. This proved very confusing, each parent disliking the other's church, I was so full of questions. 'Why?' came tumbling out at every opportunity. Even more confusing was the family relationship with my Maori Family. Their beliefs very different from any church, their faith was firmly planted in nature.

Jigsaw

My paternal relatives had married into a South Island tribe, my maternal relatives had married into The Tuhoi of the north island I watched with a child's curiosity as my Dad followed the Irish/Maori tradition of planting with the cycles of the moon. He would often be heard talking to his beloved garden. I soon learnt that when you are quiet, you hear many stories from your elders. I watched from my bedroom window as the senior men in our family would often gather around the fire pit, once a drink was in the hand they would begin to sing the old Irish and wartime Maori songs, their voices rich with melancholy. Army songs, by the score, would float around the backyard well into the night. I learnt later in my life this was a 'men's circle', a bond of understanding between them, much deeper than blood. It was a place of remembrance, where men could weep, sing, reminisce, talk of folks' passing, of famine, of the hardship and consequences of war.

When the female side of our family came over, Mum would put her dressmaking aside for the day. It was here amongst this women's circle I learnt how information can be linked to currency. Mum would read palms or tea leaves, raising their hopes of money, travel, love and luck once they crossed her palm with silver. Only once were tarot cards produced by an aunty, Mum insisted they be covered with a dark cloth, put away as far from the room as possible. I had no idea then that her experience with tarot had proved so successful, it had frightened her.

Mum was also known as the neighbourhood backyard herbalist, with many placing trust in her cures and tinctures made from plants. It ignited my curiosity as I saw plants differently, knowing they weren't just edible but that they had an energy that was able to heal. This tribe of women, sisters of all ethnicities, met regularly, my job was to babysit the young ones who came along with their Mums. I loathed it – until I discovered I was a dab hand at making up stories. I couldn't read that well, however my strengths were in oral storytelling, unbeknown to me I had unearthed

Kez Wickham St George

my DNA, ghost stories were my absolute favourite.

CHAPTER 2

There were many people watching over me as I grew up. Mum's best friend, Aunty Ruby, offered to adopt me, 'You don't care for her like you do her sisters!' she said to Mum one day. 'Look at her. She's a daydreaming raggy tomboy.' Mum told her to 'get out and never return.' Months later Aunty Marg, Mum's sister, offered to foster me. Apparently, the Nuns had reached out to her. When Mum informed Dad she was in tears, 'What are we doing wrong?' she cried. One Saturday, the full Maori contingent arrived with their cars parked up down the street. My Aunty Moana, the nominated spokesperson, offered to help my parents financially by taking me away to live with her. 'Just until you're back on your feet.' It was at that point in the conversation I was asked to leave the room.

I sat outside the kitchen window, their voices spilling out. 'We're concerned about her quietness,' 'What about her diet?' asked Aunty Pania, 'I s she getting enough good food?' 'What about the beatings? We are concerned about all the bruises on her little body.' Mum, of course, vehemently denied beating me. 'So, if it's not you, then who is it?' 'Oh 'it's just a bit of sisterly jealousy – it'll come right,' I heard Mum say. 'Well, if it doesn't I will take it one step further ,' answered my aunty. After the family meeting, Dad was more alert and on guard. His quiet voice would insist 'enough' when Cilleen's constant teasing turned into angry insults or physical abuse

The family had decided I needed something to 'love'. It was an instant love match when my Aunty Marge gave me a small bantam rooster to look after. I didn't play with dolls or girl's toys, but I loved playing in the garden. I would talk to the big fat worms I found, giving them a good home, adding them to the compost bin. I built tiny houses with sticks and leaves for the hedgehogs and their friends, so they had shelter on cold nights. Every morning I would feed the local birds in our backyard with toasted bread scraps, my face would crumple in sorrow if I saw an animal in distress. Mum, though, was terrified of birds, cats, rabbits, mice, insects or anything with four legs and fur, doing her very best to foster that feeling in me. To her they were dirty and dangerous, if I brought insects into the house she would have a fainting spell, or I would be reprimanded for disobedience.

I called my bantam, Chooken, and together, Dad and I built a pen for him, Mum ordered us to keep it far away from the house. Another aunty stole a baby lamb from a farmer for my Christmas gift, I was in heaven. I now had my swing, my Chooken, a lamb I named Beep which was bottle-fed, Dad showed me how to mix up the milk powder, Beep's tail wiggled with pleasure at feed time.

I also loved the neighbourhood horse, Blackie. When his owner was hospitalised, Dad with me in tow, would to go to the paddock to care for this beautiful animal. At Sunday School, I had been taught that Jesus loved all animals, therefore, so should we.

To me it was obvious, with Blackie's owner away, the horse needed looking after, so I unlatched the gate so Blackie could follow me home.

Jigsaw

At six years old, I thought it was the right thing to do. Mum almost passed out when she saw Blackie in the back yard. She became hysterical, slamming doors, windows, anything that was open was now shut tight, insisting the animals were diseased and dangerous. 'Get rid of the filthy beasts, or I'm leaving,' she informed Dad in no uncertain terms. That night, Blackie was returned to his small enclosure. Within the week, Dad found a local farmer who took my two pets away to live on the farm.

I had been in seventh heaven, on my swing with Chooken under my arm, Beep and Blackie close by, with the animals gone I had no friends, loneliness crept in. I found it hard to digest any food. It would sit like a huge lump in my stomach, or I would vomit it back up. One day, as Dad and I sat outside by the empty chook pen, he put his arm around me. I still remember that feeling as my body snuggled into his. It was rare for Dad to cuddle me. It must have been confronting to have an angry little girl tell him, in the only way she knew how, that she was unhappy. 'I don't like it here, and I don't like any of you,' I said, 'I want to live with Auntie Moana.' He was not one for pleasantries no Dear or Darling, it was 'Cassie, I'll do my best, if you do your best.'

True to his word, Dad asked around. A cousin needed his dog, Racey, to be looked after every Saturday morning while he was at Scouts. Dad's reasoning to Mum was that Racey would only be around for half a day on Saturday mornings, it was my job to walk and bathe him. I quickly fell deeply in love with Racey; a mixed breed with big brown eyes and a soft multi-coloured coat. Saturday mornings were now exciting. That is until one day, Mum found a group of the neighbourhood kids totally fascinated, as Racey discovered love, mounting the dog next door. His frantic quivering haunches mesmerising us all. I had no idea what was going on, I don't think any of us did. Mum came charging out of the front door grabbing the garden hose, aiming it at the two dogs, who by this time were focused on finishing the deed.

Kez Wickham St George

The blast of cold water caused mayhem to us and the dogs, to my absolute horror, they got stuck together. The female dog began to scream, Racey joining in, as the kids around me took off, with Mum yelling, 'Clear off you dirty little buggers.' I stood still, too scared to speak as I knew somehow I would get the blame for this. Yet, I was mesmerised by the scene acting out before me. Mum marched me inside the house, while Cilleen was asked to tie Racey behind Dad's shed. Cilleen was in her element of cruelty, Racey cried out as she beat him. I was washed down with cold sudsy water, Mum shuddering and muttering 'filthy animals.' I was told to go sit in my room. When my cousin arrived for his dog, he was told, 'She is too young for such responsibility. Do not bring *that animal* back here again.' The words were screeched into his face, as Mum knew no other way to get her point across without attaching a little drama.

This time Mum was adamant. There would be no more animals, no insects, not even a mention of wanting an animal. I dared to mention a budgie in a cage, surely that would not cause her to faint, but she gave me a look that would cut through glass. 'Did you not hear me, Miss?' She repeated the rules, slapping her hands together as she spoke. 'No more animals. No birds, or *anything* that requires a commitment to be cleaned or looked after.' I had no idea she had a phobia about insects, dirt and disease. I don't suppose anyone really knew what it was called back then.

CHAPTER 3

It wasn't long before Mum found a label for me. I was now 'difficult,' which meant I had learnt what buttons to press to annoy her. Mum often cooked animal offal, liver or brains with vegetables, stewed together until they were mash. I loathed what she cooked for us, making sure in little ways that she knew I did not enjoy her cooking. Whenever Dad cooked a Sunday family roast, I would eat every little scrap on my plate then ask for seconds, which would make Mum furious.

If I wanted to annoy Mum, I made sure she knew that Dad did everything better. My vocabulary changed with this small insight, I stopped using the words 'Mummy and Daddy' that a small child would say, choosing to mimic my sisters, it became 'Mum and Dad.' *I learnt a lot during this time.* I learnt if I wanted a pet to love, it had to belong to someone else. I learnt that my Folks would rarely listen to anything I had to say. To avoid conflict I began to read their body language, this family's love language was sarcastic and demeaning, laughter at another's misfortune was common amongst my sisters. I also learnt that Cilleen was dangerous. My sister's mental illness was not diagnosed or understood at the time, as she became a teenager it got worse. She knew just what to say about me to wind Mum up, I would often be severely reprimanded for something I didn't do. Cilleen was her beautiful daughter, her first born, woe betide anyone who tried to separate them. At six years I would run away, often finding hiding places Cilleen knew nothing about. Some places quite dangerous for a small child, but hiding anywhere was better than being beaten.

The offers from my aunties wanting to foster me became insistent and it was a constant worry to Mum. A welfare officer knocked on the door to enquire on the health and wellbeing of the youngest child in the Wickham household. Suddenly, I had braces fitted to my teeth, and I was taken to the optician at the hospital to look at my lazy eye. He called me 'malnourished,' so boiled Silverbeet or Comfrey was added to my plate daily, a tablespoon of cod liver oil before school was added to my health regime. Dancing was introduced three times a week; tap and ballet. Mum absolutely shone as a stage mother so every day after school it was straight home to practise my dance routine for the weekend. I absolutely loved the music, my little body feeling every musical note. Soon I was entertaining at old folk's homes and at festivals. I was entered into many country competition dancing, although if I didn't come away with a reward or prize, Mum would be unhappy with my performance. Life became busy. She was still dressmaking for weddings and balls, plus fitting in her much-loved social gatherings and soirees. Everyone seemed happy, all except for one person in the family, my paternal grandmother, Nellie.

Both of my grandfathers had passed over before I was born. My grandmothers, Nellie and Rose, were both known as Wellington's two top spiritualists, from what I was told, in fierce competition with each other. For some reason, Nellie my paternal grandmother did not like me, making it obvious by showing affection only to her other seven grandchildren. One memory was of a Christmas day our family were at her home for Christmas dinner. Nellie beckoned me over to her side. I excitedly obliged as all the other cousins had been given gifts now, it was my turn. She then asked Cilleen to also stand beside her. 'I can see why they call you an ugly duckling,' she said.

I looked around the room for someone to say something. Not one word was uttered. My grandmother's open dislike for me hurt me deeply. I began to cry big, embarrassed sobs. I remember thinking that Mum would be angry with me when she saw the tear marks on my shirt running outside. My folks were shocked at my rudeness. Mum slapped me on the legs, with each whack demanding I apologise, I simply refused to speak that woman again. I never saw her again, but I will never forget how her verbal cruelty made me feel. When Nellie passed over, I learnt that grief comes in all shapes and sizes. In our house some grieved, some did not. I really couldn't understand what all the fuss was about. Mum making sure that Dad had a splash of whiskey in his cups of tea, Cilleen cried, Lois did not care one way or the other. However, it was Dad's sobbing that concerned me. This was my tall, strong Dad. Not knowing what to do, I sat on my swing pondering how strange adults were, when I felt my Dad's hand my shoulder. "She's in heaven now, the angels have her," he whispered. I really didn't care who had *her*, I just wanted my Dad to be happy.

My maternal grandmother Nana Rose was different – we really liked each other. Rose had an opinion on everything, a loud one at that. Unfortunately, she was Mum's nemesis. Rose fascinated me but also scared me with her spirituality. She would often say, 'you have such a cheeky spirit with you today,' or 'you have angels treading before you.' It was my job to meet Nana Rose at the bus stop every Wednesday. She would stay for dinner, always greeting my two older sisters with the same comment as they came in from work. Looking directly at my Mum she would say, 'Girls, you're wearing far too much make-up for nice young ladies. Has no one taught you that make-up is sleazy?' Nana Rose would have a hot toddy with Dad, making comments on how Mum's cooking had never improved, once she had cleaned her plate of food. Dad and I would walk her back to the bus stop for her six o'clock bus, her weekly visit over until the following week. I never saw affection between mother and daughter or between her granddaughters, which were my two older sisters.

When Nana Rose became ill with pneumonia, Mum invited her to stay with us. It was a shock to us all, as these two did not even like being in the same room. Nana and I became buddies of sorts, an old army cot was pushed into the already packed room for me to sleep on. My two older sisters were asked to share the lounge for the time being, while Nana slept in my bed. She told me stories of my grandad, Jack Preston, they were both from Lancashire. New Zealand was never discussed, Nana simply refused to talk about her childhood. One memory I have of her, is her aged blue-veined hands covering mine as she taught me to play her piano. Then one night Nana Rose began to teach me how to read the tarot cards. I loved them. They looked much like the cards Sunday School gave away, only bigger. Nana said I had a gift for reading. When Mum walked in, all hell let loose, 'Never ever do that in my home again! I don't want my family involved in your hocus pocus. It's evil.' I was too young to have an opinion, the unfairness of my Mum's accusations stayed in my mind. I saw it as pretty pictures. Nana Rose saw it as a way of communication with her loved ones. Mum saw it as the devil's work. Too much confusion for one so young to figure out the ways of adults who don't like each other.

That was the first time I had ever heard Mum speak badly to her mother. The next day, Mum insisted she leave and Rose did as asked. She packed her small case, Dad ordered her a taxi to take her home. That same night, she committed suicide.

My thoughts were muddled. Was this what you did when no one loves you? Was there a purpose? She wasn't loved or wanted by her family - just like me. I was much too young to think of saying, 'Nana, you matter to me.' Mum did not grieve at all, well not that I saw. If she did, it was in private. To be honest, when Mum showed emotion it was headline news, everyone knew. That unsolved question stayed with me into my adult years; *if no one loves you, if no one cares, then what is the purpose to your life?* The following year there was discord between my folks. Mum actually became besotted with another male, Otto. He was always buying her gifts, when she ran away with him, she took me with her. I was privy to a passionate affair, which no child should be. They argued violently while I cringed on a cot bed in a side room. Mum seeing better sense, returned home to Dad. When they had made peace with each other they declared they were leaving their respective churches to join a popular cult. They announced over dinner one night, that they would no longer celebrate birthdays, Christmas or any Christian holidays.

My dancing was stopped, as it was now considered an instrument of depravity. Both older sisters were on a very tight rein; no public dancing, clothing to be up to the neck below the knees, restricted to a curfew of home by ten o'clock at night. Their boyfriend's had to be instructed on the ways of my folks' new beliefs, their make-up and clothing was now demure at all times. Mum's little teacup reading plus her thriving herbalism business was stopped, as it was considered Satan's work. Dad stopped his men's gatherings to study this cult's doctrine day and night. It was insinuated if he did, he would be a respected minister within the realms of this new church/cult in no time at all.

Everything changed in a matter of weeks. Family relationship doors were shut tight. Aunties, uncles plus any close friends were told they were unwelcome unless they became involved in this new way of worshipping, when they flatly refused, my folks made new friends in the church calling them our new family of sisters and brothers. I silently questioned why they were doing this? Why were my folks telling our family they would die if they did not follow their new faith? I had no choice but to do as I was told. Unhappiness stalked our home and I learnt once more to be quiet. I would practise some dance steps in the laundry, or hum one of the now forbidden tunes under my breath.

Then the apocalypse happened. My mother's worst nightmare became a reality when Lois announced her engagement to an Italian-catholic boy named Des. Lois announced that 'if she could not marry him with all the bells whistles of an Italian white wedding, she would solve it by becoming pregnant.' Mum went white, staggering to a chair with her hand on her chest, struggling to breathe. 'How could you do this to us?' she rasped. The wedding that was planned was extravagant, both sets of Folks arguing about money or who paid for what. Lois would sob as she heard the argument between the families escalate. We were cuddled up on her bed together when my folks finally agreed that Lois would learn the catechism and the correct conduct to be a catholic wife. Only if Des would study the doctrine of the new faith my folks now embraced, to learn what was expected from him as a good husband.

The final insult delivered to our family was when Mum suggested I would be one of the flower girls, his family said 'No.' There was no explanation – just no! Dad insisted on knowing why his daughter would not be allowed in the wedding party, the answer was, 'She's not suitable.' This was the first time my looks had been brought out in the open, however, it was not the first time I had felt shamed by my physical appearance. No matter how hard they tried to push me into the happy ever after picture, I simply did not fit. They were all pretty, slim, happy. Me? I was a chunky, straight-haired brunette, still with a lazy eye not quite corrected, now with a front tooth missing.

Jigsaw

With Dad's insistence, their permission was given. The drama, tears, stress leading up to it was awful. Mum's budget didn't include hairdressing or an appropriate flower girl dress for me. A week or two before the wedding we went second-hand shopping, she spied what she thought would work. An adult pale lemon frock that had lace inserts from the waist to the hem, after much pinning and tucking she was satisfied. I was told 'you'll do'. The day before the wedding she washed my hair, popped a bowel on my head, cutting my hair in a circle. She then permed it with a foul-smelling lotion, once that was semi-dry she applied hot tongs. What I ended up with was a tall tower of burnt split hair. On the day of the wedding, she sprayed my hair with water, as it dried it frizzed upwards even more. She gave up after a while, picking a large pale-yellow rose from her garden and pinning it to the top of my head. I could feel it wobble as I walked. Cilleen's comment, 'She looks like she's got a blob of snot stuck on top of her head,' did not go down well. My dress had been given a good washing, as Mum's penchant for dirt and disease had attached itself to second-hand clothing. It had shrunk considerably, now it was too short. I could hear the frustration in her voice as she tried to cinch in my non-existent tubby waist with a wide satin band, instead the satin band rolled up to sit around my chest.

My folks made a very attractive couple that day. Dad was dressed in his long-tailed black tuxedo, Mum looking lovely in her long, jet black dress with matching beaded bolero. Cilleen wore her blue lace bridesmaid's dress and for today only she was permitted to wear her high heels. I could see the pride in my Dad's handsome face, as he looked over his pretty flock of daughters as we prepared for the wedding. That is, until he saw me in my wedding attire. His eyes became wide as he shook his head pouring himself another whisky. The wedding went off without a hitch I was sent home immediately after the ceremony with a cousin who was asked to babysit while my folks attended the celebrations. I really wanted to dance, so Dad perched me on his shoes taking me for a quick spin around the floor before I was whisked back home. The next morning, I was surprised to see Dad removing Lois' belongings onto the front lawn. It seems that Des, her husband, had refused the opportunity to become a member of this cult my folks followed. Therefore, Lois was no longer part of the family. My heart ached watching them pack her belongings into their car, wondering how they could say to Des 'welcome to our family,' one day, then slam the door shut. Was this what family did to each other? I began to mentally question what the word 'family' meant. Would this happen to me if I displeased the people I called family? Was I also going to be kicked out and disowned? Where was this loving god they worshipped? Fear began to take the place of safety within my family circle, I felt like my days were numbered. Sadly, I was not wrong.

CHAPTER 4

My folks arranged one last party for our vast extended family. It was all under the guise to invite their family and friends to join them in their new spiritual home. For those who didn't join them, it would be a last 'goodbye'. Everyone who was invited arrived. As it was summer, the yard and house spilled over, people were everywhere. Mum had been dancing with the aunties. She was a little giggly after a few too many shandies when she introduced me to the man who had taken care of my beloved Chooken and Beep my lamb. This kind farmer patted me on the head, saying, 'Thank you, dear, they were delicious.' There was a moment's silence, before Mum gave an embarrassed titter. I was stunned then angry. 'You're a big fuck,' slid out of my mouth. I didn't know what it meant, but I did know it was one of the bad words I was never allowed to use. I had heard it at school, when I asked Mum what fuck meant, she told me in no uncertain terms to, 'Never say that disgusting word ever again.' I couldn't see what the fuss was about, all the kids said it, but I was marched to the bathroom to have my mouth vigorously washed out with soap and water. That night I thought Mum would pass out immediately as she clutched her chest. The farmer turned crimson before muttering 'disgusting brat,' he bellowed for Dad to come over to where the three of us stood, not so quietly telling him what had happened. Dad looked down at me, then said, 'You must be mistaken. My daughter does not use foul language.' I knew I was in trouble, expecting Dad to tell me to 'pack my bags', sending me off to one of my aunties. That's what you did to family if you didn't want them around anymore, wasn't it? I had seen Lois kicked out of the house plus some of the family. My legs were trembling, but as I looked into my Dad's eyes, I could only see a smile in them, 'About time you were in bed,' was all he said to me. *Did he approve?* I had used a bad word, insulted a guest, yet my Dad seemed, almost, proud of me. I was more confused than ever; adults were far too hard to understand.

By the time I was nine years old my physical appearance had changed. I had slimmed down, my once enforced frizzy brunette hair had grown to be long and wavy, my teeth were now straight and white. My lazy eye was now gone. I began to gain confidence. Despite this, my natural love of life was doused, as my early family life had affected me emotionally. I rarely laughed and trusted no one, adding to this, Cilleen continued to bully me. Any dark corner or alone in a room, my arms or back would soon be covered in painful pinched red welts. I became a loner, preferring books to people. Ironically, just as I began to enjoy school, excelling in my subjects, I was to be dealt another blow. I was still in primary school when I contracted polio.

It was well over a year of being nursed at home before I could get back to school, I had no idea how serious the polio virus was, that it could leave victims with lifelong physical ailments, or end up as a death sentence. Thank heavens my folks knew a little, doing their utmost to help me.

Every night before bed, and every morning before work, Dad would bath me in warm water, then massage my body with warm oil, wrap

Jigsaw

warm sheets around me, and tuck two hot water bottles against my spine. His empathy for me was amazing. Often he would place his hand on my forehead, asking if I was in pain. He used every trick he knew from his WW II ambulance training to help me stand and walk. He would lecture Cilleen not to enter my room under any circumstances, she knew there would be serious repercussions if she did. Mum and I also became closer. Now that her socialising days were over, she stayed home to care for me. We would listen to a radio show every morning called *Breakfast with Aunt Daisy*, singing along to the signature tune. We had many interesting discussions about God, I became her sounding board for the topics she would put forward at her weekly bible meeting. Through polio, the muscles in my throat had also become weak, Mum would administer ice water plus her homemade throat lozenges to help with this. When I lost my voice, she would make a hot cup of tea then liberally apply Vicks over my chest and throat, along with a hot water bottle on my upper chest. Mum's worst fear was that I would end up in an iron lung, like some of my school friends.

To help with my education, my folks engaged ladies from the church to come entertain me. As I lay in bed recouping, I would listen to stories of their childhood, read from the bible, I became an expert at memorising scriptures. I soon became captivated with philosophy, any sort of religious discussion fascinated me. A young teacher from my school, Miss Jilly, delivered homework regularly so I could still be a part of the class. She encouraged me to write poetry, her quick mind picking up my desire to write short stories. The first one I entered, those three sentences won a gold star. The day it was delivered into my hands, I knew without a doubt one day I would be a teacher. I found it exciting to dream of a future when I was better, this involved walking without clinging to walls, chairs or people for support. When the final x-rays were taken, before the doctors would allow me to return to school, they clearly showed the damage polio had left behind.

My pelvic bone was misshapen, one hip was higher than the other, I had a curvature in my upper spine, my jaw was also out of alignment. All of this was termed as *normal* for a polio survivor. My family were informed I was to stay home for another three months to gain strength, do some physiotherapy, along with daily walks. On the day I achieved a walk around the block without my leg muscles shaking, the physiotherapist was informed of this achievement, he declared, 'She can return to school,' advising sitting or catnaps whenever possible. No one then was aware of the long-term effects of polio, however I will be forever grateful that my Dad used Sister Kennedy's methods for helping with the muscle pain, massaging my limbs to remain strong straight. The one remaining problem was I now suffered with severe headaches and fatigue.

During this time, Mum's wedding gown business thrived, her new faith encouraged all the young females to marry as soon as they looked into a young man's eyes. Dad became one of the principle ministers within our church. He blossomed with his newly found power. It became known that Brother Wickham considered women were to be of service to God first then man.

The women in the church loved him; my Dad, the all-powerful Brother Wickham, could do no wrong. The bible was administered with every intake of air. If he said *don't* – we did not. I was not as easily convinced though, as it was me who refilled his glass, but not with the Holy Spirit. It was also me who emptied the ashtrays and refilled his little tin of mint drops before each meeting. They may have instilled in me that I was to be seen not heard, but it did not stop me from forming an opinion. The congregation had put Dad on a mighty pedestal, as if he had become the answer to their prayers. Every line they uttered had, "Brother Wickham' before it. I kept my head down my mouth shut; he knew I was slowly figuring out the fine line between respect, power and love.

Jigsaw

How I found drama class was purely accidental. Miss Jilly asked me to stay behind in class one day to show me the new year curriculum, which included drama. I remembered my dancing days thinking perhaps drama class would be fun. Dancing and singing (apart from church hymns) was frowned upon, but if drama was part of my education curriculum, surely the faith would allow it. Miss Jilly encouraged me to put my name down for the backstage crew because of the fatigue I still experienced. I was never to be on stage, I was happy with that. I fell in love with prompts, lights, camera, action. Unfortunately, Dad found out and stepped in. The Bible says, 'Do not be involved in worldly activities.' I argued my case accusing him of hypocrisy, as behind closed doors he still drank and smoked.

That day he called me some harsh names, from his daughter to nosey and backstabbing. I fully expected him to ask me to leave the family home. Disgruntled at his decision, I again voiced my opinion, 'It's so unfair. I'm behind the scenes, I just paint and prompt when requested.' My punishment for being cheeky? Two weeks of mowing the lawn. The grass was thick and tall since Dad had decided he would spend his weekends knocking on doors, growing his little circle of believers. His opinion now was that, 'His time spent in the garden was not bringing the flock into church.'

By then, I had learnt something powerful from watching drama class. I too could be charming, demure, persuasive, bargaining for a better outcome. A large section of tall grass to hand mow, with my muscles still affected by polio, was no easy feat. I decided to set up a meeting with my folks, as this was the way we now communicated, we were encouraged to have family meetings. I went about it as the cult directed, knowing if I was to gain my folks' approval to get the outcome I desired, it had to be absolutely correct. I also had valuable ammunition; Mum wanted me to become baptised to announce to the world I was saved, Dad was in the baptising team. I could see the headlines – *Our Brother Wickham will now baptise his beloved daughter.*

The congratulations and invites to speak at different cult gatherings would now blossom for them both. The day we agreed to have our family meeting finally came about, thankfully, they had the good sense not to invite Cilleen. I had made warm buttered scones with jam for afternoon tea; Dad's favourite. After all, I had often heard Mum say, 'The way to a man's heart is through his stomach.' When the tea and scones had been admired then eaten, both of them were now looking very pleased with themselves. Favourable comments flowed, 'Our little girl is turning into a great hostess. She'll make a good Christian wife to one lucky man.' I began my practised words while shaking with fear. I stood demurely, my hands clasped, my eyes downwards like the obedient lamb my folks had raised, being in a drama class had its perks. 'Dad,' I began, 'I will happily mow the lawns every Saturday plus clip the hedges once a month, for two shillings a week. Or I can go door knocking with you, but I don't feel I can do both.' There was a pause, a murmured discussion, before they both agreed I would mow the lawns. Little did they know, I would have eaten glass rather than go from door-to-door.

I was now the official lawn mower for two shillings a week. It was also agreed that I was to be baptised at the coming assembly. Dad also decided, out of the blue, that after the baptism I was to become a child missionary, the first in our congregation. Mum was so pleased, knowing they would be applauded for our family's devotion. The baptism did not go well, to be baptised all of your body is submerged. As Dad said a prayer and pushed me under, the fear of being held under water took over. I baulked, yanking his hand off my head, leaping up heaving and gasping, Dad grabbed me, trying to push me under once more. I was having none of it, I headed for the pool side. Mum rushed over with a towel, her voice pleading with me, 'Cassie, don't be silly, do this for us.' I ran to the changing rooms, my folks ignoring me for the rest of the day.

My job as lawn mower did not last long. Within six months Dad gave away his beloved bees and dug up the garden (except for the plum tree, which was now massive, bringing plenty of shade to us and the neighbours). The tool shed was dismantled and a smart, small white gazebo took its place. Dad ripped down old fences that once had strong healthy passionfruit growing over them. He paid men in their faith to build a gravel circular driveway around the house to accommodate his new car.

My swing in the plum tree was taken away as I was considered too old for any daydreaming rubbish. Our backyard was now empty. He had spared nothing. No plants were allowed to live. Mum was allowed to keep two potted standing roses, placed each side of the front door. The front yard, once a colourful garden surrounded with green hedges, was ripped up and replaced with grey bland concrete. Dad's devout worship had ripped away the very soul of our home.

Now there was no lawn mowing. I was informed I was to knock on doors selling the cults propaganda material, I was to write a weekly report of my actions, including the street, day and time. It was stipulated I was to go out for two hours during the week, four hours on the weekend. I was rewarded with time off during the week to study the Bible. I was still fatigued post-polio with very little appetite, if I even attempted to study, I nodded off. School itself became a hurdle. My body ached, I was plagued with headaches, vertigo and nausea daily. I felt like I had a head full of cotton wool. Mum would feed me two Aspro with a large glass of milk every morning. If I tried any sports at school, I would feel faint. Finally, a doctor's opinion was sought. It appeared I was a healthy child, he said it may be psychological. His prescription, to carry on with two Aspro with a glass of milk every morning, if need be Mum could apply for homeschooling. Dad insisted the doctor was a quack, he suggested an age-old remedy of eating a small nugget of charcoal every day, brushing my teeth with salt. He resurrected an old homemade iron tonic from his childhood, which I took twice a day, if I felt tired then I was to sit down. There were some days I was just too tired to answer back, tell them both how sick I felt I would swallow their potions and aspros, just putting one foot after another, it was an effort. Then steps in my saviour with a twist is how I like to put it. Her name was Pat. This woman, for some reason, appealed to Mum's mothering instincts. Pat was an ex-comedian/nightclub singer who had been in a bad relationship. Her partner had taken a knife to her body. She'd been one of the patients Mum visited while preaching at the local hospital, they became firm friends; even Dad liked her. To me, she was everything I needed in my life. Pat was not only a beautiful woman, she sang, danced, told us fantastic tales of her life in the theatre. Her imitations of people were comical, never hurtful or rude, just funny. We all loved her, she became my friend, sister, and family for which I had yearned for.

It was Pat who also encouraged Mum to stop feeding me painkillers. Her own system could not abide solid food, she was on an almost fluid diet, she asked Mum to try cook for me what she ate. This consisted of beef broth or veggie soup, fruit milkshakes, made with goats milk and a vitamin powder. I flourished, growing quickly, slimming down, my clothes and shoes became too small. My skin glowed with health. Mum had found her niche in catering – she was the best soup maker in our village. Pat bought laughter into our lives. It filled every corner of our house. Mum was smiling, singing, Dad was happy, even Cilleen was being nice. Pat and I would often go door knocking together, her intelligent conversation with strangers encouraged me to find my own voice. When Pat began to have flashbacks of her worldly life, the terror of being cut with a knife imprinted in her mind, she came to live with us.

When I found life unfair she would sense it, sitting with me at night, counselling me to see it in a positive light. Pat became my anchor in the weird world of pre-teenage emotions. She was no angel, especially where men were concerned. She would creep into our shared room waking me to say, 'Cassie, kiddo, I think this is the one.' It never was.

Two weeks later when she would try to convert her beau into becoming a member of this cult it would all come tumbling down. We would cuddle up on her bed while she reminisced about lost romance. When she passed away through complications from the knife wounds to her intestine, I was devastated. I dove into a world of silence, trying to figure out why all the people I knew or, liked, disappeared out of my life, did God hate me? Was there even a God? If so, I firmly believed he was not a very nice one. Dad would try to comfort me with words from the Bible about resurrection. It didn't help, I just wanted my friend to be with me. It had been so sudden. One minute we were all surrounded with laughter, the next she was in an ambulance, a day later, my Patty 'the Nightingale,' had passed away. I was not permitted to attend the funeral, instead I wrote her a letter pouring my love and my loss onto a small piece of paper. Life went on as we all came to terms with the loss of the very special person who had lived with us. I missed her, but I wasn't the only one. When Mum took Pat's make-up out of the bathroom, I heard her crying. Dad was pale as he packed up her belongings into a large bag to give away. I felt like I was the loneliest child on the planet, as the one person who understood me had left my side.

CHAPTER 5

I was close to thirteen when Mum went through the most traumatic menopause, she tried to commit suicide. Dad went into control mode. He went to work, he went to worship, he would go from door-to-door selling his religious books. When he came home, if Mum was not up to cooking dinner, he would cook. I was ordered to 'Just look after your Mum.' I tried, but if Mum was upset in any way, she had a habit of passing out wherever she was. The head minister of the faith asked her to stay at home while she was unwell, Dad agreed. When she heard the news, Mum had a howling meltdown, Dad put her to bed bringing her round with smelling salts. Normally he was empathetic, but that day, the look on his face was something I had not seen before. 'You will find a doctor that will help, or you are no longer welcome at our meetings of worship. You either gain control of whatever is bothering you or you know the consequences.' She did as she was told, our doctor saying she was 'menopausal compiled with a nervous breakdown' apparently it was very common in women of her age. She came home with tiny pink pills called 'mother's little helpers,' they medicated her daily with Valium plus sleeping pills.

Jigsaw

Cilleen was now enjoying a life of freedom, with no parental guidance. The congregation did try to assist, but she was 'wild,' often coming home very late at night reeking of alcohol and cigarettes. Dad would reprimand her, but she ignored him. Dad was confused and had no idea what to do. This was 'women's stuff' he realised he could not control her. If he put his foot down grounding her, all hell would let loose. Our shared bedroom was often ransacked in her temper tantrums. Wallpaper had been stripped off the walls, mirrors were smashed, clothing ripped. If I got in the way there was no escape from her fists, or sometimes her teeth. All I could do was run – hide.

At such a young age I was given the task of nurse/carer for my Mum, staying home from school for three months. I missed those carefree days of going to college. I knew education was the one way I could escape the world I was living in, the two raging women ready to abuse me in some way. During this time, Cilleen announced she was seeing a lovely man. His background was Spanish Maori he seemed to be a really nice person. His parents were part of the upper society Mum was once a part of. It was obvious that Cilleen had panicked when Dad had made it very clear that he would be husband-hunting for my sister. True to his word, he invited many young men to dinner, however, her reputation as a troublemaker was well-known, sadly, not one of these boys asked for her hand in marriage. Cilleen had changed dramatically over the years. She had gained weight, her rage shone in her small green eyes. She suffered with incredible temper tantrums that went on for hours. There had also been a small incidence of self-harm, which was hushed up. A mental health nurse came to visit us, social welfare had begun asking why I was missing schoo. It seemed my school had called to complain of my continued absence.

Cilleen saw red when she was questioned about her social life. The social worker saw first-hand the explosion of her temper. Cilleen's face went purple, her voice high and harsh, as she spat obscenities inches from the woman's face. Mum went to bed with a migraine. I was called in to look after her, keep her calm. The outcome of the health worker's visit was an official letter to my folks, demanding I return to school immediately. The health department would be visiting us again. Cilleen panicked and within a week, introduced us to her fiancée. When she admitted to Mum that 'There had been a little bit of sex.' I got the look from Mum, which I knew was *'don't ask,'* but I remember thinking, 'How do you have *a little bit* of sex?' Dad pushed me out of the room. Cilleen claimed they were in love. She threatened pregnancy, just like Lois, if their permission was not given. I had expected Mum to pass out and Dad to roar his displeasure, but instead something strange happened; they both eagerly said 'Yes. Where do we sign?' being seventeen she still needed their approval. The wedding was arranged to be held in one month. With a daughter to marry off, Mum suddenly became well, saying her medication was no longer needed. She was focused on three things; a wedding dress to make, a wedding to plan, plus ensure our family name was untarnished within the cult family.

She took us both aside, informing us the correct behaviour of young Christian women. Cilleen was told of her wifely duties, 'To be in submission at all times, to lie back and think of God,' the actual instructions were too intimate for my young ears, I was asked to leave them alone. Something must have clicked with Mum, what began as a lecture to her two daughters, grew into a weekly meeting of ten or so juvenile girls, sent to the Wickham's home every Saturday afternoon to learn the correct behaviour of young Christian women. June Dally-Watkins eat your heart out. Mum was in her element as a highly respected sister within an organisation that proudly touted; *No sex, no kissing, no dancing.* If we did feel any internal stirrings, her advice to us was to think of God looking down on you. This ever-growing group was informed there would be, 'No sex at all, not even a little bit.' There, it was said again, I badly wanted to ask that question: 'What does *a little bit* mean?'

Once again, my folks pulled out all the bells whistles for Cilleen's big day. Dad worked overtime so no expense was spared. Mum used her Saturday girls' group as volunteer helpers for the wedding breakfast. Cards were made for the seating arrangements to be correct, all the young men had a girl's name on the back of his seating card. This was his dance partner for the night. When Mum found she had a spare young man, guess who was the chosen one. Mum, of course, was the dressmaker, making Cilleen's wedding gown plus my bridesmaid's dress. My status had gone up. I was now the bridesmaid, however to our surprise, Mum insisted a young child she was teaching the scriptures to was the flower girl. Cilleen objected as the child was not part of our family, Mum stood her ground. Two weeks before the wedding, I came home to find this young child was now living with us. My introduction was, 'Oh hello, dear, nice day at school? We have a surprise for you. Meet your foster sister, Rayleen.'

Dad looked unhappy, but Mum was delighted that she had another chicken in her nest. Me? I felt devalued. *How could they do this to me? Wasn't I enough?* I had often wondered why we always had people staying over, strangers eating at the table, showering in our bathroom. Mum often giving our clothing away. There was never any doubt that Mum had a good Christian heart, she wore it on her sleeve every day – except where I was concerned. I just seemed to be in the way, always asking too many questions. I silently questioned if these weird people were really my folks. Maybe I was adopted, or swapped as a baby. I felt my status as their daughter shift as that one small piece of jigsaw I had been holding onto began to slip.

The wedding was nice, very modern and upbeat for the 1960s. I was encouraged to dance with the senior brothers in the church. The problem was, I had been taught to dance, not stagger around in a sideways shuffle. Believe me when I say, these so-called brothers with beery breaths and bleary eyes, were not past the odd boob feel. Why did these men think it was okay to slur sexual innuendos into the face of a fresh, bright-eyed Christian teenager? When the scriptures made it very clear their actions were sinful. I made my excuses claiming a headache. Dad drove me home, the house all to myself, the shower delicious, into my pyjamas, made myself a hot cocoa and into bed with a book. Heaven.

The next day Cilleen moved out of our home, what should have been a close family unit of three, was now Mum, Dad, 'the foster kid' and me. Mum doted on her new daughter and I began making serious plans for escape. To do this meant earning more money, so I became the best, most trusted babysitter on the block. My fifteenth birthday arrived but no celebrations were had or encouraged. I did not care. My little tin of money was becoming heavy. I was determined by the time I was sixteen I would be out of there. I babysat every chance I was offered. Babysitting all ages, really confirmed I did not want children, the best part of the night was reading to them once they were tucked up in bed, I read every fairy story available. Once the children were asleep, I would continue to read, losing myself in the world of adventure, *Peter Pan, Alice in Wonderland, Tarzan,* as these books of fantasy were not allowed in my home. I lived and breathed every word. My folks had begun to argue again. Dad had never stopped his drinking, often sobering up just in time for the sermon on Sunday, Mum saying, 'I'm sick of being your crutch, sober up or admit you're a drunk.'

When Mum became morose, diagnosed with depression. Her mothering duties toward Rayleen became non-existent, it was a disaster! I could see why Mum wanted my help, discovering she had fostered a child with a mouth that belonged in the sewer. Rayleen was illiterate, suffered with rickets, her teeth were rotten, this kid was hell on wheels. Dad walked away, he looked beaten, so that left me, I certainly did not want to be part of rearing this child. I was still desperately working on plans to run away.

Mum's moods darkened, the Valium gave her vertigo, when she suffered a minor stroke. Suffering with Bell's palsy, her face dropped on one side and she was admitted to hospital for two weeks. With Mum in hospital, Rayleen was sent to another foster home. It was like a breath of fresh air for Dad and I while they were away. Cilleen was a constant at Mum's bedside in hospital, leaving Dad and me to return to a relationship. It was heaven for me. We would often eat together while he talked about his day at work, I would tell him about school. Although there was always a discussion on the Bible, we became closer than we had been for a very long time. I had not known how lonely I had been for a parent to love me , I loved our conversations while we cooked together or did the dishes together, we wallpapered the kitchette together. There was a calmness in the home which I believe we both enjoyed.

Dad would light his pipe while listening to the radio, something he never did when Mum was home. For the short time I had a Dad who was not in control, just my Dad. However, once Mum came home all hell broke loose. She found a fault with everything. She hated the wallpaper, claiming it was on upside down. She hated the carpet, everything was old or tatty. She demanded they redecorate, he struggled to accommodate her demands.

Dad began to spend more time at work; overtime became his favourite word. He had become good friends with the tea lady where he worked. Dad often mentioned Mary by name, telling us what a good sport she was. We knew this Mary was a widow with two kids, it wasn't long before Mum began to suspect something. To appease Mum's ranting, I would appear at the factory on the pretext of taking him afternoon tea, I never once saw Mary and Dad being intimate. I just saw happiness and laughter when they were together. On returning home, I would tell

Mum the truth, that all I had seen was them laughing together. One day, something snapped. 'Liar,' she yelled. 'You're Dad's little pet, you've always been his favourite. You love him more than me.' Finally the dam of constant humiliation burst inside me, I yelled back, 'That's because you're an awful mother.' The woman I had called Mum caught me by the hair, grabbed an electric cord, and began whipping me, It hissed in the air as it made contact with my skin it set off a chain reaction that consumed her, with each landing of the cord she screamed, 'I wish you had never been born.' Just as those words escaped her mouth, Cillen walked in the door. I managed to escape, running out the back door. Cilleen was not far behind me. I could hear Mum calling out, 'Cilleen, just let her go,' I had seen the look in her eyes, I knew if she got hold of me, I would not survive. She had wanted me dead from the day I was born and now was her chance. I began to scream with terror just as a bus drove up beside me, the doors opened and I jumped in. Thankfully, they closed in Cilleen's face.

When you live in a small village everyone knows each other. Eric, the bus driver stopped outside my Aunty Ruby's house. Ruby took one look at me and pulled me inside. 'I've got this, Eric,' she said, not much was said between us. She ran me a bath, then she rang Dad, before calling the police. There was plenty of talking between Dad and the police, as they left I heard, 'Dick, for God's sake, you wouldn't treat a dog like this. She's your little girl!' They told him they would be, once again, reporting the incident to social welfare.

I stayed with Ruby for three weeks, her doctor making a house call. He checked me out, nothing was broken. Severe bruising and abrasions. So many questions were going through my head. *Why did Mum and Cilleen hate me so much? What had I done?* My aunt saying, 'I know it's hard on you, but thank Christ you were a girl; a son would never have survived Cilleen's hatred.'

Jigsaw

While I stayed with Ruby we talked and laughed. Every day I was given a small treat of some sort. She had not been blessed with children, offering many times to look after me on the weekends, as she knew Mum was not managing life too well. Ruby explained about postnatal blues, about menopause and how she felt it was the reason for most of Mum's mental health problems. However, deep down we both knew the real reason – I was not the boy they had both prayed for. When the day came for me to go home, she put some money in my hand saying, 'That's to be saved in case you need me again, Sweetie.' She walked me to the front door of my home, the front door was wrenched open. Mum dragged me inside, slamming the door in Ruby's face. I never saw her again. I do know she was a good friend who deserved better.

Why was I was not surprised to find my room I had once shared with many over the years, had been given over to Rayleen? I had been relocated to the lounge to sleep on a second-hand pull-out couch that had to be put away when they had guests. I don't think they knew, but every night I pushed the couch against the door, so no one could get in without waking me. I slept with the window open, even on winter nights, just in case I had to run for safety again.

Kids can be so cruel, especially when they feel or see that something's not right. Gossip adding salt to the wound, I was bullied at school. They told me my folks hated me and I agreed with it all. I had learnt very early in life if you nod and agree, they don't have an argument. I began to have night terrors occasionally wetting the bed. Mum blamed it on polio, saying it had weakened my bladder muscles. They never considered the stress and fear I was going through. Mum and my sisters never told to me about periods. I was at college, terrified when I found blood in my underpants. In fear, I informed my art teacher that day Mr Spidle that I was unwell. He put his hand under my chin, 'What is it, Cassie?' Highly embarrassed I admitted, 'Sir, my bottom is bleeding,' he took me to the school nurse, his wife. Between them they explained about my body. I was disgusted with this 'thing' that would now happen every month. When the nurse said my body was preparing for motherhood, she was surprised by my vehement "No thank you," reply. Motherhood to me meant hate, anger, pain. I never, ever wanted to be a mother. *What if I hurt the baby like my family had hurt me?* No! No babies for me. I was adamant.

Now that Cilleen was married, she did not have to answer to Dad anymore, her husband was her lord and master. She did continue to visit every day though, to help 'poor Mum'. What exactly did *poor Mum* mean? I just knew Cilleen bought with her a miasma of anger that clung to them both, which was regularly aimed at me. I made sure I was never alone in a room with her. What can you do when you look into another's eyes and see them swimming with hate. Yet Mum adored her, I had no idea why. My plan to run away as soon as possible gained momentum. I continuously daydreamed of a little shack by the beach that one day I would call home. I would see myself in my little cottage, filled with flowers, my art on the walls. I would make pretty seashell wind chimes to hang on the porch. A big dog and budgie. In my dreams the sun was always shining.

The one saving grace from all of the anger in this house, came through Rayleen, in an unexpected way. She had an older sister, Maggie, who was married to a Fijian Indian and training to be a Muslim wife. Mum saw an opportunity to teach her that any religion, other than belonging to her much-loved cult, was sinful. Maggie was always a cheerful happy woman, we got on well. Mum asked me to introduce her to regular Bible studies. So, when Maggie invited me to spend a weekend with her, as her husband was away at some sort of men's meeting, my folks agreed. It took me by surprise, but Mum was enthused, packing my bags with all sorts of magazines pamphlets, and of course, the Bible. Maggie was delighted, we arranged we would meet at the gates of Wellington Railway

Jigsaw

Station, I hardly recognised her. She looked amazing in the full regalia as the wife of a Fijian Indian. Her hair was thickly oiled, pulled back off her lovely face, with white frangipani flowers arranged through it. Her sari was orange gold. Gold jewellery hung from her ears, surrounded her throat, and entwined around her wrists. On her forehead a small red dot sat proudly announcing her status within the family. I was mesmerised.

She took me to her in-law's home, introducing me as her cousin, simply to define our relationship. For the first time, I ate samosas with curried vegetables that tasted sweet. We had a perfumed sweet dessert, rich in coconut and Ghee, the tastes of another country teasing my taste buds. I was welcomed with open arms, it did not make a difference that I was Caucasian with a Christian upbringing. That night I walked down the main streets of Wellington dressed in a beautiful blue and silver Sari, my right hand hennaed, my auburn hair slicked back with oil of lily, flowers were threaded through my hair. These women had dressed me in their national costume, my eyes surrounded with Kohl looked huge, silver bracelets jingled on my wrists. I was tall for my age, the sari slimming me down even more. When the Hari Krishnas began to sing and dance, Maggie encouraged me to join in. I loved it. We rejoiced, we clapped, we sang, danced and laughed. The God I had prayed to every night since I was a tiny child, had not heard my prayers, hopefully this Krishna would.

I had the best night in my young life, one I will never forget. Any racism, religion or any differences were replaced with a respect of love for all. It was so weird to see the Marigold Laden Hare Krishnas beating out a tune, dancing with such joy, while on the opposite corner, the cult my family cherished were praying loudly for all the sinners. When I returned home on Sunday, I had been scrubbed clean. The tell-tale stain of Henna on my hand, explained by saying we were practising their art. Maggie never became interested in my folks' faith, she stopped visiting her half-sister Rayleen. She lived with love, so why would she ruin it? That night remained a secret with me for a very long time .

My fifteenth birthday arrived when my best friend Maureen informed us that her and her family were returning to their home in Fiji. I adored this Fijian family of five; they knew how to love and live with peacefulness. Maureen and I were close, I was always a welcome guest in their home. When they invited me to go live with them for a year, to help Maureen settle into a new country, they followed the protocol of the cult. First, they approached Dad who called a combined family meeting. My folks were on their best, welcoming behaviour. A lovely morning tea was made for the adults while we, the two girls being discussed, were told to go to the lounge room study a passage from the Bible. We disobeyed, sitting outside the kitchen door, we hugged each other listening to every word.

I was fizzing with excitement. Her parents were generous, if my folks agreed to my being part of their family for the year, I would have a continuing education in a good school. The religious instruction continued and my folks agreed to consider this arrangement. Once the guests had gone I waited for my them to call me. My head was full of palm trees, blue ocean and white sand. When they sat me down informing me of the discussion, they told me their decision was that I could not go. The reason? They would have to pay for my return fare of over one hundred pounds. I jumped up saying 'I can help.' I had put all my babysitting money in a tin, in my drawer, but when I went to check, it was empty. It had not occurred to me that when they had changed the rooms around, they would have found my stash of money. I knew that tin was full so where had the money gone? My folks just shrugged when I stood there crying, 'But this tin was full of my money.' I looked at Rayleen, I knew it wasn't her.

Then, I looked into Mum's face. As soon as Dad had left the room,

Jigsaw

I simply said, 'Why?' She answered me so flippantly, 'What does a silly little girl like you need with all that money?' That was my first real lesson in disappointment. I just couldn't express how I felt. I knew I had no trust left in my heart for these people I had to live with. It was a moment of feeling incredibly lonely and abandoned by the people who were supposed to love me. If there was a way to leave, I would find it. I had learnt by then that disappointment is so much worse than dislike, or hate. Disappointment is different; it means you never trust again. By the time I was sixteen, Mum had laid the ground rules of our relationship, a mutual feeling of dislike had grown between us. She had made it very clear I was not what she had wanted as a daughter. I was mouthy, always asking questions. I was always touching things or undoing things just to find out what made them tick. In an argument between us she made it clear I was not pretty, attractive or cute. I was a tomboy, I was not her cup of tea.

    She did not see me for who I was or how I had twisted myself inside out to accommodate them all. Cilleen was now pregnant in her second trimester. Mum, Rayleen and Cilleen were a team. There was no place for me in this house, that was made obvious as the three of them would laugh chattering with each other. Until I entered the room, then silence. Cilleen's pregnancy did not suit her at all. She hated it. As she grew rounder, she had many health ailments. I grew tall, slim and healthy. I loved softball and swimming. I adored creative writing, poetry and the arts, I did not bother to inform my folks of my passions at college there was no point. Now that Maureen had left New Zealand, I had no friends in the church. To be honest I had no desire to make any, as everything I said or did was reported back to the family.

    I threw myself into the arts, well what was considered acceptable. I would doodle with a pencil or make up lines of words, often tapping my pencil to the rhythm. We all knew, if any breach of behaviour within the church rules was reported, there would be an investigation and possibly a demotion. So, when Dad hung the swing back in the plum tree, which by now its branches were reaching up high into the sky, he knew he had bought my silence. One sturdy branch now had two big, strong ropes with a small wooden seat attached. Summer, spring, autumn and often on a winter's day, they knew where to find me. Lonely? Very.

The head minister of the cult was brother Charles and his wife Katherine, both were kind, caring, enthusiastic and empathetic. They encouraged all the young people in church to be passionate about their faith. They encouraged kindness, consideration. Their motto was to encourage growth in all ways, to study other religions, challenge our own truths. Once or twice, I was invited to dinner after Sunday church. The teens from the congregation would sit around the dinner table where American hot dogs were served. We philosophised, talked scripture, discussed life itself. The Mormon doctrine plus other religions beliefs were openly discussed with us, there was no shock, horror or repercussion. It was discussed with interest, my young mind responded with absolute joy. I wondered why my family could not practise logic or an intelligent conversation without them feeling harshly critiqued, instead of in the drama-loaded dogma they persisted in delivering. Their behaviour confused me. Both of them were educated in the teachings of Christ, yet they did not trust me or respect my exploring mind.

All they wanted was total obedience from their daughters, enforced into our lives by any means, to make them look good within the church. Dad was up for eldership that year, he had hid his drinking well, or so he thought. My time was nearly up at college. University did not seem to be an option, there was no money to do so. However, with Mr Spidle's encouragement, I had applied for an education grant to gain a teacher's diploma at Wellington University. My folks were aware of this, as they had to sign the papers for the grant. Mr Spidle had rung them discussing the opportunities this education would open for me. Nothing had been said, though they both seemed amenable to the idea. All was going to plan with three months of college left, I sat and gained my fifth year certificate. If I the grant came through and I was accepted, I would attend university for two years followed by employment. It meant everything to me.

I had also found myself a part-time job working in the local fish and chip shop four afternoons a week for twelve shillings a week. Mum announced, 'You're earning money so you can now pay your own way.' I mirrored my father every Thursday night, as we handed over our sealed pay packets. Mum would count it out; ten shillings for Dad's beer and cigarettes, I was given the remaining two shillings from my wages. I saved what I could. Rayleen was now touted as the family's true blessing as she was the up-and-coming missionary, loved by my family and congregation. One morning Dad surprised me joining me for breakfast. He was normally at work by then, I asked if he was unwell? He gave me the strangest look.

My Dad had striking blue eyes that spoke volumes. My stomach lurched in anticipation, hoping he was giving me the green light to go to training college. He announced, 'You're leaving school this Friday. We have discussed this, prayed about it and feel any further education is unwarranted. You do have a choice though. Join us in our missionary work or find a full-time job for your keep, we are not a charity.' Since when had I fallen from daughter to a charity? I was stunned. Deeply in my core I knew their God, who was supposed to be of love compassion, was not for me. Who could I trust now? Lois, Maureen and Pat had gone. My heart still missed them. My folks preferred their two obedient daughters, Cilleen and Rayleen. This God I was told to worship felt like a farce. If he loved me, would he not want me to be educated? I was under the impression that any education was part and parcel of becoming a mature adult, if I was truly one of his children as the scriptures said, then why? Why did he allow this to happen to me?

That day was my last day at high school. I did not say any goodbye's, there was no need. I cleaned out my locker. The school nurse alerting her husband Mr Spidle, both wishing me well. I would often feign sickness so as not to attend any cult meetings or go from house-to-house. When my folks got tired of me claiming sickness, Dad informed me I was committing a sinful life of laziness. Study the Bible, get a job or get out. There, he had finally said those words I knew one day he would say. It struck me that this was how much I meant to them, it had come down to a choice of their God or their daughter. I soon found a job in the city working as a window dresser/ticket writer. It was there that I was introduced to my first gay person. He was a Rarotongan, his name one I will never forget, Ronan. He was the shop's head window dresser. We hit it off straight away. I loved his funny stories. One Friday night when the shop closed, he requested that I stay back to assist him, to further my training. Ronan taught me how to dress a window, how to dress a mannequin for the windows. In the weeks that followed he also showed me how to smoke like Audrey Hepburn, walk like Marilyn Monroe. How to mix a martini like Dean Martin with a caution to sip it only.

He taught me how to tease my hair like Bridget Bardot plus how to apply Mary Quant make-up. We would stagger around in our super sexy super high stilettos, trying on clothes that only a super star would wear. He swore like a sailor but forbade me to swear, 'well-mannered young ladies of high quality should not impress with foul language.' He taught me to use and watch body language, use facial expressions. And suggested I used my Dad's tricks of sucking peppermints on the train home to hide the odours of alcohol and cigarettes.

Six months into this fabulous new world I was enjoying, I was asked to attend my manager's office. I entered with a smile thinking of

Jigsaw

promotions, only to see Mum sitting there. My scandalous behaviour had been reported, by whom they would not say. I was fired immediately, so was my lovely mate from Rarotonga. At home, I experienced another lecture of what a failure I was. I should be more like my sisters; nice obedient Christian girls. Funny how they had forgotten Cilleen's outrageous behaviour when she was around my age! Her husband had left her, she now had a son, and had come home to live. Her behaviour toward this baby boy was nothing but vicious. My dad crowed he had a grandson, Mum was besotted. And whenever I could, I would creep into their room and cuddle this beautiful wee man. When Cilleen found full-time work, my folks happily took over parenting him. I too fell deeply in love with this baby who always greeted me with a smile. I was hired by the local carpet factory, I almost ran to work every day. I settled in, worked hard and within three months, I was made a senior on my floor.

The floor manager said I had a real talent for mixing wool colours, with a promotion I was given a wage rise. Within that year Cilleen was divorced, claiming loudly it was not her fault. Rayleen was diagnosed, complications from the Rickets she had as a child, so no more going from door-to-door with bibles etc. Dad became distant, Mum? she seemed to cope well, her grandson always came first but still a shoulder for those not coping well in this world. And I had begun looking for a one-bedroom flat.

However, Cilleen's ex-husband also worked at the factory. As I listened to his story of their separation, I believed it was more truthful than what I'd been told by the family. Knowing Cilleen's personality and what she was capable of, he offered to help me find accommodation. All was going well, until through the factory grapevine my intentions were discovered. I was severely lectured, apparently I was up to mischief once again, Dad announcing it was time for me to be groomed to be the perfect Christian wife.

He began vetting the young men in the church as future son-in-law. Boys in the age range of nineteen to twenty-five years old were now at our dinner table on a Saturday night and I was the prize, but only if they passed the interrogation about their intentions. If they loved the church, whether they were gainfully employed and more importantly, could they support a wife? I actually felt sorry for the entire acne squad; they were all so very young.

I dated a few, there was a curfew to be home at nine o'clock, nothing but a luke warm handshake was offered as we said good night. I longed for someone to sweep me up in his arms and carry me off. Making passionate love did not enter my innocent brain, all I wanted was to get out of this tomb they called a home. Marriage was one thing my folks could not force me into, or so I thought. How I had reached sixteen with such naivety about sex and marriage, I have no idea. They finally settled on a young man of nineteen to be my husband. He was worldly wise, had an excellent job, he was one of the local cult, showing such promise to be part of our family. Soon, I was an engaged teenager. Mum chose and bought my engagement ring, then placed it on my finger in front of my fiancée, 'It looks lovely,' she cooed.

A huge engagement party was planned, with everyone rejoicing that Cassie had found a husband. To be honest, I did not like him. This uneasy feeling happened every time we were together, but I saw it as an easy way to leave home to make my own way in life. Mum was once again in her element as a wedding planner. I was very surprised to see my aunties, uncles, cousins and old family friends at my wedding party. She had really turned it on for all to see. Her youngest child, was not pregnant, was being married in white satin and lace to a dashing young man. This was Mum's swan song. If there had been a crystal ball to tell my fortune, hopefully they would have sung a very different tune. The saying *from frypan to the fire* is very true.

CHAPTER 7

The person I was now married to, I cannot call him a man, even to call him a psychotic bully is too good, showed me the ropes of becoming married in the cruellest of ways. Beatings and marital rape became the norm. Out of desperation I asked my family for help, they showed no remorse for marrying me off into a perverted immoral family that practised sexual depravity. When his taste for sex turned into paedophilia, I entered a whole new world.

I had no idea that grown men could groom an innocent child into depravity. His interests were aimed at any female under fifteen. Twice he bought a young underage girl into the house, his excuse 'I'm driving her home for a mate.' When I threatened to report it to the police he returned the threat by bringing home the barmaid to live with us, apparently she was homeless, their sexual activity paraded before me. I knew my life was in danger it was time to run. The only place of safety I knew was my parent's house. Dad ordered me to return to him or the church would be looking into it, which would mean a demotion for him. My husband's dislike for me turned into a vendetta.

Kez Wickham St George

In four years I had two children eighteen months apart, a girl who adored her dad's every breath then a boy who was my boy from the day he was born, they were both good kids. I did my best to hide them from the lifestyle of shame forced upon us, but what child would be proud to know their mother was being auctioned off at the local pub for alcohol. My two children had it rubbed in their faces at school daily. Thankfully, I had a friend who would warn me to lock up, to keep the house in darkness when he was in one of his moods. I was sold to his turps drinking younger brother, who informed my husband that I had welcomed his sexual advances. A neighbour intervened the beating, driving me to hospital. When the doctors informed my folks, as they could not find my husband, they insisted there was to be no police involvement. The church must never find out. A cracked rib with a bruised thorax was the medical report written up and given to my Dad. I lived in fear and shame for eight years as there was nowhere to run, no one to turn to, not family or church. No one wanted to admit the obvious violence I lived with daily, I was in danger of my life. When the government brought in the single mother's pension, I was the first to apply. What had I learnt? Never love another with your entire heart, as you need to leave a whole lot of loving for yourself. I was finally free. Or was I?

Now into my twenties, I was a single Mum on a government pension, haunted by an ex-husband who would turn up out of nowhere threatening me with harm or with taking the children At that time, police intervention was not an option. When I asked for protection, I was informed to, 'Go home, *dearie*, cook him a nice meal, spread your legs you'll be okay.' At twenty-two years of age, I had still not discovered my inner core, my crone, my womanhood. I had found a pro bono female lawyer, she disliked my husband with every fibre of her being, my divorce was soon on its way.

Moving to a small fishing village up north; a twelve-hour road trip

Jigsaw

separating me from my folks, it suited me. The farther away the better as far as I was concerned. But life was about to turn a sharp corner, my father was demoted from his position in the church. This 'so-called' church of love that they had committed their lives to, demoted him because he couldn't control their foster daughter. It seemed Rayleen had also threatened pregnancy without marriage if they did not give her their blessing, taking it one step further she informed the elders this was her wish. Dad had nowhere to hide. Mum in her sixties was a hollow-eyed shadow of her former self. Dad confided in me that the doctor had warned him Mum's health was failing. They sold up, moving to my northland village, living a short walk from my home.

We began to form some sort of friendship. I would often visit, clean or cook for them, without interference from other members of the family, our differences put aside. It was around this time that I decided if you can't beat them then join them, my make-up lessons with Ronan now came into play. I liked what I saw in the mirror, as did many others, I would go so far with flirting, then it was time to stop and go home. First and foremost I still had two children, they were my main priority, life was hard enough for them as it was.

My Dad had a harsh opinion on my lifestyle calling me an ignorant alcoholic, 'You'll be dead by the time your thirty,' When I took no notice, he once continued with, 'You don't deserve the good man we found for you.' My retort staggered him, his face greying when I answered back; 'Old man, I'm nothing like you! I'm not a drunken fool. I put my kids first and at least I won't be giving them away to any man I deem as suitable because I'm sick of parenting or because I want to look good for a power seat in some cult. You should be ashamed of yourself for what you allowed to happen to me. That person you happily married me off to is a cheating liar, a narcissist and a bully, he tried to kill me, has put me into hospital, you knew yet you did nothing. What does that say about your so-called fatherly love?' There it was, finally out in the open. Relief rushed through me. He demanded I leave their home. Mum had sat passively through my accusations, however when Dad ordered me out, she spoke up. 'No! Richard, our daughter is not to blame for our choice of faith. She has a right to live as she wants.' Wow! I was stunned. That was the first time she had taken my side, for once I had an ally.

Life became busy, I found work as a café manager. My kids were growing up fast, the two years I had waited for my divorce day arrived, it was not a pleasant divorce nor did I expect it to be. I will simply say, he left the court with a smile, his bank account very healthy and I left the court with custody of my two children, and what we stood up in. I met Larry and we gelled. After a year of courtship, he proposed. With all my insecurities still not dissolved I said no, bless him, he persisted until I said yes. For the first time in a long time, I began to trust again. When Larry moved in with us, my two children were not happy. I thought it would be plain sailing as Larry was a good man, but with no experience as a father it was trial and error. Our parenting skills very different from each other.

My two children rebelled with their father's encouragement, they were rude to Larry whenever my back was turned, the eldest began to spread a web of lies about Larry and I. With my rose-tinted glasses on, I did not see it. What do you do or say when the Christmas wish of my eldest was for her parents to live together again, while my youngest was scared of his own shadow. The wedding was planned, I told Mum she was my VIP guest, 'Just get prettied up and enjoy it, Mum. It's a party.' She understood, both of us knowing she no longer had the strength to plan another wedding, though she took it upon herself to invite Cilleen and her family. Thank heavens I had found a man who went with the flow, he did not give a damn about my family. He wanted to marry me. If I thought I was secure though, I was mistaken, as my husband to be and his family had emotional issues of their own. I delayed the wedding twice, then I settled on a summer's day in November.

Life once more surprised me, as three months before the wedding, I discovered I was pregnant. At Larry's insistence, we gave up the little two-bedroom Villa I had made our home, for a larger house in the suburbs. The day we moved in, full of joy for a new beginning, Larry lost his job. I was in my second semester knowing I would not find work. With no money to pay rent, we were soon told to move out. Larry had borrowed money from his parents to pay for our wedding, they kindly offered a very small one-bedroom cottage across the road from them that his mother owned. Our wedding day was a day to remember, a soft warm wind slowly stirred the lime green leaves of the majestic ancient oak tree we were married under. I felt beautiful, Larry looked very handsome. Our families and friends surrounding us in a horseshoe pattern, my Dad walking me down the gravel walkway. My Mum looked perfect, dressed in a long, peach-coloured cocktail frock. My own gown? I had never worn anything so beautiful, an oyster crème chiffon with crocheted lace bodice. Applause filtered through the air when it was announced 'you are now man and wife'.

Moving into the offered rental cottage two days after our wedding, it was cramped, damp and cold. Larry was there for just one night before he was offered work on a fishing boat, he would be away for three weeks. Although I thought this family might be different from my past experiences, I was so wrong. The women did not want me in their family and were very direct about. I was shunned, except when Larry was home on break. His mother inviting us over for a family dinner, where their dislike for me and my two children was made very obvious. I would leave that house feeling lost, what had I done to deserve such blatant rudeness? Why did Larry not speak up or at least clear the air.

I lost myself in that tiny damp cottage, questioning everything. At night I would go to sleep wondering why no one liked me . Was I supposed to feel this lonely? Was I a horrible person? I was trying so hard to please everyone, I could not believe this was how I was supposed to live my life, disliked and alone.

Every day, my eldest daughter and I would argue. She wanted to live with her father, she hated it here with us, accusing me of being a bad mother. I should have stayed married to father, he was a good man, she hated her life. I wondered if my insecurities were contagious. Finally, she ran away to live with her Dad. Was I scared for her? Yes, as I knew what he was capable of, however she adored him. I felt guilty at the feeling of relief that rushed into the small cottage when she left, I certainly was not surprised by Larry's reaction.

'Thank God she's gone.' Soon, my son began to miss his sister, deciding he also wanted to go live with his father. I encouraged phone calls between them not realising the consequences when she would regale tales of wonder and happiness where she was living, how wonderful her new family was, the big family home they lived in, she had no curfew, she was loved. She belonged there. I tried to phone, however any conversation between us was interrupted by his new wife. It wasn't long before my son left to have an extended holiday, with what he termed 'his family.'

I became unwell as my pregnancy progressed, my new doctor advising that I was stressed, recommending a councillor, a professional mental health person named Miz Damon. Her pen busily made notes to my answers to her questions. She reminded me of a startled bird, yet when we were finished, she looked at me, then at her notes, then back at me, saying 'How the hell have you survived all of this bullying? My God woman, don't just sit there, get bloody mad. This is wrong.' I replied meekly, 'It's not wrong. It's just my life. No one actually likes me, and I don't know why?' She showed me her notes in black and white. They were an eye opener; parental control, church or cult control (acceptance

Jigsaw

of marital rape, violence and emotional control), remarriage, financial stress, plus my new family's dislike of me. Her advice was to journal, learn to meditate. 'Join a women's group, make some friends,' she said, 'leave the eldest two where they are for now – you have enough on your plate with moving plus trying to find your feet in a new relationship. You also have a baby on the way, that will be taking a toll on you.' I was grateful for her compassion and understanding. I joined a women's pregnancy dance group, gaining confidence in my mind and body.

I must admit being a daughter-in-law did not come easy to me after my last experience, so I decided to pay my Mum-in-law a visit; try to mend fences if I could. It was a cool summer day. I had dressed up, made a fruit cake, however when I knocked on her door she was talking on the phone. So I placed the cake on the table, thinking I would do what any good daughter in law would do, I began to make us both a cup of tea, in her kitchen.

I was certainly not prepared to hear my mother in laws description of me as she spoke to her daughter. 'Dear God, she's an awful woman. She's been married before, with God knows how many kids running about, she has two of them with her. Most men I know, would have steered clear.' I was shocked. I don't know what she thought I was or who I was, but I did not deserve that sort of judgment. I walked back across the road to the tiny, damp blue cottage in tears. I was having her grandchild and I was married to her son, yet she was talking about me like I was dirt, why?

The two women in Larry's family, his Mum and sister, made any sort of relationship uninviting; the more I saw and learnt, the more I wanted to keep my distance. When Larry was home from his sea trips, I tried so hard to be part of the large family I had longed for. When they were all together, they laughed, played silly jokes on each other, his Mum would cook big meals for them all. His brothers were fine, we all got along, but the women remained aloof. It resurfaced memories of my grandmother

Nellie: 'You're not one of us, so why are you here?'

Our baby girl was born, cute, chubby and a brunette like her Mummy. When she laughed, we all smiled. She was a blessing and I loved being her Mum. It didn't seem long before she was in kindergarten. I began to look for a part-time job to help save for a house of our own. Life was very different in the suburbs of Auckland, I was not a fan. I wanted a place to call my own. I saw an advert in the paper for a three-bedroom house. We took one look, I could see my dream of the white picket fence coming true. It desperately needed a good clean, the gardens needed work, but I knew deep inside this place was going to be ours. Larry was not impressed. All he could see was the money it would take to achieve my dream. I honestly did not see it his way. He thought of it as a lifetime of commitment, watching his money dwindle away on mortgages and bills.

There were days I did not really know him. He seemed to flip from 'I do' to 'I don't' very quickly. Maybe a longer engagement where we had a chance to discuss each other's dreams would have been better. Any savings added to the $5,000 divorce settlement which was tucked away in the bank, using that as a down payment on this small home, we were informed we needed another three thousand dollars to complete the transaction. Larry saying, 'No! I can't afford it.' I knew this house was my home, I found a job, working weekends, I was delighted. Larry was home on the weekend so he could look after our baby – it was perfect.

For two years, I worked the weekends holidays or when staff were unwell, On weekdays, I worked in the home being a Mum/wife. I was exhausted most days. The old adage 'happy wife happy life' was not in Larry's vocabulary. It was a pure light-bulb moment when I was journalling one night. The house was very quiet, as my baby and husband slept. I began to write what I wanted in my life, I was thirty-one years of age and accomplished very little apart from marriages and children, my brain loved education, so where to from here. When I miscarried at eight

Jigsaw

weeks, there was little time for grieving, home and work called for me to be focused on the future not the now. This is one lesson I will never forget, take that time to stop, grieve and smell the roses today, tomorrow is not known. One year later I gave birth to a five week premature baby girl, once she was placed in my arms, I had never seen a baby so small before.

If I thought I was tired before, this one tiny human certainly claimed every ounce of my energy. She had chronic colic, nothing we tried to settle her worked. Larry and I both spent hours in the rocking chair gently rocking her little body while she screamed. Doctors, specialists were sought as she was now having trouble breathing, her tiny face grey with pain. One doctor suggested we put her into hospital, so they could sedate her and perform x-rays plus other tests. Our baby was released the next morning, the doctors looking puzzled as they could find nothing wrong. The specialist suggested she might just be a bad-tempered baby, I smiled; I had never heard of a bad-tempered baby.

This tiny babe would sleep with exhaustion, wake up and repeat the screaming. I couldn't put her or my three-year-old into care while our home was so unsettled. I left my job becoming a full-time Mum once more. When Larry came home one night feeling unwell, I suggested a doctor and was told 'no quack for me.' I suggested a herbalist I knew. I was amazed that he kept the appointment, he came home with many pills and potions. The diagnosis? He was stressed and needed a sea change. I was tempted to say, 'we all bloody do,' but if he had an extended holiday, how did we pay for our food and mortgage.

Funny what life teaches you. Larry's paternal granddad had passed away, my mother-in-law knowing we couldn't afford it, bought Larry the return airfare to attend the family funeral. I was told ' no children were to attend' hence I was not invited. Larry just about fell over himself with joy, as he left with his family to fly out the following week. My two babies, my son and I happily became a unit. We worked well together, for a week we relaxed the rules. Yes, the baby still cried, my son still whinged about a life with his family up north, my little girl of three loved me being at home, but what amazed me was that we all got on as a family. I admit, the house wasn't spotless, with no demands we all relaxed without being grumped at or an opinion added that would fire up arguments.

Dinners were in front of the TV, we ate what we wanted when we wanted, not the regular regimented meat with two veg. When my son learnt of his step-father's return, it was like watching a snail curl back into its shell. He became surly, the feeling in the house became different. However, Larry had a spring in his step regaling stories of seaside walks with his cousins, family meals, lovely times re-connecting with his family. When I was informed that his Mum had paid for all his family including small grandchildren to attend, including families living overseas, I knew then, no matter what I did or said, I was not going to make one blind bit of difference; they did not like me or my children. So be it. I had done my utmost to give the best of me to all I knew. It was time I set some boundaries.

While Larry had been having family time at the funeral, I had been thinking. My son had admitted that he preferred the country life and hated the suburbs. I had an idea that perhaps this family would do well in the country. Hopefully, it would be just what the doctor ordered. I too wanted to return to country life, simple, quiet. I made a decision. I would sell this house we had made from a run-down shell into a lovely comfortable home. It was my money that had paid the deposit on this home, Larry would simply have to 'like it or lump it.' Our home in the suburbs sold within two weeks. Finding a place to rent close to my son's school was not hard. We settled in planning a camping holiday over the Christmas holiday, then looking for a home in the country, I was okay with spending a little of the money from the sale of our first home. Life was good, our two little girls thriving.

Jigsaw

My son decided that Christmas was his opportunity to go up north for two months to live with his family. The fare was paid for by his father. I waved him off knowing I was losing him. I loved him so very much and it confused me as to why he preferred his family up there. What did we do that was so different? I had asked many times why my two older children preferred living with their father, especially from what I had experienced with him. He had remarried twice, with many children to different women. His unstable lifestyle was very different to what we offered them both; an education, a stable home life, plus a good role model in Larry. Larry saw me struggling with a decision to give my boy his wish; a life with his father. He offered to adopt my son so he would have our name, a name to be proud of. When we approached my son with this offer, after discussing it with his father and hearing the roar of displeasure, my son declined Larry's offer of adoption.

CHAPTER 8

While on our camping holiday, we ate dinner off paper plates, swam in the camp's pool and collected seashells from the rugged shoreline. We ate ice-creams for lunch, took long walks in the country, Larry bonded with our two daughters like never before. It was a magical time for all of us. On Christmas Eve, Larry rang his folks to wish them a merry Christmas, however when he returned, the news was not good. My father-in-law was very unwell, they had decided to sell the three properties they owned in the small country village of Stillwater, on the coast of Whangaparaoa. In a heartbeat, I knew this was a chance for us all to have our sea change. Asking Larry to look after the two little ones, I almost ran to the phone box, ringing my in-laws. My mother-in-law answered the phone. I wished both of them a merry Christmas, then said, 'I believe you're selling all the Stillwater properties? That green cottage in Stillwater by the estuary, are you selling that one?' She said, 'Yes.' I immediately made her an offer of a large deposit, paid into her bank account once we had returned. I knew, I just knew she would not decline my offer.

Jigsaw

By the time we got back to the suburbs of Auckland, the paperwork of ownership was waiting for us to sign. To my surprise, Larry's Mum offered us a mortgage for the remaining twenty grand, with very minimal interest added. We accepted. It meant no bank to apply to for a mortgage, as well as leaving a little in the bank for any renovations. Larry was also excited about his Mum's generosity, I treated it purely as a business transaction. I did not like her and she did not like me, yet money talks. There was no drama, no fuss; here's your deposit, mortgage papers agreed to then signed, insurance papers signed, here are your keys. Done. Simple. She wanted to sell, and suddenly I saw my childhood dream, a cottage by the sea in the country.

Any money I had put aside soon disappeared. Having to rewire the entire house, every switch was live, the taps and oven giving off shocks if you touched them. One wall in the lounge had been torn apart by the axe left embedded in the plaster, this had to be completely replastered. The ceiling in what was to be our girls bedroom was sagging with damp, that was replaced. The bathroom toilets were outside, both needing instant fixing, they were filthy. Her generous offer of a minimal interest was a farce, she knew exactly what she was selling.

Still, I called it our home from day one. It was pure joy, I adored every year I lived there. We had half an acre with our little cottage by the sea. I loved saying those words, 'My home is a small cottage by the sea.' Our two baby girls were happy there. For me, it was paradise. Slowly, over the seven years we lived there, we had quite a lot of renovations done. Larry's trucking business in Auckland kept him busy, I hardly saw him, as the hours travelling back and forth six days a week were horrendous.

It was in this home that I relaxed enough to release all my frustrations and disappointments, I finally got to know who Cassie was, acknowledging my strengths and my weaknesses. However, If I had known the road of awareness ahead, I wonder if I would have ever taken the first tentative step. The catalyst of becoming, growing, finally knowing one's self is a hard road. When you remove the blinkers, you rediscover things you have covered up for many years and it can be extremely painful. It came about because of my Mum's death. We had survived so much, with our relationship improving in her later years. We had become close friends, not so much mother and daughter, but in her words, 'I've already got one of those dear. You can't choose family my dear, but you can choose your friends.' Point taken, Mum.

It was in this home, in Stillwater, that my road to a major healing took pace. We grew close, both confiding in each other as girlfriends do, giggling at our men's behaviour. When my folks visited, they would spoil our two little girls, the laughter in the house was infectious. Some of her confidences included her sorrow around Cilleen's mental health, for allowing her behaviour towards me. She opened up to me. Her heartache about the mental unwellness in our family, apologising for the attacks on me.

She also apologised for insisting I marry my first husband. She admitted she knew what he was, what his parents were, 'I just wanted you safe.' I had to disagree, 'Mum, let's be honest. You wanted me out of the way so you and Dad would be highly regarded in the church. I asked too many questions, I rocked your boat too much, didn't I?' She nodded. I hugged her tight. Tears always spill before healing can began. Her grey tear-filled eyes looked so sad, as her aged hand held onto mine. 'It will always haunt me, what we allowed in the eyes of the church. You were such a naïve child,' she said as her arms went around me. She then expressed sorrow that the in-laws didn't want me as part of their family. 'They don't know what they have dear,' she smiled through her tears, 'you're the best of the bunch.'

That day, Mum and I sat at the very back of our block, the spring grass had grown high under the old elm tree where we sat under its green leafy branches. We laughed at memories of the old swing when I was a child, how I would hide in the branches when she was angry with me, at last, it felt like I had a Mum. When she passed over, she took a large bit of my heart away with her. It took a while to adjust, my heart wept every time I saw a photo of her. I would see her face in a crowd or hear her breathless laugh. I worked through it. I still had a family to raise, a home to keep. I looked to Larry for that extra cuddle or empathy. One day, feeling a little fragile missing Mum, I asked him to spend Saturday with us. His words will remain etched in my memory: 'Pull yourself together – she's gone.' It was like ice water in my face. I went numb for weeks after, everything I did was through a fog. *How could he say that? He had loved my folks, hadn't he? Did he love me?* His words were hurtful, his harshness affecting me in many ways.

Once I acknowledged I needed guidance with the heaviness in my heart, this time from a neighbour who was a hypnotherapist she had put flyers in the letterbox. I went through her front door as a scared young woman but I thrived under her care. Much of the trauma I was carrying, calmed down. I realised I was living once more with PTSD. I began to learn a very big lesson in my life: Firstly, responsability was mine for my actions only, of course, I had a responsibility for my two little girls, but everyone else could bugger off. I began to retrain my emotional brain, acknowledging that I was a capable mother/wife. Because of my abilities to budget, we were home owners in what I called 'the most beautiful place on Earth.' My family thrived. Acquaintances began noticing there was something different about me. Well, yes there was. I finally believed in myself. I joined a belly dance class for relaxation. Life was good, but I kept getting the feeling that it was the calm before the storm, my hypnotherapist saying it was all the old stuff trying to re-emerge. I would book in for a monthly session, within ten minutes of going under I could feel a soft change in me. I was growing stronger than ever before.

I made sure the mortgage and bills were paid religiously. If we kept it up, we would be mortgage free in a few short years. I did backflips to make sure everything was as smooth as possible. I saved and bought myself a car, a second-hand 1967 Mini. it may have been an old car, however it brought so much joy to our family. Now with transport, my life became busier than ever. I joined a group of young school Mums and became a teacher's assistant, loving every minute of the role, with my two girls in preschool next door – happy days. When my sister was finally diagnosed as bipolar, alcohol becoming her closest friend. Her husband found her unconscious one morning, shit hit the fan, huge conniptions with their church. That was when Dad reached out to Larry and me, asking if we could help by having our two older nephews come stay with us in the country. The church had offered to look after the three youngest.

I loved both boys dearly, although I'd had very little contact throughout their lives. We agreed to have them live with us. *What could go wrong?* The eldest nephew stayed just two weeks then decided he wanted to find his own way in the world. I will admit I had something to do with it. I would often say, 'If I had your life, I would certainly not be hanging around. I would be living life to the fullest.' He left with a cheeky smile, some money in his wallet and a backpack. The second nephew stayed with us for over a year. We loved him, and he loved us. There were no rules, except to be respectful at all times. We told him he could talk to us about anything, he became like a son to us. We celebrated his twenty-first birthday, then he decided to go home to start where he had left off. Full of confidence, Larry and I both knowing he could charm the bees from trees, we encouraged him to do so.

I don't think he considered the terrible backlash that occurred when he happily informed his parents that I practised ethnic dance and believed that motivation plus self-care were the keys to personal success not religion. If this was not enough fuel to add to Cilleen's dislike for me, he also added that I did not practise any religion or encourage it in my home. It was true. I taught/practised motivational thinking with my family, hoping somewhere, somehow, once they were teens, they would understand the positive effect it could have as they grew.

Cilleen's jealousy must have simmered deep, now armed with this information. She decided I was possessed with evil, she took her concerns to a meeting of the cult elders. Dad beseeched me to attend this meeting, I agreed but only to make him happy. I was sat before the elders; all four men judged my life as sinful. I was immediately disfellowshipped. My Dad was demoted in his role of bookkeeper for the church, as I was his daughter. My nephew rang, full of apologies. Cilleen rang to inform me, 'we are no longer related, *my* father no longer wishes to call you his daughter.' Not again! I gave up. Let them stew in their own juices, I was over it. It's fascinating how a so called 'Christian' environment can be so toxic. If I had known that the insidious unwinding of a happy home would begin with the next phone call, I would not have answered it.

Not for the first time, my eldest daughter asked to visit us. Larry was reluctant as he didn't want her influence for our two girls. For my sake, he agreed she could 'pop in' for lunch, our girls were thrilled to meet her. I had never been secretive about their siblings, I wanted my family to be 'whole' as much as every mother does. I had left them all playing a card game inside the house. It was a beautiful day and I was hanging out washing, when I heard my husband yelling. He never yelled. I saw my eldest running down the driveway, getting into a car that her father was driving. When I asked what happened, Larry replied, 'I heard her tell our two girls that *her* Daddy still loves Mummy.'

Two days later, as I opened the curtains of the lounge room windows, greeting another sun filled beautiful day, I saw my ex-husband sitting in his car on the roadside staring up at me. My blood went cold. I immediately locked all the doors. Our two girls were eating their breakfast, both ready to go to school. Memories from my old life of violence and heartbreak reared their ugly head once more. I rang the police. There was nothing they could do, it was a public road. He could pull over where or when he liked. I rang Larry's workshop; he was out on deliveries. I put the two girls in my car, drove them to school. My hands were shaking all day, my concentration gone. The bell rang for home time and I stayed back. I decided to talk to the principal about my situation. She was shocked at my story, even though she lived in a town over an hour away, she insisted on following me home in her car to make sure he had not entered the house. Everything was as it should be, she offered to stay with me until Larry's truck headlights shone down our driveway. As I cooked dinner, I informed him of the visitor we'd had that morning. He didn't say much, as I was helping our two young ones into their beds. He made a phone call, informing me once his conversation had finished, 'We would not be bothered again.' When I questioned him, his reply was, 'Cassie, I still have friends that live close to that family, so believe me when I say, 'He won't bother us again.'

CHAPTER 9

My confidence went to zero as self-condemning thoughts plagued me twenty-four hours a day. I had trusted my eldest daughter because I wanted my family to be whole once more, look how that had turned out. My thoughts wandered to Cilleen. Perhaps she was right, maybe I was not the positive/confident person I claimed to be. My thoughts questioned why my folks had more or less, put me aside, then married me off. *What if Larry's family was right – I really was the gormless idiot they saw?* I soon found it hard to get out of bed or find beauty in the world. I knew I had to act before it became depression. The doctor's advice was sought, he prescribed a holiday, 'some time out' as he put it. The school found me a young mum of two little ones the same age as our girls, who was willing to board them for a week. Her interview went well, so I hired her for five days with Larry's approval, I was good to go! I had rung an old friend, Carla, who I knew lived in Wellington. She was delighted to have me stay. However, when I boarded the plane instead of feeling excitement I felt really low, knowing I left behind an unhappy husband, and two little ones who did not like me out of their sight.

Kez Wickham St George

The flight to Wellington was wonderful. I was spoilt. The hostesses were very considerate, it had been a long while since anyone had been at *my* beck and call. Within two hours, the plane arrived and I was greeted by Milo, my friend's husband. A huge warm hug enveloped me as we picked up my case from the baggage claim area. I felt a surge of excitement to spend time with Carla again, greeting me with a huge hug. Lamb chops with salad was served for dinner, plus a coffee infused ice cream for dessert. We watched a little TV before I claimed tiredness, but truthfully I wanted to just bury my head in my pillow and cry. I missed my cottage and family, sleep soon overcame any emotions or overthinking.

The explosive argument between Milo and Carla woke me at two o'clock. Barging into my room, they requested me to be their sounding board. By four o'clock, I'd had enough, suggesting we go back to our beds and discuss it in the morning. I slept badly till morning, thank heavens the argument between my hosts seemed to be forgotten. I caught the tram two or three times into the city, each time wanting to explore places I hadn't seen for many years. Carla would escort me, complaining about her marriage every minute of the day. I had many thoughts, the main one was, why do people stay together. when they make each other unhappy.

The time to return home could not come quick enough. A quick hug goodbye with Carla at the airport then I was on the plane, excited to be going home. I was soon sipping my first cup of tea in my own kitchen, noticing how nice everything looked; Larry had even picked wild flowers to greet me. When he asked, 'Do you want the good news or bad news?' My heart sank, *what now*? It seems my professional child carer, had delivered an invoice for the five days of childminding to my husband, the amount was five hundred dollars for five days – double the price I thought we had agreed. I should have asked her to write it down. My husband had packed the girls up on the fourth day asking his mother to stand in for one day. My mother-in-law had had a huge hissy

Jigsaw

fit, complaining about me being an irresponsible mother. Larry had paid what we owed to the childminder, then he informed me he was expecting me to put the money back into our bank account.

However, the universe had not finished moulding me, not yet.

What I did not see was that when you keep giving away so much energy to help others, you sorely need to keep some energy aside for yourself. In my mid-thirties this body had borne four children, it had worked like a steam train; it had never let me down. I ate the right food, exercised regularly, cooked, cleaned, looked after my family, worked when there was employment available, yet deep down in my deepest core, something was missing. The tiredness returned with a rush. It was not just the fact I kept forgetting to take some time out for myself. It went deeper, so I sourced a local herbalist, her examination proving I was not physically exhausted, it was my adrenal system on the verge of collapse. My energy, mentally and emotionally, was at an all-time low. Her advice, 'If you can, you need to take some time for you.' I knew she was right. A small voice whispered, 'They can't call you a failure if you work hard enough.' Unfortunately, the primary school did not need my services, so the house was cleaned like never before.

I had to prove the only way I knew how that I was neither stupid, nor a failure. First, I sanded then washed every single outdoor board up to the roof, I primed it then painted the outside of our cottage. I cleaned the gutters, mowed the lawns, clipped trees and bushes, cleaned the inside of the two tin water tanks. One month later, while buying my weekly shopping, I had an idea. I would approach the local motel to ask if they needed a cleaner. The motel hired me immediately, all the hours I wanted to work were mine. Once more I joined the mice on the treadmill; eat, sleep, look after family, work then repeat. The more money I earned meant life was better for everyone. No more outstanding bills.

Larry was over the moon. We now had a little amount of savings in the bank with a very small mortgage. I worked until all I saw was fog. I had been getting severe headaches, my lower back hurt every day, but I put one foot in foot in front of the other. Finally after many months of the stress, the one feeling that had sat in my heart for a while, began to scream at me – *If this is my life, I don't want to be here anymore.* I battled any thought of asking for time off from the busyness of my life, always feeling I was never good enough. I craved for Larry and his family to respect me. At night I prayed for it all to end. The doctor prescribed sleeping pills. Yes, they knocked me out, but it didn't help. Every morning, I would wake, go onto auto pilot; look after our girls and my son, plus Larry. Work at the motel, clean house, cook. I made sure our house along with the large veggie garden was perfect, so Larry wouldn't have to work on the weekends. I focused on what my family needed, wanted and asked for.

Work at the motel grew busy, I was called in every day to work from 10am to 2pm. When it was public/school holidays I was allowed to take my girls with me and the motel owners, being childless, loved having them around. Every day I worked, she would plan something for morning tea or lunch for the girls. She played children's videos, sitting with them, enjoying the movie as much as the girls did. They loved going there. On the days I was not needed at work, the girls would ask repeatedly to go and see them. I became uncomfortable with the relationship beginning to occur, deciding it was time to leave. Applying to the local council, I was offered employment as a campground cleaner. It was weekends only, so Larry would have the girls while I worked. Though the wages were great, the hours were brutal, starting at 4am in one camp then 7am in the other. Some days the tiredness in my body was completely overwhelming. I would be up predawn to clock in by 4am. For four months I worked, cleaning up after some 'very grotty' people, who did not seem to understand to defecate in the shower or a

Jigsaw

bathroom floor was against the law, until one day as I drove to work in the predawn, I woke to the bellowing of horns. I had fallen asleep at the wheel barely missing an oncoming truck. The sleeping pills had not worn off. The police/ambulance was called.

CHAPTER 10

When I woke up in hospital, strapped to a bed, all I could see was anger in Larry's eyes. He still didn't understand how overwhelmed I was, my entire body saying, 'no more.'

I was so over being a Mum, a wife, a worker, cleaner, cook, nurse, taxi, councillor, with little reward, life seemed pointless. Life for me at that point was just too hard, constantly trying to find money to pay the next bill and keep everyone in my family circle happy. The nurse who had bought me a hot cup of cocoa with biscuits encouraged me to talk to a professional counsellor. How do you explain to a stranger you are over life. I was too drugged to cry but I knew I had to sort it out before it all became too much. Being a peacemaker/worker had been implanted in my DNA since I was in the womb, no matter the cost of my own emotional and mental wellbeing. I was released under strict instructions to seek mental health care.

As Larry drove me home, not one word was exchanged between us. In the past any argument was met with silence or him walking out. I was happy to sit there in silence, the hum of the car wheels hypnotic, me trying to push all the negatives away, bring in the positives. I knew Larry would not be at all happy when he heard what I had decided. I was not going back to work until I figured out what I wanted to do with my life.

I was slowly figuring out for myself that we could not continue as we were. I was closer to forty, with no training in anything except cleaning and motherhood. To date, all I had achieved was a feeling that I did not belong, no how much I tried to fit in and be accepted. When asked for my opinion I was called blunt, rude, even cruel. My achievements to date equalled two older unhappy kids who preferred to live with their father. I finally understood why; they did not like Larry. The feeling was mutual. Although to give him credit, he tried. I knew I had lost them to their father's lifestyle, it crushed my heart to acknowledge this, however I could not change it.

It was back to the drawing board, making an appointment with my neighbour and friend Collette. The sun was warming her office as she read the hospital report and lifted an eyebrow. She looked at me asking, 'Why?' My answer was, 'I can't do what I'm doing every day without knowing there's more out there for me than cleaning up for other people every day. I'm always defending everything I say or do, with no support, no uplifting conversations. I want to learn how to work smart not hard. I want to find what's out there for me and who I am. Surely, this can't be all there is? 'You already know the answers, Cassie.' She was right, as I spoke they popped up like corks, what I wanted was to be loved, appreciated for myself not for what my wages might bring in. I had wanted to give my kids a smart Dad, a good family home to help them grow into engaging, responsible adults. I had thought that marrying into this well-to-do family would allow me to relax, study, be involved in intelligent conversations. It seems my expectations of them were misread, this family was not interested in my growth, all they wanted was for their son to be happy.

Collette, always the patient one, explained one simple rule of life; 'Cassie, working without reward, will eventually cause emotional harm. If you don't enjoy your life, or do something you love to do, you *will* wonder what it's all about. You prayed for a marriage you would do well in, right?' I nodded as she added, 'well, you have a healthy family, a man who is loyal and a lovely home that you prayed for. Some would say you live in abundance. It's not about the money or who likes you, it's about recognising what you have, look at the opportunities. Use this time to study, dance or do whatever you want. Forget about the people you crave respect from, are they really worth your time?' She took a deep breath. 'Yes, life is going to give you mountains to climb on the way to finding your purpose or your mission in life, but, Cassie, think of the joy you will feel as you climb to the top, then cry out, 'What's next?' I really feel you haven't seen what life is showing you. Learn who you are learn to recognise your own beautiful spirit.'

She then advised me that if my older children were really happy where they were, to let them go. She was the second person to advise this, so what was I missing by insisting my boy live with us. Looking from a different perspective, if he was truly happy with his family then why was I standing in the way of him feeling he belonged.

As my health improved, walking the beaches, breathing in the warm sea air, my thoughts became more positive, it showed. My home was filled with a happiness I hadn't felt in a very long time. A flower garden appeared, pots of flowers bloomed all around the cottage, the girls and I made hanging seashell windchimes, my mind became settled. I sang, danced, played with them, we built a swing in the back yard. I began attending sewing classes, as well as knitting. A friend lent me a spinning wheel, I learnt how to card wool, spin and weave, and loved every moment I was at the wheel. I spent time journalling. My neighbours began to ask what I was 'on' and why I was so happy. I pointed them Collette's way. The one thing that did not change was my constant migraines. Memories of Mum and her fainting with migraines haunted me. My mantra became, 'I am not my mother.' The doctor and I looking for a solution, the prescribed painkillers made me sleepy or nauseous. Finally, he ordered scans of my spine, bingo, the curvature in my upper spine was causing pressure in C1 /C2 in my neck.

I had three options: 1. For them to operate, placing metal rods into my spine. 2. Massage, physiotherapy. Or 3. Take an addictive painkiller that contained opium. I first went for the painkillers, but they affected my liver function, so I threw them out. I then tried massage with physiotherapy. It was in the physiotherapist's office that I learnt about the healing oils, the power of crystals and kinesiology. She used a pendulum over my body and it directed her to where I needed attention. She also used reiki. It was so wonderful, I felt like I had found a home. She was willing to teach me, and I was a willing student.

Once I had stopped the driving force of 'work till you drop,' the blinkers fell off, I became a student of life. The local library was a mine of information on personal growth. I remembered the doctor's suggestion about marriage guidance, so I enrolled into a marital guidance course run by the Salvation Army. The meetings were in the city, as I enjoyed the written exercises, I could study at home. I decided to enrol in a diploma as a couples counsellor. it just felt right to be working with couples, especially women. I began to dream of running my own health business including workshops.

However, to succeed in the diploma I still needed to work on *me*. That meant I had to have a mentor, who else would I choose but Collette.

Soon our notebooks were full of handwriting on the benefits of counselling. It was in one of these mentoring sessions I learnt some important lessons. I had been taught all my life, by my folks, by their faith plus watching my aunts uncles, cousins and friends, that women expected to be 'roughed up a bit.' They were also taught to remain silent, accepting it when confronted with abuse. Church dogma also came into it. I believed I was unworthy, as *complete obedience* was drilled deeply into my core. I awoke to the knowledge that *I was not responsible for other's insecurities or their actions.* I had two children to love, to guide with my refreshed outlook in life and that was all I was responsible for. I started a vision board – Larry calling it 'mumbo jumbo.' My first handwritten sentence pinned to the board was, *one small step after another.* My husband was not a willing convert to my new-found awareness. His downtime was fishing. He had discovered a small beach, the only way to get to it was by boat. He also designed a scuba board that could be held on to as you skimmed above the water, or you went under water when it was aimed downwards. As a family, we spent hours at the beach. Larry taught us how to snorkel, he took our two toddlers out on a donut ring, driving the boat very slowly in the shallows. We all became golden with the sunshine, growing lean, glowing with health. Often we would end up having dinner on the beach.

   I taught our girls how to dig for pipis, a local shell fish, their Daddy would dive for a crayfish or two. A fire would be lit as we ate our seafood dinner, both little ones wrapped in warm towels, falling asleep on the journey home. Once or twice, we took a pop-up tent to spend the night there. As the girls slept soundly in the tent, Larry taught me how to read the stars, showing me how the old seafarers found their way home. Our lovemaking was more intense under a moonlit sky as the ocean quietly lapped the shore. When I look back with a heart full of gratefulness, I call them our halcyon days. If only time had stood still, allowing us to live in some sort of time warp, happy and healthy forever.

   It was the beginning of what promised to be a glorious summer. Everything was as it should be. The veggie garden/fruit trees were producing an amazing abundance of produce, the air was clear and pure,

Jigsaw

Christmas was a month away. All my studying had come to a halt, I felt at a loss for a while, busying myself with hobbies, enjoying teaching my two youngest that making their own gifts cards was much better than shop bought. By Christmas we had my son plus our two nephews staying. Then on Christmas Eve, Dad showed up with his new fiancée Mavreen, a little part of me cried, 'She's not my Mum.' But the adult in me emerged and I gave her a hug, welcoming her into my home. Dad announced they would be staying for two or three days.

Christmas day arrived, the kids ripped into their gifts while Dad and his fiancée sipped their way through a bottle of sherry, both passing out on the couch before Christmas dinner, as all good members of this particular cult do. The cries of joy from the boys and girls, the noise of packing up boxes and xmas paper, or the making of a Christmas dinner did not wake my Dad and his fiancée. When I was woken the next morning by strange noises, I discovered Mavreen and Dad were busy making out on the pull-out couch in the sitting room. She was on top of him rocking back and forth, her head thrown back, calling out his name.

I was shocked. I was no longer the little girl who obeyed him. I found their behaviour insulting, asking them to leave. Dad knew why, with his grandchildren in the next room, what were they thinking? Dad was a respected pillar of the church. Yet here he was acting like a horny teenager. How bloody rude. Well, it was not happening in my home.

Maybe I was overreacting or being judgmental, but it hurt to see him slobbering over a stranger. Larry was also upset once I had explained why I asked them to leave. They did as I requested, Larry driving them to a local bus depot. I did not expect, nor did I receive an apology from Carla and Milo. I also knew our two nephews would be reporting this to their parents. I could have asked that it be kept between us, it was my Dad who taught me to 'be responsible for your actions' that 'every action has a consequence.' I felt it was time he listened to his own advice.

The days ticked over nicely with everyone doing their own thing, but again, it was the calm before the storm, as they say. We were having a beautiful summer. The family was down by the estuary, swimming or fishing every day. My two nephews stayed for an extra week. My son had already left to live with his family up north. All too soon, Larry was back at work, the girls were in school. I was looking at more study, not only in couple counselling, I was leaning towards the metaphysical side of life. Everything had settled back into a routine, the house was peaceful. I enjoyed some me time, when Larry began to show signs of being fed up with his job. He said he wanted change, one suggestion was that we sell up, move back into the suburbs. My gut turned over at the thought of it, to be fair to Larry I mulled it over for a week or two, my gut saying no! However, Larry was persistent that he needed change. His Christmas gift from our family had been a scuba diver's course, he fell in love with it. He joined clubs, he began to spend his weekends away with groups of divers. More diving equipment was purchased, then a small boat was required.

CHAPTER 11

Larry was insistent, we should sell up and move on, he had begun to advertise the trucking business for sale. He began talking about a diving business he knew was up for sale. I insisted we check it out with an accountant first. The accountant advised us the business was not looking healthy, but with some hard work it might pay off. I was against it, but Larry's attitude was 'I want it, so I'm buying it.' The man I lived with was now grumpy, impatient, unkind in many ways. I felt alone, the new self-confidence that bloomed inside me began to wilt under his demands. He now spent most of his time at his parents' house, or with a new group of commercial divers he had met in the city. When Larry was home, it was uncomfortable. Both our girls were growing fast, the eldest was being bullied at school; we now had one very unhappy little girl. I went to the school to see if we could do something, but all she wanted to do was stay with her Mummy. Around this time our youngest became very ill, diagnosed with chronic asthma, requiring many hospital visits over the next few months.

My decision to sell up and move was not for Larry's ego or his demands, it was that the hospital was an hour's drive away, sometimes two in busy traffic, which could have proved fatal for our youngest. So, I made a decision that our little one's health was too important to ignore. I put the house on the market, Larry became enthused about where we could live next. What he did not seem to understand was Stillwater was MY home that I had manifested. I had fought long and hard to get there. When the 'For Sale' sign went up, my hands were itching to tear it down.

The truck business sold first. I thought we might add another room to the cottage to help it sell, but the mother-in-law who knew everything we did or said via her son, asked for us to repay immediately what Larry had borrowed for truck repairs. So there was nothing left from the sale of the business. The extent of what he had borrowed shocked me, Larry was adamant I knew everything, I knew differently. It took close to two years to sell our home, we had subdivided our large block of land, the top section with the old elm tree on it was the first to sell.

Our new neighbour made us an offer over the asking price and I don't think the ink was dry on the papers when his bulldozer ripped out the tree where Mum and I had mended our hearts, or where our family loved to picnic. A new A-framed home was to be built on the soil where I thought L would build our forever home. My heart hurt when I saw the huge carnage caused by one small machine. That left our small cottage for sale. I looked at it with love every time I drove into the driveway. All Larry could see was a run-down cottage badly in need of renovating. A young family made an offer and we accepted and sold. We now had a large amount of money, Larry immediately buying the dive business he hoped would make us wealthy. Then a phone call from my mother-in-law, 'Pay me what you owe on the mortgage.' This time I had words with my husband, he was not to relay anything that happened in the house or any other home. We paid the amount owed, seaside cottages sold for a high price even back then, and it still left us with a healthy amount.

Jigsaw

Gratefully placing this large amount of money we now had into the accountant's hands was a relief, as I was very aware after many years of marriage my husband and I did not agree on my budgeting.

Now we were totally debt free, it was a fabulous feeling. Around the same time I was invited to finish off my marriage guidance counselling diploma. We had found a family home to rent in a quiet cul-de-sac; a pretty house with fairly large grounds for our family, plus our assortment of animals . I enrolled the girls into a local school, our youngest making friends easily, our eldest not so much. The owner of this rental house was becoming a problem. It was obvious she didn't understand the rules of renting. She would appear at any time, so in my own way whether she considered it blunt, rude, she was asked to stay away unless there was permission or an agreement given to her to be on the property. Her attitude was shocking, however it worked, we did not see her for quite a while after that.

I was so excited when the letter arrived from the head office of the Salvation Army. I had spent over a year studying for my diploma, not missing one meeting with Collette or in the city chapel. Larry had agreed to me taking the four hundred dollars out of the bank, to pay for the counselling retreat with three night's accommodation. There were two days of classes, we were in two groups of five, it deeply challenged our personal belief systems. I had already learnt a lot about other aspects of emotional upheavals in marriages, I loved it. I was on fire. Day three, diploma day arrived. Our families had been invited to attend the graduation evening. I peeped into the dining room as I went to my last class of the day, the dining room looked like a Hollywood production. I was so excited I was going to be a professional marriage guidance councillor. I was going to receive a diploma, my first educational recognition ever.

Ten of us sat in a semicircle, for the last day of the class, it was a debate on abortion. I was the first up to take the lead, to give my stance on abortion. I knew my topic, I knew my answer was from the heart. I explained, 'I would want to be advised on the mother's physical and emotional health first, then ask the people involved to seek a mental health counsellor's advice.'

I added that, 'Sometimes this decision is caused by fear of the unknown, that there are birthing clinics with trained midwives who were more in touch with the spiritual side of birth, who could help with such a difficult decision.' Ending my speech with, 'I would be guided by the mother's medical team, plus the parent's choice.'

After the class, I had lunch with my other excited colleagues. I went to pack my case, shower, sort out my party dress and shoes for the dinner. Larry arrived looking handsome, both our girls were dressed in pretty dresses; they looked so cute. We were all very excited about the party. As I zipped up my overnight bag, the phone in my room rang. It was the Salvation Army board of directors asking me to attend a meeting, *immediately*, in the study room. Larry asked if everything was okay, I admitted I had no idea. Perhaps there was something I hadn't signed. 'Wish me luck,' I whispered as I kissed his cheek. 'Meet me in the dining room in half an hour.'

My excitement was soon extinguished when I was met by three very grim male faces, who informed me I would not be receiving my diploma after all. In fact, I was to vacate the premises straight away, any re-application for the diploma would not be accepted. I was, of course, devastated. They explained they had a complaint from another student. She felt I was too smug about my opinion on abortions. She had found me too lighthearted about a serious topic, which could be life-changing for any woman. If I received my diploma that night, she would seek legal advice to have me dismissed. I stood there stunned, my mouth open and shutting, wanting the ground to swallow me up. As I began to protest, one of the older men spoke; 'Our view on this matter is closed. A serious

Jigsaw

complaint has been issued against you. We have considered this properly, and a formal letter of dismissal will be sent to you in the near future. Please vacate the premises immediately.'

Walking to the dining room, I felt completely numb. *How? Who? Why?* Larry saw me in the door he became alarmed at my pale face. 'What's wrong Cassie? Is your dad okay?' I nodded. I watched my two little girls as they joined another family, playing with balloons scattered around the dance floor. Larry grabbed a seat, pushing me into it. Sloshing water into a glass, he wet a napkin placing it on the back of my neck, waiting for me to speak. 'I failed Larry. I'm not getting my diploma. I've been asked to leave.' He didn't say anything, just grabbed the girls, pushed us all outside towards our car. I still couldn't believe what had just happened. Larry was furious, 'Look around you, hun. It's all about the jet set, the posh club. We're just not rich enough. I knew it was all too good to be true.'

CHAPTER 12

I kept the tears inside until the girls were in bed. Then, I sobbed until I vomited. No amount of Larry's comforting helped. Without adding any drama, I repeated word for word what had been said. As I repeated each word back to Larry, I felt all my hopes disappear for a future in helping women and or couples, my new found confidence melting away. The letter arrived, the reason given not much more than what had already been said on the night I was asked to leave. I considered taking it to a lawyer, although I knew no amount of fixing this would delete how they had made me feel. I found distrust in my own words once more, becoming a silent onlooker, speaking only when questioned or spoken to.

My belief that life was full of lessons was obviously warped. Where was the lesson in this? I had failed once more. Unbeknown to me, Collette had argued my case. She was disgusted by their reply, they felt I was not a confident student. When she told me what she had done, I was grateful. When she said, 'The problem is not you, Cassie. It is because abortion is a law made by friggin' men, who would not know what an abortion is.'

Jigsaw

It did not make any difference to my situation, although I felt she was correct. Where to now, Cassie?'

The stocks and bonds the accountant invested for us grew until we had more than enough to buy another home. The dive business, though doing okay, was not quite paying its way. The bills began mounting up for boat repairs plus diving gear. Larry suggested that we take some money from our investments to help. The accountant strongly advised against it. He told us, 'If we waited for two more years, the way the stocks are going, money won't be a problem.' We would be mortgage free. I saw relief sweep across Larry's face, I also felt we had done the right thing. For the short-term, though we were not coping financially, Larry suggested I find work.

I found a job as a cashier in Woolworths. It wasn't me, however I was grateful as the wages filled the cupboards, paid school fees, outings and paid for the little things every family needs; dentist, doctor, school books, uniforms, and so on. My work was mind-numbing. Larry was totally invested in his business, he had become president of the local dive club. He was now giving public talks on diving and water safety around the North Island.

He was invited to be the safety diver for a major film company. Two movies were being made in the Hauraki Gulf – *Hercules* and *Xena Warrior Princess*. Larry was the man in charge of safety for the actors, he was the one to go to for any safety rules, laws etc. After all, he had assisted in writing up the safety rules so why not employ the expert in his field? Every day I would make his bookings or fill out his diary with bookings on the answer phone. He was busy and popular – he loved it. Our two youngest filled their lives with clubs, friends.

Me? Well, since I hadn't received my marriage guidance diploma, I had a huge empty spot inside that I didn't know what to do with. I developed the spiritual side of my life, completing a course on the healing power of crystals, receiving a diploma. I then joined night school, learning energy healing with reiki. I received a diploma to say I was a qualified in reiki, still it wasn't enough. I joined a long-distance correspondence school on the healing powers of oils, completed another course on foot and hand massage. This was a year of part-time studying. When I received my gold-edged, red-ribboned diploma as a therapist, I was thrilled. Attending classes on crystal scribing, on meditation, I learnt the art of Indian head massage. I was recognised for my skills and knowledge, receiving invites to give talks in some very popular venues, to large groups, with well-known healers. But public speaking was not for me. For some reason, with all my studying I had not uncovered why, when giving a public talk, I would lose my voice. I had tried, but after ten minutes I could no longer speak, often having to leave the stage with a coughing fit. It had proven too embarrassing, so I declined.

A metaphysical college in the USA wrote, offering me a place studying quantum physics. I received honours with my diploma, I was offered a position as a correspondence tutor. I was thrilled, I very much wanted to accept, but that whisper entered my head; *your opinion is not worth it.* That was the crux of the problem. I had been told this many times by those I loved, those I had worked for and those I had trusted. It had sunk so very deeply into my core. So where did I fit in? Who would listen to me if I did not believe in myself?

Yet I also knew, deep down, that I could not escape public speaking if I was to become the person I saw in my dreams, professional, confident, respected. Speaking on the phone was okay, if I wrote a thesis or manuscript, the words flowed. With all my studies of spiritual healing over the years, I had prayed for the answer. When would I be able to stand in front of an audience to guide and speak as an authority with all the knowledge I had accrued over the years? The answer at the time was, 'I would rather eat glass.'

Jigsaw

When my niece invited me to accompany her to Fiji for her twenty-first celebration, I was delighted to accept. With Larry now doing well in his business, I decided the girls and house were all his for two weeks. It would give me a well-earned break. Just before I left, I had seen a small advert in the local paper; a four-bedroom cottage on two acres, with four milking goats, two beehives, a small orchard with a variety fruit trees, plus two small guest rooms on the property. My heart warmed to the idea that blossomed. Perhaps I could have that passive income, my dream of a country home, workshops, plus a B&B could be realised once more. I circled it, asking Larry to look into it for me while I was away – 'Don't forget the advert, Larry, please,' were my very last words before I boarded the plane.

Fiji was so beautiful, but very expensive. My niece had booked us onto an island. I toured wherever the charters were going, spent half a day in the hotels dugout canoe. The men rowing were chanting as we dipped and swayed in the challenging massive waves, which was scary, breathtaking and exhilarating at the same time. I explored two or three islands. I was served with whatever I desired, being a non-drinker, the bar staff made me glorious fresh fruit cocktails every day. I was massaged daily, I swum daily, once or twice taking a dip in the pool at night, generally I felt spoilt. My niece? Well, from the quiet little mouse I thought I knew, I was suddenly holidaying with Miss Party Pants.

The available men, some not so available, were paraded before me, the tell-tale sign of a removed wedding ring did not seem to faze her. I kept thinking of the demure Christian niece I knew in Auckland. It was like she had thrown off her everyday mask along with her panties. She was determined to have a good time. I minded my own business had my ten-day restful fun holiday, quite happy to go home when the time came.

Once through customs in Auckland, I searched the crowd for Larry's face. He just stood there, not a smile or a wave. His face looked grey;

his eyes were red-rimmed, my first thought was that someone had died. The drive home was silent, my niece and I wondering what the hell had happened. We dropped her off at her place. Once we were home, Larry told me of the stock market crash while I was away on holiday. We had lost everything.

He showed me what we still owned; a fifty dollar share in the pine forestry. We had lost it all; many thousands of dollars, the very day I had boarded the plane to Fiji. What can you do, but accept it? I put my arms around him, asking him to see what we had; our health, two great kids. We could start over – *we were both young enough, surely?*

It gutted him. He became morose, not flinching when we were told the news of our accountant committing suicide. Friends began to tell us they had lost their farms, businesses, cars and homes. We read about hundreds of suicides. People had invested in the good times they had not prepared for the bad. New Zealand was in a financial mess. The life I had once dreamed of was slowly falling apart. Larry's depression became insidious.

It crept into every corner, attaching itself to our lives in so many ways. It took a while for our loss to completely sink in, that is until I found the small advert of the two-acre holding, including B&B with goats etc. stuck in between the phone directory pages. As it fluttered to the floor, I saw the blue circle I had put around it. If only we had bought it outright when we could. It was then that I released the tears of what might have been. My dream of owning my own studio, teaching massage and oils, plus a cabin or two would have been perfect. I could have held seminars. I had dreamt of teaching my two girls about farm life. It had all gone, I became overwhelmed by another dream smashed to pieces.

CHAPTER 13

It took five years trying to hold it together, both of us discovering strengths we did not know we had. Many homes were rented, Larry repeating the same story like a record, 'we can't afford the rent.' I had insisted on staying in the same area for our girls to continue their friendships at school while they grew up, but I was aware we could not live in the suburbs another month. There was no reason to stay in the suburbs any longer. My son now lived in Australia, I'd been informed I was now a grandmother. My eldest daughter, who still lived with her father, she had given birth to a daughter.

I had just turned forty, I felt like life was just about head down, bum up. There was no other way to live. When attending a tarot card party, my cards were read. 'You're moving, to a beach,' the reader said, 'it's a tall yellow house, with palm trees growing each side of the front door. It awaits your love and attention.' She was not wrong, two weeks later our rental contact in the suburbs was terminated, the housing agent giving us two homes to look at.

One was in the country, the other by the beach. We liked the house in the country. It was a sweet little, aged cottage, but just a little too run down for a family of four. As we drove up to check out the house by the beach in Tindal's Bay, all I could see was old seaside shacks, then, as we turned the corner, there stood a two-story yellow house with two palm trees each side of the front door. The ocean was across the road.

Perfect, we signed the papers, paid the deposit, were given the keys to five years of beach living where our two girls made deep lasting friendships. Larry also loved it. With his knowledge of the ocean, its currents, boats of all shapes and sizes, he was soon employed by the local council as harbour master for the local bays.

It was in this small seaside village, I was given a challenge. A friend asked me why I was I not doing anything with my life. I replied that I felt like I was waiting for a door to open. But her comment made me ponder. In the local paper I read adult student classes at the local high school were being held, with enrolments in ten days. Two of the classes available were English Literature plus a Creative Arts class. I rang enrolling immediately, spending the following year studying. I was so proud when I passed with honours. I loved the academic side of life. I then enrolled again for the following year in Creative Arts, studying art, philosophy, psychology, mental wellbeing.

My English Literacy tutor, Diana White, was a godsend. We just 'clicked', she soon had me writing short stories to enter into competitions, magazines and newspapers. She grew a love of creative writing in my heart that I never knew I had. I will be eternally grateful for the creative soul she saw in me, begging to be set free. We would often sit together after class to discuss how we saw the world. I had a deep spiritual belief Diana was more logical. We both enjoyed each other's company, not friends exactly, but comrades, two opposites that agreed to hear each other's point of view.

For various reasons, Larry and I still struggled to pay rent, moving once more. However this proved to be life-changing, moving into to a lovely house that we made our home for the next nine years. I loved every minute of it. This home was beautiful; French doors in our room and the lounge would open up wide to a panoramic view of the Pacific Ocean. A balcony wrapped itself around the house, life consisted of teenage barbeques, my two girls regularly bringing their friends over. It was during this time that my brother-in-law passed away. He was the youngest in the family, Larry was filled with grief. My girls were unsure of what to do, missing their kind uncle, so I made sure we grieved for him as a family. Not left to wonder about the grief filled vacancy he had left in our lives, working through it together. Cilleen also came back into my life, now a different person. Her phone call to me began with uncertainty, both of us unsure how to speak to each other, but finally she told me she had been diagnosed with grade four cervical cancer. I began to cry with her, a small healing began. So many years had been wasted disliking each other, when we could have accepted our differences.

It was, in this home, I began a journey I had never thought possible. With the certificates in English literature creative arts, I applied for a position advertised for a tutor with an ESOL (English as a second language) company. Diana had seen it first, saying, 'This is so you, Cassie.'

For three years, every four months, a group of fifteen young Asian students would arrive, starry-eyed at the wonders of New Zealand. We would begin with vowels and consonants, the class would be in hysterics when a certain letter was mis-pronounced. We had days attending other schools to take part in singing or dancing, we would take day trips to farms, plus an overnight trip to Rotorua or lake Taupo.

I loved this job with a passion, making deep and lasting friendships with students and host families. At the farewell ceremonies, host families students and tutors would be in tears. During the Christmas holidays, a group of ten senior Asian students would arrive for art and craft classes.

Kez Wickham St George

We toured the many artisans throughout Auckland's city and countryside. My enthusiasm for ESOL classes was noticed. I was honoured by the Japanese Ambassador to New Zealand at a small ceremony. He then visited my home, to personally thank me for my work with the people of his country. Unfortunately, the position ended when the company went bankrupt, but I had loved every moment of my role as a tutor. Up to date I had worn many hats; head tutor, mother, nurse, teacher, journalist, public relations, international tutor, crafts administrator. When lethargy took over my body I thought that what I needed was a good rest – maybe a holiday somewhere quiet. But many tests later, I was diagnosed with fibromyalgia, the percussor to post-polio. It was a slow journey to regain my health. I was only partially in recovery when I needed an urgent hysterectomy. Once I was well enough to consider part-time work again, I found my physical strength was not what it used to

I had been at home for approximately three months when Larry was diagnosed with grade-four bowel cancer. After several operations to cut away the disease, he spent eighteen months recouping from his many operations, the harsh chemotherapy treatment taking its toll on his body. His surgery sites regularly turning into hernias, more than once he had to be cut from breastbone to groin. I have no idea how he managed to get through it all or how he regained his health. It was here I soon learnt the important lesson of teamwork. The medical team, they were truly inspiring, I could not thank them enough. We were in urgent need of money, during his time off work we were made aware of peoples generosity, often a casserole was sent over from friends, or an offer to mow the lawns was given. I figured someone must have been listening to my prayers when I found employment in a local newspaper, as a part-time sales representative.

After six months, even partly subsidised by the government, we were only just getting by, as medical bills were so expensive. Larry was on a

Jigsaw

mix of specific protein food whizzed up with a fruit or veggie puree. We hung in there. The tiredness in my body was always there in the background, I knew something wasn't right, but I didn't have the time to sit to go deeper. When I did find a quiet moment, I would sleep

CHAPTER 14

Larry had been at death's door. We had all been very scared, as any family would be when we were told he only had four weeks to live. I was informed to 'go home to prepare our family for the worst.' I had taken those words literally, trying to make some preparations. However every one's dislike for my actions amazed me – I was called heartless and uncaring. Though no one saw the jittering mess I was. No one heard me cry, and there was nobody to hold me close when I needed help. I smiled while drying our daughters' tears, while listening to their fears. I refused to simply cower in a corner begging for help. The dislike intensified from our youngest when she realised I had arranged everything, including a funeral service.

Why could they not realise that I was doing what every other wife would do? 'One step at a time, Cassie. Don't let any emotions out, till it's all over.' Physically, Larry healed, but his emotional healing was much slower, his attitude towards life the main reason. He had lost his job while he was recouping, so his ego had taken a beating once again. Although he had stopped smoking, his temper was on a hair trigger. When I suggested he

Jigsaw

try counselling for his mood swings, I was told no!

Many months later, I fell on my feet when I was accepted for employment with a New Zealand tourism school. This job meant I was to be trained as a tutor. I soon picked up the pace, I needed daily painkillers including massive amounts of B6 with a vitamin B, swallowed religiously to keep me on my feet. Within a year, I was head tutor with my own department, encouraged to teach my favourite subject of all – self-motivation. Using everything I had learnt from study, I collated the information to teach, it was greedily inhaled by this school, their client success rate went through the roof.

Unfortunately Stan, my employer, was everything I disliked in a person. He was a pompous, obnoxious bully, opinionated in all ways, he did not tolerate discussion. If he said something was right, then it was right. I never knew what sort of mood he would be in. His office door always locked. I added him to the list of unhappy men in my life. *Is it me, or are men generally unhappy?* It was a topic Diane and I had discussed once or twice, always ending in laughter, as she too lived with an unhappy partner. In this position, I had requested that all teaching certificates required be included in the contract. He was agreeable, and also offered me use of the school's vehicle. I received my tutor's certificate, my first aid certificate, plus my minibus license, all within a three-week period. All I had to do was put up with the boss's daily verbal abuse.

Every time he would grumble about the expense, I would practice that valuable lesson of, 'you can't argue with an empty space.' I needed the job, so I stayed. I had a love for learning, I thrived. It was here I was reintroduced to the power of positive thinking; feeling confident plus looking after my mental health was part and parcel of what I taught. I absorbed every word, reading anything I could find related to the topic. I loved philosophy, attending as many off-campus groups as I could. There were pluses to staying with this job, even though the manager was deep into narcissism I had a very nice car to drive around in for two years while I worked there, and an education. It was close to the Christmas break when I was rung with a better employment offer, a higher position as a certified tourism tutor. It seems my reputation as a tourism tutor had been noticed, I jumped at the chance.

My new sun-filled, comfortable office was in the centre of Auckland. My wages were the most I had ever been offered, in my entire working life. Larry was supportive, but insisted, 'that I did not include him in my beliefs of positivity and self-love.' I buried my head in my work. Our oldest daughter had already left home, and our youngest was invited to spend the Christmas holidays with her best friend. Their home was magnificent, their lifestyle one to envy. Larry and I discussed it, agreeing it would be okay. She had her bag packed and picked up within twenty minutes, leaving without a hug or a wave goodbye.

Larry had been offered part-time work through the holidays. I was looking forward to some me time, catch ups with old friends had been planned. I had saved up enough to buy my own car, so invites to meet up were readily accepted. I had six weeks ahead of me to relax, refresh, journal to create some motivational quotes. Christmas came and went. It was peaceful not having to listen to our youngest's temper tantrums. She reminded me of her colic days when she had screamed nonstop. Now she complained constantly, this young one was simply unhappy, extremely bad tempered or as my dad would say it, she had a good dose of dung on the pluck. If I said no to her going out, she would scream abuse, coil up in a fetal position, sob until she had an asthma attack, or bang her head on the wall in her room, resulting in migraines. At first, when she began her tantrums, I would run to her room, trying to soothe her, nothing worked until I agreed she could go out. After several months of trying to calm the situation, I had taken to ignoring it.

Sadly, her relationship with me was fading. She made it obvious she did not want to come home. She loved being with her friends and her parents at party central. I had no idea they encouraged smoking, drinking and drugs. My little girl was just fifteen already addicted to the party life that these two adult morons encouraged. School was about to begin, so I drove to their house to pick her up. She had gone for a walk, or so I was told, they would bring her later. As soon as she arrived, she complained of a headache going to her bed.

I recognised the smell of stale alcohol as I sat on the bottom of her bed in the dark room. The smell of booze was emanating from every pore of her body. She was so pretty, with long blond hair to her waist, green eyes, olive skin, a petite build. I had so many wonderful memories of this little one as a baby, as a toddler, a little girl, just like her big sister, I loved them both. *Why did they want to leave home?* I gave them whatever I could, whenever I could. Larry was a good Dad, not always involved, but he was there for them both. I wanted to pull her into my arms to cuddle her, feel her wriggle into my body her arms go around neck. 'I love you Mummy,' was all I wanted to hear. I missed our times together as a family.

Within those six weeks of holidays, my Dad passed away, he was ninety-five and very ill when he died. My bother-in-law rang to politely issue an invite to the funeral. A private wake was to be held at their home, to that one I was welcome. However I was not permitted to call into the funeral home or the congregation hall to say goodbye. I don't condone hypocrisy and I was very aware this was what it was. Of course, I missed his presence in my life. We had grown apart since he remarried, his wife causing nothing but unrest and dislike. She had asked for money more than once, I had refused each time. The last time I rejected her request, she became abusive, forbidding me to see him again. If I did approach her home, or the rest home he was in, she would have me arrested then escorted off the property. Alone, in my lounge I said goodbye to the man who was a major influence in my life. I lit a candle, placed it by a vase of my garden flowers. I placed a photo of them my parents together, then whispered, 'Safe journey, old man. Thank you for all you have taught me.' I could have sworn he was in the room with me. I caught just a flicker of him standing in the room, then he was gone. I sat and shed a tear for this man who sired me.

When I received a call that Larry's old bowel operation had herniated, it was serious he was in the emergency department in hospital. It felt like someone was saying, *You've had enough peace, you've even had some fun, now time for some reality.* The surgeon phoned to ask for his medical details, saying not to bother visiting as he was heavily sedated after a three-hour surgery. I was in shock. I rang my eldest girl requesting her to stay overnight with me. I've always liked my own company, but this was very different. I felt very much alone.

To my surprise, when I rang her the two girls were together. I asked if they would come home to stay a night or two with me – there was a pregnant pause, my intuition kicked in, it didn't feel good. Knocking on the front door, no one answered, so I went in to find both our daughters stoned. I had never been so angry. All I could think of was all the crap I had taken over the years to keep a roof over their heads.

All the shit I had swallowed from family friends to protect them. All the heartache I had shoved deep inside for what? I had sold precious things I loved to put food on the table to keep them in school. Yes, things had been tough at times, but no matter what I had always been a mum first and last. I had always been there for them, come hell or high water, only to be told, 'You should have a smoke, Mum. Relax.' In my anger all I wanted to say, ' Sure, why not? No one gives a damn. Let's all get pissed, smoke pot.' I guess working at a school with kids who have terrible home lives because of addiction had shown me a thing or two. When I got home, I emptied every ounce of alcohol that was in the house down the sink. There was now

Jigsaw

a strict 'no smoking' policy in my home, but as I emptied the last bottle of alcohol into the sink, I had a crazy urge to light up again, just guzzle back what was left in the bottle. No one actually cared if I was a raging drunk, smoked pot, beat the kids or became unfaithful. The bills would still roll in like clockwork, Larry would still be a grumpy man. I heard my father's voice quite clearly, 'be aware that all actions have consequences. Their life was up to them.

Larry had become unhappy with his employer once more, mentioning he wanted a change. As it happened my son had recently told me he was having amazing success as a boat broker, so when I saw an advert in the local paper for a boat broker, I showed Larry. 'They won't go for me, what do I know?' But he couldn't hide the hope that flared up in his eyes. Now, I was in my field of expertise, along with tourism and motivation, I was experienced in work placement teaching my clients how to write a CV that was creative. As I saw it, Larry had been in the boat business for the past twenty years. What he did not know about boats was minimal. I wrote the email, made sure every word and sentence I used was motivational, promoting his skills. He began his new job two weeks later, his boss admitting his age was against him, but his CV was exceptional.

Larry then wanted a new car to drive potential clients around. I grudgingly handed over my keys, my car being the more modern of the two. His first sale was over the ten grand mark I was gobsmacked. Larry crowed, 'I've made it, Babe.' His computer skills soared, he taught me a thing or two, his attitude was so much better. Life looked promising; he now went to work smiling. Success was in the air between Larry and our two girls I rarely saw them, speaking to me only when I rang them. I often wondered why my life had turned out like it had, four children, a grandchild I did not know. I knew they all rang and spoke to each other regularly. It seemed I did not count. I had to be happy with what I had, I had always done my best. If that was not good enough, then so be it.

CHAPTER 15

Work for me became busy. When my father-in-law suddenly passed away, Larry spent every hour with his mother. Our home became lonely. One night on an urge, I rang a friend I had not seen for some time. We had become friends through our girls being at clubs together. They had left the district, we still occasionally shared a phone call. I asked if I could pop in for the evening to catch up. She was delighted. 'Of course, why not stay over?' The night turned into a weekend as I poured my heart out to my old friend. Her advice was 'to seek God.' I willingly went to church with her, however, I felt drained by their need for me be touched by God, Pentecostal was not for me

If I wanted to be shown God, it came the following week as I left work. It was part of my contract to work late every Friday night. To be honest, it was not such a good thing to do in central Auckland, as by seven o'clock the homeless and addicts had found refuge in the many shop foyers along the main street. It was here I learnt another valuable lesson, that was these people were family. They may not have been blood related, but they had formed a tight relationship looking after one another. I would see a small city of bed rolls or pop up tents emerge as night fell. Locking up the main foyer door to my office, three or four homeless people were already there bickering about who owned what small space. They began begging me for money. I was a little nervous as they pulled at my coat and satchel when I heard, 'Yoo-hoo, darling, want some company?'

Six transvestites walked across the road to surround me. One of them was an ex-student of mine. They were all tall, South Pacific lads, with fluorescent wigs and clothing you could wear on a red carpet runway. Their high heels added to their already six-foot height. All of them were made-up, with sweeping false eyelashes, iridescent eye shadow, bright-red pouting lips, their smiles so beautifully bright. I was escorted to the bus station, a good ten-minute walk away, where the same sight of the homeless fighting amongst each other greeted us. So, these lovely people stayed with me, chatting away like it was a completely normal Friday night. As I stepped onto the bus, my ex-student grabbed hold of my hand: 'Thank you, miss Cassie, your words changed my life.' Who says angels don't send messages through the unexpected. Knowing that somewhere in this madness called life, my words had added value to another's, it was so empowering. It may not have been within my own family, but it was right there in front of me. I had helped another see a brighter side of life. It dawned on me then, that through all the ugliness of life, here was God showing kindness and gratitude in the strangest of places.

The bus had only two young passengers and myself, the ride home quiet. I actually snoozed for a good half hour on the bus, the walk from the bus stop to home took only five minutes. It was velvety dark . When I stood still, I could faintly hear the sound of the waves washing onto the shore. The air was still as I soaked it all in, enjoying the quietness. Looking up at the bright half-moon, I gave thanks that I had been a small part of another's healing. My heart was full in many ways.

Larry had not been home for a few days. He was still staying with his family to help them with his father's probate. There had been many loose ends to tie up with all his father had left behind. Larry had called every day to say hello and informed me that his entire family of siblings had arrived with their partners. I had not been included, nor had Larry invited me to attend, our two girls were invited to attend the funeral. Having no expectations there were no disappointments, at last I was at peace with it all.

Around this time, alarm bells were starting to go off in my head about the education college I was working for. Some things did not add up financially, I decided to leave. Once again, I emailed my CV to other schools, a beauty academy in Auckland rang. I had an interview within two days as they were interested in my skills as a motivation specialist. The interview went well, the job itself was excellent and so were the wages. After three months as a tutor the beauty academy I was invited to a board meeting, I was intrigued. I was questioned on my ethics plus records of any training in the field of wellbeing. A little niggle inside said, 'you're not qualified to teach positivity, look at your family.'

I expected to be dismissed as an imposter, however to my surprise, they invited me to write an instruction manual on the power of self-motivation. If it was approved it would be published under the academy's name, with myself as the author. They were also planning to submit the manual to the New Zealand education board, again, if approved, it would be used as part of the school curriculum. At last, I had been recognised for a skill that I practised and taught daily. Now, I could actually write about it and be published. I was amazed. I floated over to the table, to the three women who ran this school, they held out their hands to me. I was being treated as an equal I signed a new contract then floated out of the office. I was to spend three days at the academy teaching, plus two days at home, writing.

I adored those days, researching deeply into the wellness we create inside us when we practise self-belief. I was manifesting the dream I had journalled two years ago. Excitement coursed through me. I did not know who to tell or where to start. I knew the girls were not interested and Larry was busy with his family, so I rang Grace. She was delighted for me, congratulating me then asking to meet for coffee in town after work one day soon. I wanted everyone to know. I rang two more friends, one saying, 'Well, why not? You are very passionate with this subject, it was bound to happen.' Another saying, 'I'm so proud of you. When you love what you do, the universe rewards you.' My heart glowed with such praise from these women who were fully supportive.

This was a different road for me. I had always written, journalled often joining in many discussions about the power of positivity. When I informed Larry he was not fussed about it all. As long as I was still earning, he was happy. It took six months before I had finally finished my manuscript of one hundred fifty pages, which included exercises for clients to practise. I had it edited plus proofed by Moana, the academy secretary. After all the corrections were made, I went over it with a fine-tooth comb, nothing was to be missed or misinterpreted. She also assisted in formatting before printing. I loved the direct communication that went on between us.

Once I was happy with the outcome, an appointment was made to deliver my finished manuscript. I was so excited. My hands shook as I delivered a copy to each board member. They flipped through a few pages saying they would get back to me once they had read it completely. It had not entered my head that this could turn sour, I'd been having too much fun. It took two weeks before I was notified that the board wanted to meet with me. Huge grins and congratulations were offered, it was a big thumbs up from the academy and the education department.

They put on an afternoon tea for me, placing the finished, beautifully, polished book in my hands. It looked amazing. I was so proud, soon signing copies as they were passed to me, my face ached with happiness. Then I realised my personal logo had been replaced with the academy logo. My name had been taken off the front cover replaced with theirs. I searched for my name, finding it under a long list of the many departments coordinators of the academy, and the board members. *Why would they do this?* Moana took my hand saying, 'Congratulations, Cassie, you did it. Wow! You're an author of a tutorial book that will be used far wide. You should be very proud.' The head of the academy board came forward to shake my hand. 'We are so proud of you what this book will do for our clients. Your strength as an author is powerful. Thank you.' My hand was pumped by so many in that room my name mentioned as an author/tutor so many times, so why did I feel deflated? I should have been revelling in the praise but something was missing. Was my ego bruised because my logo wasn't there or because I had been listed in the book under a long list of names. That afternoon, I met Grace for our catch up. As I slowly walked to the open-air café, it came to me. I was waiting for the other shoe to fall, memories of being expelled from the marriage counselling school had gone deep. I was expecting a big 'but' from the beauty academy, there had been none. I was being celebrated, what a difference it made.

Grace stood up as I approached, 'I've already ordered,' she said, she knew I loved a pot of English breakfast tea. It was one of those days when the warm sun filtered through the leaves of the old elm trees. The air was warm, the city quiet for this time of day. She enquired about my day, I was about to tell her when she said quickly, 'I have to tell you something. I wanted to before, but …' I stopped drinking my tea carefully placing the cup back in its sauce, saying, 'Is it about Larry?' She nodded lowering her eyes. 'I'm so sorry. My marriage was in a mess and when Larry worked for us, he would listen to my worries. He was a dependable shoulder to cry on. Then I got to know you better, well, I couldn't do it.' 'Do what?' I asked. 'Did you have an affair?' 'No,' she replied, 'We shared our worries, he would often pat me on my shoulder. He was always sympathetic but that was it. Honestly, Cassie, he's a good man your Larry. I gave him so many opportunities. He was either blind to my flirtations or he's one of the good guys.'

I had a desire to empty the pot of tea over her head. I walked away. What really hurt most was that Larry had never been interested in any of my concerns. He had often accused me of being a drama queen, meeting my questions about most things with anger. It also made me wonder if that was why our daughters were so callous and rude. They had seen that Larry had never shown me any real attention, so they had followed suit. My brain hurt, my heart hurt; everything was too hard to figure out.

I sat on the front porch watching the sunset its long red gold fingers peeking through the two large ferns I had growing there. Those ferns were a present my girls had bought me for my forty-fifth birthday. I remembered the fun we had potting them. As I sat there, Harry and Fred as they had been named, were now overflowing the huge pots, their fronds gracing the wooden boards. They were so beautiful, both in competition for the deepest colour of green. Lilly, the biggest of peace lilies, complimented the ferns with the purest of white flowers. When Larry found her, she had been on the second shelf at the garden centre. Larry was not an emotional man, so when he gave Lilly to me saying, 'I just knew she would be happy with you,' I was touched. Lilly, like the ferns, had grown to be stunning with some tender loving care. My eyes strayed to another large pot, where there grew another rescue plant.

Two years before, Larry had been working across the road from a hundred-year-old church, which was being demolished. When he told me about it, we had both felt sad. The history of the once-busy early 1900s village was being destroyed, and Larry and I were both looking for some way to preserve the memory of the old broken-down church. Sadly, the council had their way before we could do anything. The ancient gardener asked Larry to take home the hundred-year-old rose bush that was in the church grounds. I was honoured to be the custodian of a plant that had seen so much change in our society. Today, it sat proudly in the large terracotta pot on our veranda. It too had been bountiful in its blooms, the sunset gilding the pink petals with golden orange. As I sat on the veranda that day, my mind wandering, remembering good times, I knew that whatever lesson life was trying to teach me, for whatever reason had not quite sunk in, not yet.

CHAPTER 16

Why could I not accept that I had been applauded as an author. In front of me sat the bound book I had created. I loved it, so why was I not celebrating? I should have been grateful for the news of Larry being faithful and ignoring the advances of a beautiful woman like Grace. I must have sat for an hour or two recalculating our daughter's claim, that I was too harsh and demanding. I also considered my feelings about Larry's family. *Were they simply rude boorish or was it me taking everything so personally?* Their dislike for me very real from the day we announced our engagement, after fifteen years of marriage nothing had changed. All I could think of was to breathe, place one foot in front of another. I wanted Larry to walk through the door to hold me so tight that I would lose my breath in his arms, the way I used to. I wanted to hear the laughter of my four children around me. I ached for my family to be wholesome, caring for one another. *Was that asking too much?* How could I teach or write a book full of motivation, when I could not motivate my nearest and dearest? Even my Dad had conceded to another's wishes; agreeing to never wanting to see me again.

Tomorrow was another day, so I went to work teaching my students about self-love and motivation, to me my words felt like sawdust. Once home, I would make the two of us dinner, watched TV then went to bed. Larry who was once more home, after burying his dad and waved his family goodbye. He also would eat dinner, mutter, 'How was your day?' watch a little TV then climb into his bed. There was not a lot of conversation, we now slept in separate rooms. It had been my suggestion, as Larry's snoring had become chronic. Our conversations were limited to 'yes, no, thank you.' I could feel my marriage breaking down until there was nothing left but goodbye. What had happened? Where had the laughter, the joy, the fun gone?

The day came when I woke, no longer feeling my heart beat with love or gratitude. I rang work, taking the day off. I showered, looking at my fifty-year-old body in the mirror. I was a little unfit through childbirth, I had silvered stretch marks. I could do with losing five kilos. Strangers often still complimented me on my looks, but no one saw that my heart was dying in this healthy body. My energy had gone. The brightness in my eyes had left. All I wanted was peace, I was beginning to feel life was all too much. I may be an educated, successful author/teacher, however, here in this house, my heart was the loneliest it had ever been.

Opening the bathroom cabinet, I sorted through Larry's assortment of medication. I knew if I swallowed the majority of the painkillers he had accumulated, it would end the hurt. All the feelings of being unwanted, the tiredness, the deep sadness would leave me. I would be free, so would the family. I took my time. A weird sort of relief, mixed with joy, settled over me as I put the smallest of pills into a pile. I added the cancer medication into the palm of my hand, there, nestled a very colourful cocktail of pills. *Would they end my pain, making everyone else happy? Should I leave a suicide note?* I decided they wouldn't care.

I left the pills on the bench for one more look around my pretty garden. I had fought this rock filled clay to plant many plants, today it was showing me a beautiful display of autumn blooms. The porch, full of greenery from the ferns and potted shrubs looked beautiful. The day was warm, so I decided to sit under the blue sky, my face turned to the sun, knowing once I had swallowed the pills my spirit would rise feely. It was time. There seemed no point to life if no one loved me. With the pills in one hand a glass of water in the other, I was more than ready.

When the phone rang I automatically answered.

My eldest was calling, wanting to visit. She had some news. I closed my hand around the pills, these would keep, agreeing to the visit. When she arrived, I could see she'd been crying. I made us both a cup of tea. It was a very polite situation as we were now strangers in each other's company. 'It's nice to see you honey, what the news?' I asked. There was a minute of silence. 'Mum, I'm pregnant. I don't want it. What am I going to do?'

My heart answered immediately, 'Sweetheart, when you have this baby, why can't we look after baby together?' Buried in the grounds of the house, may still remain a small plastic jar full of the many coloured pills I had been about to take. My heart began to overflow and a feeling of joy began travelling through my body. This baby was a gift, one that I could hold, love and cherish.

Unbeknown to anyone else, the news of a beautiful baby joining the family was the glue that held me together. It was also the catalyst I needed to visit the doctor requesting for some professional mental health care. I smiled when my doctor looked surprised, 'But you're one of the few I know, who has got it together, are you sure?' 'It's all smoke mirrors Doctor,' I said. My next journey into self-help mental health care began. I may have written a book on the power of the positive word self-motivation and had taught on the subject for many years. However what I hadn't included in the manual or in my everyday life, was that we should never be ashamed to ask for help. Life often has some huge stepping stones, sometimes we need help to navigate them.

My first session began with Mr Graham, a young forward-thinking psychologist. Two hours shot by, his questions were to the point – nothing was left untouched. He broached everything from the day-to-day life to the often taboo subject of intimacy between husband and wife. His one request was for me to be honest, not to shy away from the more personal questions.

My first job was to go home denying myself access to harmful or mood-altering medication, though I was allowed to keep a month's prescription for migraines for when they occurred. He requested that I journal my thoughts three times a day, keep busy and productive to keep channelling positive motivation. This was all written down in black ballpoint pen across his prescription pad which he handed to me as I left his rooms.

His advice was powerful. 'I feel the problem is that you have never found out who you really are, Cassie. You've been married for many years, you have raised more than your own kids. You have actually raised two men, your son and husband. Do you realise you have worked since you were twelve? To put it plainly you don't feel validated by your existence. Let's find out who *you* are, it's not a label of wife or mother, lover or teacher.

Be prepared for tears and upsets as we uncover who you were, who you are now, who you see yourself today, as well as your dreams and desires. If you're up to it next week, we'll begin with some hypnotherapy to unwrap your emotions from when you were young. I did as I was asked. I knew I had a supportive professional, who had my best interests at heart. It felt good to feel I could leave my problems with him. Like a ball of twine, each week we would unwind it a little bit more. I flushed any medications away. I realised this felt different. I was about to go on a journey to discover *who I was*, not what I could do, teach, apply or write for someone else, or helping others heal their pain, this was my time.

Our eldest had moved back in with us. Her news to her Dad, 'You're going to be a grandfather,' was not well received. Adding to his angry frustration, I had quit my job, there would be no financial help from me. Larry did his best to cope with all the new arrangements, my mantra was 'if you can't be honest or kind, then find somewhere else to be.'

My weekly appointments with Mr Graham were working well. Together we waded through years of bullying. *Why had I allowed myself to be bullied?* We covered my disappointments, my folks and my children, we discussed celebrations, the power the cult once had over me, employment opportunities missed and gained, and most importantly, my creative side. Since I had written the motivation manual, I had begun to write a children's book.

When my grandson was born, my heart blossomed with love. I was honoured to cut his cord, wrapped his tiny body in a blanket blessed him with words only a grandmother would know. I wished for him to show compassion, to speak wisdom, to practise kindness, to give with generosity. Every day I poured as much love and care into this beautiful boy as possible. It took a while for his Grandad to warm to him. In Larry's words, 'They're not interesting till they can do things.' He obviously did not see this child's eyes take everything in.

It took a while until the wonder of having a little boy in the house worked its magic. Larry became enamoured he wore the name of 'Grandy' well, taking pride in this baby who was our legacy. Slowly we became a functioning family once more. I realised how much I missed having little ones around. Larry would often take our grandson for outings, a bond growing between the three of us. His Mum would often leave for three-day weekends with her friends. I would almost pack her car for her. I adored spending time with this little blond baby boy with the huge brown eyes who looked at me with such trust and love.

Kez Wickham St George

An entire year sped past, my time with Mr Graham was nearly over. He had turned my self-disappointment into self-love. Despite our grandson building a bond between Larry and me, I felt my marriage was always going to be a rocky road. As we had grown older, we both had different wants and needs. Most of the time we were cordial with each other. I had come to terms with three of my children not wanting to speak with me, as this was their choice not mine, occasionally my son would ring. He also preferred his father to his stepfather, there had been cross words between my son and Larry, now it was a bitter silence.

My son and I had become polite strangers within a half hour phone call, he would tell me about how successful he was, in fact, he was well on his way to becoming a millionaire. My eldest daughter called once, demanding I apologise. I wasn't sure why. 'Because I left your father?' I asked. When there was silence, I put the phone down. She could practice her abuse on another, I was not interested. Something clicked listening to her demands, she was very much like Cilleen my sister, a bully.

Our youngest daughter had flown out to Australia. Larry had been asked to drive her to the airport, there was not a lot she could do when we both showed up. I was not spoken to, not even as she walked towards customs holding out my arms to hug her. I ached to hold my baby girl, her eyes green just like mine, looked back at me, but there was no love in them. She hugged her Dad, "I'll be in touch Dad,' she said as she walked away. Gulping back tears, I tried to remember what I had learnt, the lesson in that moment.

It's their life, their choice. When the time comes they must face the consequences, so do not wait for the apologies. Fill your life up with the love offered to you now. Yes, it hurts, you may never understand why, but you have raised independent children. Just know you did your best.

As my grandson grew into a cheeky, gregarious little boy, it was soon time for kindergarten. I was now into my early fifties, he was so lovely

Jigsaw

to spend time with. He would play jokes on me, the laughter so contagious. His mum found a house for them to live in and I missed them both. I made sure I still saw him daily. I had found some local part-time work with an aged care company. I learnt many computer skills there, enjoying the position. I was the 'go-to' for pensioners plus disabilities, often sorting out medical welfare papers. I wore many hats in this job, the one I enjoyed most was in public relations.

Although physically tiring, it was exciting and certainly stretched my skills. For two years, I worked for a minimum wage in a full-time job. I did not mind as it was close to my home, close enough to pick up my grandson from kindergarten. Larry was now in full-time employment, we were getting along, our lives had a sunny side most days. Life was good, our daughter seemed happy enough. Until an old injury in my lower spine began to worry me, the pain at times stopping me in my tracks. Our doctor ordered scans. A winter's day in New Zealand gets dark very fast. I was about to leave work at five o'clock for the day, it was already dark when my doctor rang my mobile. 'I'd like to see you tonight if possible. Can you be here by six o'clock?' I agreed, thinking how unusual it was for him to call. The thought struck me, *maybe I have cancer, maybe I'm really sick.*

The news was not good. I had chronic arthritis in my lower spine, the nerves were pinched, the bone did not look good. More bone scans were ordered, as was six weeks of bed rest. No prolonged sitting or cleaning, no lifting, no extended walking. I was scheduled a half hour session in the pool with a physiotherapist three times a week and that was all. The post-polio had certainly done its work, the scans discovering I had scar tissue on my spinal cord. There was nothing they could do. My only option was to attend pain management clinics or take medication.

CHAPTER 17

I came home to a dark, empty and cold house - no one there but me. Larry was at his mother's place. I sat at the table sobbing like there was no tomorrow. There was still so much I wanted to do, see, so many places I wanted to, visit people I wanted to meet. Yet here it was, my lower spine was not in good condition. The pain I had ignored for so many years now let me know it was time to put my feet up. I went to bed, trying to sleep, hoping it was all a bad dream.

I made an appointment with the physio the next day, we had known each other for many years. He sympathised after examining me then suggested he fit me into a stabilising back brace. It pinched, hurting me in every place possible but I was determined to wear it, no matter how uncomfortable I was. Larry had no idea that I was unwell. That night, he came to my bedroom door enquiring if there was any dinner being cooked. I flipped back the blankets introducing him to the metal/bone corset I was wearing.

I was the one shocked when he took my hand, held it tightly, saying, 'You don't deserve this. You don't deserve any of the shit that's been dished

Jigsaw

out over the years.' I wanted to say, *will the real Larry please stand up.* Just like that I had his support. Could it be that we still had some love for each other? Larry could not do enough to help. He had always been adverse to getting a cleaner, often commenting, 'I don't want some nosey bag going through our private stuff,' but now he welcomed one with open arms. Dina was her name, her wages were paid by our health insurance. All I had to do was rest. She was wonderful. My house shone, our clothes were washed, ironed dinners were prepped, cooked then frozen for the week. Thank heavens for the microwave.

She also asked her husband to maintain the lawns and gardens. Larry thought she was a miracle worker, as did I. The only thing I could not do, even after six months rest, was pick up our grandbaby. The clever wee man knew something was amiss. He learnt to climb up, to sit on my knee, always concerned for Nana's sore back. With my grandson by my side I began to play with my art. The conservatory in this house a perfect studio with the light, it took a while to find my style, finding time to rest, obeying the rules from the doctor, through Larry bringing a client home I sold my first piece, with her recommendations I soon had clients loving my art, ordering commissions for their business and homes. I was in seventh heaven. Life had become exciting.

Unfortunately, I was in for a shock, our daughter had received news of a work and housing opportunity in the South Island. The day her and our grandbaby waved goodbye, it tore my heart out. Yet, those words of Mr Graham's wandered through my head, 'You have done your best. Be proud of what you have given to others.' Our grandson had pulled this wavering mess of a family into one that could laugh together again. My heart was full of gratitude. 'Bye, my beautiful boy,' I knew we would see each other again, when? I had no answers.

Life went on. I was now able to swim on my own, do menial housework. I was standing for longer plus writing regular articles for the post-polio magazine. Once I was more or less up about, the corset came off a large, a webbed belt took its place. The Arthritis Society asked me to hold a meeting at my home for people with chronic pain. They advertised it in the paper. I was inundated with phone calls, having to move it from my lounge to a small hall, ten minutes' drive away.

I had no idea thirty or more people would attend, from the age of eighteen to their eighties, people in wheelchairs, with callipers, back braces, crutches, walking sticks. I had invited the chaplin from the hospital to speak with the Arthritis Society, providing supper.

To see the response was mind-blowing. My phone rang constantly with people wanting to know when we would hold another one. It became too big for me to manage, so after a meeting with the Arthritis Society, the group from my home was dissolved. It was a shame though, as so many people had a need to find a better way to control their pain.

I was growing stronger every week, when I hugged my lovely caretaker Dina goodbye, she had been part of my wellness journey for over a year. My daughter and grandson seemed happy with their new life in the South Island. We spoke via FaceTime fortnightly, we shared special occasions, my fridge door remaining festooned with pictures our grandson had drawn in kindergarten. I never heard from our youngest in Australia, only knew she was alive through conversations with my son, whom she rang occasionally. All I wished was that they were both safe happy. We decided to move back to Northland, where Larry and I had met then married.

At this time, Cilleen my older sister welcomed me into her home with open arms. A relationship began which I never expected. We talked a lot, once when she told me of her disappointments in life, how she was envious of me with all my different successes.

I had to stop her in her tracks. I was incredulous. 'Why would you be jealous of me? Look at what you have; your own home, a beautiful garden, a pool. You have a husband who loves you, plus four children who actually talk to you regularly. You have friends in your church calling in all the time. Cilleen I have had none of those things.' Her answer staggered me, 'You're right, I do have a lot to be thankful for and I'm grateful.

However, in the end you had Mum's love along with Dad admiration. You are smiling and positive, even though I know you've had hardships. Cassie, at least you can walk, write do the things you love to do – look at me.'

She pointed to her lower body , I almost cried. My sister's legs, wrapped in blankets, were so swollen. The medication she was on had filled her full of fluid, the osteo arthritis had crumbled her knee caps. Her ankles, fingers and toes so horribly swollen, they were practically non-existent. Her teeth had rotted away due to a lack of calcium. Her face had yellowed, so swollen with toxins that the skin was taught like a drum. Her painful disappointments were grinding her life away. What had not changed, were her green eyes that still held a spark of anger.

She pointed to an old folder under her bed, 'Would you like to look at these?' she asked. I pulled the aged folder out. It was dusty, dogeared, but inside her poetry was beautiful, poignant, melodic. As I read some of the pages feeling the tears slide down my face. 'See how fortunate you are Cassie?' I suddenly saw my life with a new perspective. Yes I had experienced abuse and ignorance from others, yet sitting next to her ruined body, I felt blessed. 'You are everything I wanted to be. Look at me; I'm just a fat useless Aging blob'

Her weight had skyrocketed to over 160kgs her temper tantrums had not dissipated. On some days she would rage about her disabilities, her husband would phone, saying, 'It's not a good day today, Cassie, leave it till next week.' I understood. How alike our we both were, connected to a female DNA, we both loved crafts, now the beginnings of a poet had begun to emerge

It had been a busy week. Larry was now working part-time for a local boat broker, while I had found work in an antique shop. Once more I knew Larry was not happy in his job. He was making excuses not to go in, claiming he missed living close to the Auckland city. I loved where we were living, I was enjoying my new relationship with Cilleen. Plus, all my old friends were showing up, the ones I had spent time with when I was a solo Mum. Jen, Val, Rose all called in regularly for a cuppa or we met in a riverside café. I felt completely at home, Larry claiming, 'There's nothing here for me.' He wanted more, stating he loved the bright lights crowds of the big city. He wanted to catch up with his old friends; he was homesick.

I suggested a fun weekend in Auckland to catch up with friends. He was all for it. Money was still tight, so we stayed at a friend's place overnight. She was into talking about religion and government protocol, my husband being opinionated also loved controversy, they both had a ball. It was fabulous fun. We both enjoyed ourselves immensely, Larry found it hard to leave, while I couldn't wait to get back to my home. Cilleen had been on my mind for the whole two days we'd been away.

I had also wanted to visit my friend Collette. She had two teenagers who had adopted me as their aunty when they were toddlers – what a privilege. We were both made to feel very welcome, an afternoon tea was prepared especially for us, everything was perfect. Collette had become very spiritual, practising tarot palm reading plus aura readings. Of course, my interest was piqued. I agreed to her reading my palm. I will never forget her words; 'New Zealand is not for you. You are going to live overseas far away from us all. Your life will change, your skills will be honoured, you will find your tribe.'

Larry playfully held out his hand, 'What does mine predict?' he asked. Collette stared at his hand for a sometime before replying, 'Cassie is going to leave before you. You have affairs to take care of first.' A faraway look was in her eyes as she said, 'Your need for money will be the end of you

Jigsaw

if it's not curbed, travel will follow you.' When it was time for us to leave, we hugged for a long time. She whispered, 'This is your dream, Cassie, don't waste a moment.'

Both of us were silent on the drive home both saying, 'I wonder where we are going?' My thoughts like bees in my head mainly why I would go first and why I wasn't to 'waste a moment.'

CHAPTER 18

Four occurrences happened in the three days after we returned home. I received a letter from Mr Graham, the clinical psychologist in Auckland. Inside the envelope was a document from the American university study with the results of *'successful people, a study by a Missouri university,'* which Mr Graham had asked me to be involved with. He had sent all material including recordings of my hypnosis sessions, all which I had agreed to. I had forgotten all about it. The document was impressive, with lots of large gold titles, then my name written in script, I was classed under the title of **Ambivert**, according to their studies. Under my name, birthdate plus my study file number it read:

'An Ambivert *works very hard to achieve. They have amazing energy if spent in the right direction, if the energy is not replaced or acknowledged, they can become depressed. Ambiverts are dedicated to family and friends. An ambivert can be counted on to ask the question, 'Why?' They are polite, considerate, loving, can be gracefully disruptive, they are never happy with the status quo. Ambiverts do not hesitate to speak up. They are successful people but keep it very lowkey. They are clever when it comes to critiquing their*

Jigsaw

work, they have a sense of detachment that allows them to receive negative positive feedback. They are convergent plus diligent. An Ambivert *is the quiet cheerleader, they will happily promote others. The* Ambivert *is a forward thinker with a creative outlook. They are a born artist in many genres, interesting conversationalists They lead a life of generosity. An* Ambivert *naturally engages in a flexible pattern of listening and talking, adjusting easily into many situations especially creative sources. the career outlook was creative Author, Arts Tutor, Art Therapist, Arts Educator, Travel Co-ordinater.'*

I had been employed in all of these roles including some art therapy. This paper described me in a nutshell. I had to agree, I rolled the word ambivert around in my mouth. It felt right. The second occurrence was a huge shock. Carla, my friend who I had stayed with in Wellington many years past, had done some detective work on the internet finding our landline number. I was over the moon to chat with her. She told me all about her life in Queensland, where she had moved over twenty years ago.

She and Milo were still together. Once owning a pub, they had travelled around Australia and now owned a home, as well as being Mum to a ten-year-old boy they had fostered. They'd moved to Perth, they had bought shares in a mine in the Pilbara, owned investments, he was what they call a FIFO worker.

I had no idea where the Pilbara was or what a FIFO worker was, but she sounded happy they were living life to the full. She asked about my family where we were living. I spoke about where I was, being very content with friends and family close by. My job was okay; 'It paid the rent!' Larry? She asked, 'Larry is Larry.' She had known him for a year or two before we met. It was lovely to hear from her, so when relaying the conversation to Larry, who was now working from home, I forgot to add that I had applied, that day, for the position of a trainee art therapist at the local hospital.

It was my day to have the car, as we now shared a vehicle. After my shift, I drove to Cilleen's for a cup of tea with her, then headed home. The phone was ringing as I walked into the house, it was Carla from Perth. 'Mate, it's me. Do you think Larry would like a job with my man? We are looking for a driller who knows what water can do and where it can hide.'

Larry certainly did have the expertise, having worked as an underwater stuntman many times in his diving life. He had learnt about the ocean currents, assisted police in body searches, worked in the Navy home guard, plus in the local search and rescue team. He certainly had extensive ocean experience, however water from a mountain? I left it with Larry to discuss with her. He had left the diving world when he lost hearing with a burst eardrum. It was extremely painful which no operation could ever replace. I asked her to speak to Larry herself. They chatted for a while, then I heard him say, 'You'll what? Okay, I would really appreciate that – it's a yes from me. See you in four weeks.'

Yes, that quickly, it was settled – or so it seemed. They had offered to pay his fare over to Perth. He would be working in the mines. He could live with them, while he sat for his many different tickets which would be paid for from his first wage. His face shone with happiness, he had always wanted to live in Australia, now here was his opportunity. I did feel a little hurt that he was ready to up go immediately, without discussing it with me, or without thinking of the consequences. On the other hand, if he made a go of it, well done. *See you in six months, I'll come over to visit.* He was a bit flustered when I told him I was happy where I was. One very excited Larry began to make plans. My wage would pay the rent, he would sell all of his gear for his expenses, he then announced my meagre income would have to do until his wages kicked in. He rang his friends in Auckland. They all wished him well. One sarcastic comment was, 'Yeah right mate, see you in six months. We all know you Larry, you won't last!' It was supposed to be a wisecrack between mates, however Larry took up the challenge, 'I'll tell you this much, mate, if I'm back in a year it'll be a year too soon.' Preparations were made, his plane tickets were emailed over, a suitcase lay open in the sitting room. Larry packing then packing. I told Cilleen, my friends, as well as ringing Collette. 'He's off, just as you predicted,' I said. But she corrected me; 'No, Cassie. I said you were leaving first.' I pointed out that I hadn't been invited I was happy where I was. *What if I don't want to go?* 'It's not up to you, Cassie,' she replied, 'it's up to the universe.' Here we go again, the universe had plans for me. Maybe this was the universe saying, 'Here's some peace and quiet, enjoy some time on your own.'

The third occurrence was that the mining company Larry was going to work for had rules. This was not a job for the fainthearted. They wanted a rock-solid employee, so company policy was that the spouse must accompany the employee. When Larry read this, his eyes pleading with me to say yes, I looked at the small single suitcase, looked at him, looked at the email, I began to shake my head. I should have said, 'No Larry. I'm happy here.' Instead I nodded, saying, 'We best get another suitcase out.' I wanted to clap my hand over my mouth, deny any such words. *What the hell had just happened?* I have no idea why I said it, but I know I did not want to say those words. *What had I done?*

Larry began to jig around the room, while I wanted to vomit. 'Thanks, gorgeous. We're off to Ozzie.' I sat there with my insides churning. *How could I take it back?* Larry would not listen when I tried to explain I'd made a mistake. I was happy where I was. I went outside sitting on the front steps, my neighbour, Marge was sunning herself. She took one look at my face, 'problem halved, pet?' I began to cry.

I told her what had just happened. Marge was at least twenty years older than me. She was definitely old-school but kind, I often felt like I had met kindred spirit. She knew Larry was a 'grumpy old bugger,' as she kindly put it. That day she advised me; 'Think of it like this, Cassie. Go with him, support him, salt a little money away, then in three months say, *Enough, I'm going home.* It will be enough time for Larry to prove his worth. Once you're home, you won't have to put up with him until he decides he's had enough, if he returns at all. It might be what you both need – some space.' Marge was priceless with her no-nonsense attitude, loved by her family, with so many grandchildren I lost count. She reminded me of my Nana Rose.

It seemed like we were off to Perth Australia, that is until the following day I received a letter from the hospital where I had been scheduled for an interview for the job of Art Therapy Trainee that I had recently applied for. Showing the letter to Larry I said, 'Hon, I feel I should stay here to complete the art therapy diploma. I could work for a year then join you, what do you think?' His face became mottled with anger. 'I think you want me to fail and ruin my chances. I'm not getting younger. This is my last chance of putting some money together, and you want to ruin it. You said yes, so keep your bloody word . I'm sick of you ruining everything.'

So, this is what he thought of me. *I ruined everything?* Sparks of anger ran between us. "Hey, I'm not the loser here. I'm the one who has saved your bacon over the years. So bloody much that I've had to go into therapy. You want to go to Ozzie be my fucking guest. You're not worth my happiness, now get out and don't come back.'

I had screamed the last sentence. I'd had enough. I was shocked at the way we were speaking to each other; it wasn't us. We never screamed at each other. I freely admit I had raised my voice many times over the twenty years we'd been married, but I could not ever remember screaming at him. My throat hurt; my head hurt; *What was going on?*

With sleep had come the conclusion I was happy to live peacefully on my own. I could do what I wanted when I wanted. This was my chance to say *I prefer the single life.*

Whatever was happening, perhaps this was the way it was supposed to end. What concerned me the most was that I was happy to let it end right there. Normally I would cajole, plead, bend over backwards, whatever it took to bring peace.

Between Larry and our girls I could talk common-sense till I turned blue in the face.

As I shut the front door, he turned to face me. 'What's going on, Cassie? First you say yes you'll come with me; next you're saying you would rather stay here. Are you having a breakdown?' *God almighty.* This man was winding me up, he knew it but what he said was true. His attitude was crap, but I had agreed. Then Marge's words hit home. *Three months, keep quiet, once he is secure in his work you can do whatever you want.* She was right, I had to be clever with this idea.

Larry's face immediately brightened when I agreed, 'You're right. I panicked. I do love it here, but I did agree to go.' He held out his arms to me. 'Can we kiss agree on this and settle it?' I walked into his arms. They went around me holding me tight, his hands finding my breasts, his mouth searching mine, nuzzling my neck. He whispered, 'Cassie?' My body saying yes but my mind saying, 'Be clever, Cassie. Now is not the time to declare undying love.' I gently pulled away, 'I'll put the jug on, shall I?'

CHAPTER 19

I had to tell Cilleen that I was leaving. We were getting closer every time I visited. How could I say goodbye to my friends, leave my job, give up my home? I began to list what I needed to do who I needed to contact. Larry's smile never left his face. Every day when I finished work, he would say, 'Well? Did you tell them they can stick their job?' or, 'told anyone the good news yet?' When I informed my manager, they were sorry to see me leave. Apparently I was the only one who was keen on coding each item, attaching history files to the photos. I assured him there would be plenty to fill my shoes. I was given a lovely morning tea with a small bouquet of local wild flowers. My visit to Cilleen went well, greeting each other with hugs as we began to chat she knew I was there to tell her something big. One bloated hand reached for mine; 'What's up, Sis?' I blurted, 'I'm going to live in Ozzie for a little while. I can't say when I'll be back, but I will be back.' She smiled, saying, 'Go, enjoy. You've always been the gypsy in the family .

I'm glad we had this time together.' The way she said it was unexpected and I realised I had been given a blessing from my sister for the first time ever. It was not to be taken lightly. Her husband met me as I left their home . 'I don't think it wise you return. You've said your 'goodbyes.' This will hurt her immensely. I hope you realise the damage your news will cause.' My brother-in-law was an elder with their religion. He had made it to the top, a position my father had dreamed of all his life.

We had never seen eye to eye, he obeyed his faith. His opinion about family was bring your kids up like dogs – 'It makes them obedient.' I remembered only too well that scripture, *spare the rod spoil the child*, then being a smart-mouthed teenager, I had replied, 'Thank heavens I'm not your child.' His hand whipped across my face, when I looked into his eyes, I saw his pleasure in my pain. All I had to do was cry, he would have won. I should have kept my mouth shut at the time, but I had muttered 'tosser'. Cilleen had chased me through the house for being rude to her beloved. However, he did practise what he preached; their sons were beaten like dogs into obedience.

This time I was older wiser. 'Thank you for allowing my sister and I the space to heal a wound, I truly appreciate it.' I stepped forward to hug him but was more than surprised when he crushed me to him, his loose wet mouth seeking mine, his hand behind my head mushing our lips together. *What the?* He just as quickly pushed me away, slamming the door in my face.

I got into my car so quickly, finding the handwipes, my face getting a good going over. My skin crawled. Larry greeted me with, 'How did it go love? Was Cilleen okay?' I dare not tell him about the farewell with my brother-in-law. A good strong coffee was needed, as I waited for the coffee machine to brew, a scene filtered through my mind. When both nephews had stayed with us, we'd been having dinner, when the youngest of the two boys had said, 'You know that Dad loves you, Aunty.' I had stopped eating replying, 'Don't be silly, that's not true. We barely get on.' The eldest nephew interrupted, 'It's true. Every chance he gets, he reminds Mum how clever or how smart you are. Every time she has a meltdown he says *why can't you be more like your sister.*'

I told them to stop being silly, saying such things only bought heartache. I had forgotten about it until that moment. I had known that feeling well. It hurts deeply to be told your husband prefers another woman. Tears slid down my face. Larry put his arms around me. 'Missing your sister already?' I nodded. I knew how she felt, dishonesty hurts deeply, your heart never forgets how others words or actions can make you feel.

The next day, as we sorted out our wardrobes, I felt sick. I still had no idea where we were going to live. Two second-furniture dealers walked through our home, writing lists, giving us a price. I was shocked that twenty years of living came down to $600, which was the highest amount offered. We just looked at each other. Only the lump in my throat stopped me from crying. Larry accepted the amount offered, signing the papers. In a week or two, everything we owned would be gone. Antiques were next, the highest offer from my ex-boss, another three hundred dollars added to the bank. The next item was the car.

Friends had offered a small amount of fifteen hundred dollars to which Larry agreed. With everything totalled up, we would leave New Zealand with just over $2,000, plus the bond we had paid for our rental property, another $1,000. Not a lot, when you look back and see what you have worked most of your life to accumulate.

I asked for half of the amount to go into my bank account, I needed some sort of backing. Everything was moving way too fast. I began to falter, asking, 'Larry, what if I don't leave first? What if you go to Australia first? What if I find nowhere to live? With no money to live on.' I had given up everything. Asking him to split the money between us. 'Why don't you keep the money from the car, leave the rest with me?'

Heated argument number two began. Larry was stunned by my

Jigsaw

request. He began to complain that I was being selfish. 'It stays in my bank account,' he said. 'I have so many bills to pay off, there's power, water.' The list went on, some bills I had never heard of before, a petrol card? A second credit card? ending with you. 'You'll just have to wait.' Larry's financial generosity had never been one to rely upon, he loathed commitment. He didn't like the fact we, like everyone else, had to pay for household expenses , hence we were always in arrears. He disliked parting with any money, except when it came to *his* needs. I'm no saint, but have always believed *give then you shall receive*. I willingly shared, though that had been called a weakness. I was no fool though, budgeting was my expertise. I had learnt that paying your bills was freeing. You gained respect plus a good reputation. Being generous was in my blood, not just with money, sometimes a cup of tea and listening to another's concerns worked just as well.

The sun on the front doorstep looked inviting, my body welcoming the warmth, better than trying to make sense of my husband's chameleon personality. My neighbour invited me in for a cup of tea. 'Problem with his bloody lordship again?' was the greeting I received. It was obvious Margi had a real dislike for all men, unfortunately Larry was in her sights. Her comments were often sarcastic, bordering on rude, until I reminded her that he had always been polite to her. I may not agree with most of his hair-brained schemes, his temper was always on a tight trigger, but he had not been unkind to her in anyway.

CHAPTER 20

I was not simply toying with the idea of my return in three months' time. I made a pact with myself. Perth for three months; making sure Larry had all his mining tickets and was enjoying his new life. I still felt I had a responsibility towards him as my husband. I was up at the crack of dawn when Larry joined me, his arm around my waist as I made tea with toast. 'Want to come back to bed for a while?' Now everything had been settled Larry was charmingly persuasive. 'Not today love, too many things to do,' I said as I edged away. 'You never used to say that, it was always the other way round,' Larry sighed. That was true. There had been many days when I would have loved a cuddle. There had been days when the empty nest I lived in had seemed too big and I would suggest we both have a nana nap together. Sadly Larry usually disliked it when I suggested intimacy.

Today he was making all the right moves. I was quite surprised as he had not suggested we go back to bed for years. I let myself relax into his arms, returning his kisses. But the memory of my brother in-law's tongue pushing itself into my mouth crept into my mind and I felt nauseous,

Jigsaw

pushing Larry away. 'Honey, I have a lot to do. Just let me get on with it, I have an appointment to keep. I expected questions, his reaction was sulking, stomping into the lounge, slouching on the couch, flicking through the TV channels. I offered him a kiss as I was leaving which he rebuffed, by turning his face away. Oh well, nothing new there.

The walk in the summer air was invigorating. My mantra was, 'Breathe deeply, Cassie, don't let them see how nervous you are.' I arrived for my interview at the hospital, on time and waited for five minutes before my name was called. Two women and a young man sat in a semi-circle, I was asked to join them. It was the nicest interview I'd ever had. Dennis was the hospital chaplain, Ben the head physiotherapist, Olga the head of the mental health department. Our interview more like a friendly chat over morning tea. Many questions were asked. They often referred to my CV saying it was remarkable, pointing out how I had achieved so much. Finally they agreed the job was mine. I could feel the tears burn the backs of my eyes.

They asked when I would be able start training. Sucking in air, I blurted, 'in three months if that's okay with you?' They looked at each other in surprise, Ben saying, 'Well, we wanted someone to start training straight away, why three months Cassie? The requirements were stated on our advertisement to begin training immediately.' I could have lied or reached for an excuse when Olga stood, offering me her hand. 'We'll need to discuss this between the three of us, Cassie. We will ring you with our decision. I knew my chance to live life on my terms had gone. what was I supposed to do now do now? with no job or home to return to? There wasn't much I could do but wait it out. I sat in silence for an hour when the phone rang. Eagerly, I scrambled to find it, my heart in my mouth, my brain screaming *please let it be Ben with 'the job is yours, see you in three months.'*

It was my son. He and his wife had been living in Melbourne, but growing sick of the city, they had bought a property in the country. The last time we had spoken, they were building guest accommodation on their property. 'Have a look at your emails, Mum,' he said excitedly, 'I've sent photos, tell me what you think.' He was not surprised when I told him of our plans to move to Australia. 'Wondered when you and Larry would move across the ditch.' As we spoke, I opened my emails looking at the photos. The little villa was lovely, colour co-ordinated, spacious, bright it looked comfortable. 'You really like it Mum?' he asked. 'Well, why don't come you over? Stay with us till Larry does what he has to do. Stay with us for a week or two. Love to have you visit. Christen the accommodation, so to speak.'

You will go first whispered around me. Why not? 'Our shout, Mum,' he said. 'Just pack your bags and spend some time with us, I'll make sure you get to Perth on time.' Suddenly there was nothing I wanted to do more. I received my e-tickets that night, leaving Auckland for Melbourne in three days. When I told Larry what had happened, he began to question why my son had bought me the ticket; 'Why now? He's never been that generous before.' Suddenly his eyes widened he stopped mid-sentence … 'Oh, that's right you are leaving first!'

It was time to ring our eldest girl in Christchurch, her boy, now a young man of six, answered the phone. We talked about his new dog and the goldfish his Mum had bought him. He had grown up so much, we could now have a conversation without him wanting me to constantly blow kisses to him down the phone. His mum took the phone, 'When were you going to tell me, Mum?' Of course, her brother had spilt the beans that I was leaving to live in Australia. I apologised, telling her I was unsure about going, that nothing had been settled until he had rang offering me my fare with accommodation. She was hurt that I hadn't confided in her. Maybe I knew she would talk me around to staying.

My one thought was, *I hope I'm doing the right thing*. I spent the

Jigsaw

afternoon adding bits and pieces to the already over-full suitcase. We had decided on one big suitcase each, otherwise we'd be paying a luggage tariff. Larry texted. He was at the doctors having his health check done before we flew out; *would I like him to make an appointment for me?*

CHAPTER 21

Our doctor congratulated me on our decision to move to Australia. Larry had already told her I was leaving in two days to stay with my son while he was going to wrap our lives up here, then follow me in two weeks. She did the normal things doctors do; blood pressure, her assistant running blood tests in the next room, the doctor asking me about the migraines I often experienced. She suggested I have a lower back x-ray to take with me, so when I found a new doctor in Perth I would have all the information.

Her diagnosis was that I was fairly healthy. 'You're in your early fifties so menopause may continue for a year or two. Your records show you have arthritis in your lower back, I'm putting that down to the polio you suffered as a child. You also have a slight bend in your upper spine, again polio would have caused this. It wouldn't be a bad idea to contact the post-polio society once you are settled. I think your healthy lifestyle will keep you going well for a while yet. Good luck with it all, Cassie. If there's anything untoward in the blood tests or x-rays, we'll be in touch.' That was that. I had my 'good to go' pass.

Jigsaw

Larry had been talking to our friends in Perth. It all looked good, everything was in place. Once in Perth, he would have to sit his rig tickets, forklift licence, heavy truck licence, plus much more … the list went on. I had to ask, 'Larry, do you know how much this is going to cost?' he flicked my question off. He was determined to go, no matter the cost. The only stone in his shoe was me, I was still concerned about the amount of money.

Being summer, we opted for fish chips at the beach for dinner. When I realised this would be one of the last sunsets here in Whangarei until I returned. When that would be? I had no idea. The tears I'd been holding back for so long finally escaped. Larry for once understood. His arm went around me, hushing my sobs, 'It's going to be alright, Cassie. I've got a gut feeling that this is my chance to buy us a home, do some travelling, do whatever we want to do. It's what we've always wanted. Come on now, you're going to have to trust me on this.' The tears slowly stopped. 'How can you be so sure, Larry, it's not exactly been a hay ride between us, has it?' He laughed out loud, something I hadn't heard from him for many months.

'Cassie, listen carefully to what I'm going to say, this job is perfect for us both. I know you've not been happy with me working from home. I know you've not been happy with me full stop. What you don't know is, I've not been happy either. I didn't know how to broach the subject. You're the best wife and friend a man could have, but to be honest, I feel the spark has gone out of our marriage. We are together mainly because there's nowhere else to go.' By now my mouth hung open, not so much with surprise, but because it felt like he was reading my thoughts. I went to speak but he held up his hand, 'I've not finished, honey. It's about time we were completely honest with each other. I did not want a divorce,' he chuckled as he continued, 'Who the hell would put up with me, but you, Cassie?'

I was dumbstruck. Had he read my mind? I certainly was not expecting a confession or the word divorce. *What the hell was going on*? 'What are you saying Larry?' Once again, he held up his hand. 'I'm saying, I'm going to be away from wherever we settle in Perth for four weeks, then home for two weeks. It's called FIFO work (fly-in-fly-out). I will be earning up to perhaps over fifteen hundred dollars a fortnight or more, which I will be expecting you to manage for us both, so we can buy a small villa, in time, buy that caravan we've always wanted. I want to have so much fuckin' money, the queen will be asking for a loan. Give it a year and if you're not happy then I'll happily send you back here, with my blessing. If you decide you want to buy a little place, I'll make sure you get what you want. No matter what the outcome, Cassie, I'll look after you. However, Cassie, you should know that once I get all my mining tickets, no matter what happens, I'm staying in Australia. I don't ever want to come back here.'

I sat staring at him for a good five minutes. 'You do know I will hold you to this don't you?' Larry looked at me, 'I love you, sweetheart – always have always will. I know you don't feel the same. I just want this one chance, no stuff ups, no excuses. I'm happy to share some what we have in the bank. Please, Cassie. One last chance to save of what we have left of our marriage.' I could not argue with that. 'Let's go home, finish packing, you have a plane to catch tomorrow. Australia, here we come.'

Larry's hand reached for mine, the feeling of frustration had gone. I would give Larry his chance, his year as he requested. If I was completely honest, what was there to return to? My family that spoke to me were sparse, there was no job or home to return to. Maybe it was time I stopped thinking of all my disappointments. As a wise person once said, *look forward not backwards, you're not going that way.* Larry was right, it was up to me to make a new life for myself, in a new country with new beginnings. We were leaving at three o'clock to be at the airport to catch the seven o'clock flight, which meant I'd be in Melbourne by midnight.

Jigsaw

One close friend rang before I left. I knew she was spiritual, as she never hid the fact that she received messages from the other side. Her words were, 'Cassie, I feel you should know I have a message for you. You're going to go to places you've never even dreamed of. You will lead with new knowledge, you will have everything you could wish for. It's your time now. It won't be an easy road but it's yours to walk. I love you my friend.'

Larry had put my case in the car. Margi stood on her front porch to wave goodbye. There was one last stop to make; the crematorium where a large glade of trees grew. Each tree had name plates attached to them, pots and vases of all sizes placed around tree trunks that held the ashes of the departed. Some pots were so old they had broken apart. A flash of fear went down my spine, it was with relief when I found my folks' tree. I had not been there for the scattering of ashes for Mum or Dad as I saw no point, they had gone. This was where Cilleen had put their ashes. The old chrome plates on the trees were very old, I could barely see the inscriptions.

The glade was so quiet, all that could be heard was birdsong, the whispering of wind through treetops. The sun was warm on my back as I stood there for a minute, placing my hand on the tree, my chaotic thoughts calming. I offered a prayer; *where ever you are, thank you for giving me life.* Larry gunned the car as soon as I had my seat belt on, 'Auckland airport here we come.' When the airport came into view, my stomach did a huge flip. My suitcase was soon on the luggage belt, my tickets confirmed. Larry walked with me to the departure lounge. He ordered tea, coffee, plus a few snacks, but I could not eat a bite. Everything I owned, all my worldly possessions, were in a large blue suitcase somewhere in the stomach of the plane. Was it too late to say, 'No! I've changed my mind'?

My flight was finally called. Larry held my close. 'I'll see you soon

Cassie. I won't forget my promise. I know what you've given up for me.' I walked through customs, waiting the longest thirty minutes before the flight gate was open. A smartly dressed hostess scanned my ticket, her white teeth with ruby red lips flashing me a smile, 'Hello, Madam, enjoy your flight.' I was shown to my seat as I was in business class, which meant more leg room, silently sending a prayer of thanks to my son for his generosity as I settled in taking a huge breath. I felt slightly faint, sick and nervous. 'Ladies and gentlemen, this is your Captain speaking.' The hostess did her bit with the emergency information soon the plane began to taxi down the runway, the lights of Auckland city fading into the distance. I knew from that moment on, a very different life was about to begin.

CHAPTER 22

I woke to the soft thump of the wheels descending from the undercarriage. I'd had a very tasty dinner, I even had a white wine spritz to celebrate the beginning of a new life. Melbourne never turns its lights off, it buzzes twenty-four seven, an amazing light show greeted us as we flew in. Grabbing my bag from the baggage carousel, once through customs the door opened into a sea of smiling faces. There to the right was the one smile I knew and loved, my son. It's such a weird feeling when you know you haven't seen someone face-to-face for many years. He looked older – when had the spiderweb of wrinkles begun around his eyes? He grabbed my case, gave me a half-hearted hug saying, 'Let's go, Mum, it's late.' We drove for an hour without much conversation, stopping off at a gas station to refuel. He bought us both hot drinks a sandwich each.

The more we drove away from the smog of the city into the country, the darker it got. I tried to draw him out in conversation, but he was intent on driving, so I just let him be. There was plenty of time to catch up later. We pulled in to the property, he opened the boot, pulling out my suitcase. 'Follow me, the villa is around the corner.' I did as requested but there was still no light or happy conversation. My accommodation was lovely. It smelt of fresh paint and air freshener. My suitcase was put on the luggage rack for me, with a swift kiss on the cheek he said, 'See you in the morning.'

Had I done something wrong? I went over the conversation in my head; *Come over, Mum. I'll send you the tickets.* I hadn't imagined it, had I? Should I ring Larry, tell him there's been a mistake, I don't think I'm welcome? Then I thought it out. Larry could do nothing. The time difference making any conversation difficult. I showered, slipping into bed. Everything here was so new, totally built for comfort. There was a small kitchenette with the tiniest fridge I had ever seen. I thought about making a nice hot cup of tea, however sleep was more important.

Waking to the raucous sound of crows, magpies and galahs, very different to the sweet bird song of New Zealand. It was still early when I peeked out to see if anyone was stirring in the house. There was no sign of life, so I settled down with my book making myself a ginger tea. An hour later my daughter-in-law tapped on the door, entering with such a welcoming smile. 'Morning, Cassie, so good to see you again, join me for breakfast?' I was more than happy to. As we ate, I asked the one question that was haunting me, 'Is my son okay?' She smiled, 'He's a workaholic, Cassie. Even when he has four weeks paid leave, would he take a break? Oh no, he built the villa. I'm so proud of him and all he's achieved.'

I had returned to my room for a shower when heavy footsteps stopped in front of the door, then two heavy raps on the door, 'You decent, Mum, can I come in?' The next hour was spent listening to my son; the story of a man so emotionally spent it was a wonder he was breathing at all.

He told me of the fire that had burnt down their previous home, their dog dying in the fire. His wife had been badly burnt too, when she had tried to rescue it. He had been to counselling including hypnotherapy,

Jigsaw

together it had helped. Life had been hell for them both.

There was so much I did not know; through our distrust of members in our family, he had decided not to inform me. I had no idea what he was going through. All I saw was my little boy with red hair, big blue eyes and freckled face telling me he had hurt himself, my heart ached to make it better. There was nothing I could do.

Ten days in Melbourne went fast. I loved the countryside, but the city I wasn't so keen on. We went in by train, twice, to see the sights. They insisted on showing me the chapel where they were married. It was so beautiful, with stained glass windows streaking the sunlight into prisms over the centuries old wooden pulpit. We stayed just one night as my finances did not permit me to stay longer. The scenery in the area was breathtaking. On the journey back, I spied a bush gondola, begging to try it out. My son and I climbed aboard while my daughter-in-law was to meet us at the bottom of the hill where it stopped. It was not a fast ride, we trickled along at a relaxed pace. I reached across gently holding onto my sons hand, if only he knew how much love I carried for him. He was the boy who knew my heart more than anyone else, he had laid underneath it for nine months, listening to my heart beat, listening to my words of love.

St Kildas was fabulous, the main street full of French patisseries. We stopped off for lunch, I will never forget the extra-long chocolate éclair – absolutely divine. We also visited a small township called Smokey Town, where the original steam trains were built; the quaint houses built in a 1900s style. Now and again my son would ask how different family members were. He had loved his Auntie Val, so I told him what I knew of her story. We spoke of his cousins and Cilleen he admitted he had never liked her. He agreed it was good to hear we had mended any anger between us.

I met his wife's family, going out for dinner with them. I could see they adored him. I could also see that he and his wife were a very happy couple. My son and I did not look alike, he had his father's looks, but there was one thing we shared: our humour, plus we both loathed goodbyes. He dropped me off at the airport, I assured him I would be fine. As I left, I had such a weird feeling. The whole time I spent with them, I had felt like a guest, not really a Mum or even a loved one, more like a casual friend. I didn't know when we would see each other again, but I walked away knowing I had born and raised a good man. I was grateful he had found a wife who loved him, I was proud of them both.

It was midday on 27 February 2004. The land of the long white cloud, black sandy beaches and deep green forests was far behind – Perth my destination. I would meet Larry again in the land of azure blue skies, gum trees, endless red roads, the plan I was told before I left Whangarie, we were to live with our friends for a few weeks while Larry was away work training in the Pilbara. Apparently, I was to be the big surprise for my friend. I was uncomfortable with this at first, it felt wrong to me. When I questioned it, I was informed our finances would be stretched, as a six week stay in a motel would prove too expensive. I had to agree. There had also been a problem with the promised purchase of our car. It seemed our valued friends had changed their minds, offering half the amount on the day of Larry's departure. He had argued with them, but they had said, 'take it or leave it.' We had no other option. We had thought of them as trusted colleagues; however, I had seen first hand how they ran their business and there had been times when I had mentioned their shortcomings, to be told mind my own business, so be it. We had left New Zealand with very little. It still puzzled me how little our lives meant financially. Hopefully, Larry would get a wage before the amount dried up. I felt completely helpless.

The plane landed smoothly into Perth. Once through customs, I saw Larry's face beaming at me through the crowd. Milo also welcomed me

Jigsaw

with open arms. As we left the airport, the very first thing I saw were hundreds of tiny beautiful fruit parrots sitting in a tree above the car. The noise and colours were amazing. *I was sure this had to be good sign.*

I was then informed that Carla knew nothing of my arrival, I kept getting a sense that all was not as it seemed. I put it down to tiredness. So far, it had been a very long emotional journey. Despite having a bad feeling, I was still not prepared for the welcome from Carla, who had been such a stalwart of friendship in my younger life. Dropping my suitcase to the ground, I held out my arms to her for a hug. I knew immediately I was not welcome; she literally looked me up and down, then turned her back on me. No greeting, no smile, nothing. 'You could have told me,' was all she said. That sinking feeling I'd had earlier was right. For some reason, all was not well. Their foster son, Mitch, showed me to the bedroom. It had obviously been a junk room of some sort. I cleared some floor space to get to the bed, then cleaned the bed of all sorts of old stuff just to sit down. The room smelt like something, or someone, had died in it. My case was quickly shoved in behind me. I felt completely disempowered, I had nowhere else to go. Larry due to fly out to somewhere in some God-forsaken desert, to places I had not heard of before, let alone try to pronounce its name.

I curled up my tears spilling into the rank old pillow. We had dinner; cold greasy chicken soup. It was a silent affair as Carla was furious with Milo for inviting me to stay without giving her notice. She was so very different from the friend I once knew. The next morning the two men took off to the shopping mall to buy a phone for Larry, our savings already being gobbled up at a super pace. Carla stayed in bed for the day. I chatted to their son, read a book, wandered around their garden. The pool looked inviting, as it was a hot day, I quickly changed into my swimsuit, preparing myself for a lovely dip in a cold pool, only to find I had been locked out.

A padlock was now secured to the pool gate. I just happened to look at the window where I knew Carla was sleeping and saw her son holding up the key he was smiling at me. How weird! Walking back into the house, I tapped on her bedroom door. I was met with an angry tirade on pool safety, snakes and redback spiders lurking unseen under the pool edge. *Did I not care about her boy's safety?* Who was this person? Certainly not a friend. I apologised knowing my stay was going to be a very short one, Carla was acting unstable. If that was the wrong word to use, then I had no other to describe her behaviour. When the men arrived home, I was sitting in our bedroom, sweat rolling off me. The aircon had been turned off, all the windows closed, except in our room. Carla had pointed to the open window saying, 'If you get bitten by a redback, don't complain to me.' I could not take my eyes off the window track in case the deadly spider made an appearance.

If that had been my only concern, I would have been grateful, as once the men arrived back, Larry looked terrible. I asked what was wrong. He said, 'It appears, I'm not hired yet. Cassie, you could have stayed back in New Zealand until I was actually on the pay list. I've just met the real boss of the drill rig and it's not Milo.' As he began to explain, all I could hear was 'blah blah blah,' my thoughts shouting *Dear God, why me?* I had given everything away to fly here; no job, no home, certainly no friends. Larry continued to tell me there were so many tickets to sit for plus a huge amount of paperwork to fill out. There was no contract and no job until all the tests were completed with a 95% pass rate.

I was gobsmacked. It took a while to sink in. Dazed, I repeated, 'So there's no job, no urgency that I had to accompany you. We have little money and we're stuck in this dump.' I could hear my voice getting shrill, with Larry shooshing me with his finger against my mouth. 'Not so loud, you'll just upset everyone.' I came to a halt, 'Say that again, I'll what? What about me being upset?' It felt like he had once more fooled me into trusting

Jigsaw

him. He then said, 'Oh one more thing, I'm leaving in the morning. They have me flying up north. My training begins there.'

We heard shouts of glee water being splashed. Larry gave me a hug. 'Come on, sadsack, we're having drinks by the pool tonight. Come on, let's join them.' 'I was told that the pool gates are locked, Larry, something about snakes, I don't get it.' 'Well, Cassie, they're all out there now. I'm joining them. No good sitting here in this hot box. It's up to you.' He was right. It was sunset they were all out there playing in the pool. Kentucky Fried Chicken had been ordered, Milo threw Larry a cold can of beer. Everyone was happy, smiling, except for me. My brain replayed the information I'd just been given; no job, no contract. I did not have to be here right now. I could have sat my Art Therapy job, he's flying out early morning. To where? I was gutted. He was cavalier about it all when we went to bed, I asked how he felt about the news. 'Oh well, we're here now. I guess all you have to do is relax just enjoy it, Cassie. Stop stressing.'

CHAPTER 23

At 2am, Carla drove Larry out to the airport. I was told there wasn't enough room for me in their car; not with Larry, the bags, their son, and the dog. Larry nodded in agreement, with a quick kiss said, 'See you in a month, love.' I wondered why the dog was included in Larry's farewell. It felt like I was in a crazy dream, maybe the heat and exhaustion had taken over. I woke around ten o'clock with my head throbbing. A migraine was forming, now insistent that I take painkillers. When I went to the kitchen to get a glass of water, I found myself in semi darkness, the curtains blinds had not been drawn. They had obviously come home and gone to bed, the jug was still warm. I fumbled around, finally finding tea bags and milk. A much-needed hot cup of tea was soon being sipped. It certainly helped the headache, but did not stop the silent tears. What a huge gamult of emotions raced through me: I was pissed off, hurt, angry I felt abandoned. About time I put my big girl pants on, I was an adult and could come and go as I pleased. First I would find a motel, then book my fare back to my home New Zealand. Then it hit me, there was no one in this house but me.

Jigsaw

An hour later as I finished my shower, Carla drove into the driveway. Milo had also flown out to join Larry in the Pilbara. She had just dropped him at the airport. She went straight to bed, taking her wallet and her car keys with her. Their dog was also ushered into her bedroom. Their foster son was also told to get back to bed, he obviously didn't have to go to school that day. Any plans I had of finding a shopping mall to arrange a flight or find a motel were squashed. She obviously heard me rummaging around in the cupboard for a phone book. I honestly thought she was going to hit me, the look on her face was thunderous as she emerged from her bedroom. Suddenly her arms went up, I ducked, however her arms went around me, hugs then a hot tea with honey on toast were offered. The reason for her behaviour, as she explained, was stress blaming it on her portfolio of Aboriginal clients who badly needed her help. She was trying to help a friend whose marriage was in shreds; she felt it was taking its toll. But of course I was welcome. *We were old mates, right?*

My intuition kicked in. This woman was too ill to advise anyone, let alone the Aboriginal community she claimed to be working with. She was no councillor, her so-called experience came from having to attend psychiatric assistance herself. I may be naïve but I'm not a fool. My experience in life had taught one thing: 'Don't lie, don't pretend. Be and do you.' As we talked throughout the day, I kept getting a surreal feeling. I took note of how unhealthy she looked. Apart from the enormous amount of weight she'd gained, she had a grey look to her, her eyes heavily bloodshot. Her trembling hands were swollen while she lit one cigarette off the stub of another. She told me a little about why she had a foster son, nothing added up. Her son sat beside her looking bored, not leaving her side. While we talked, he would often empty the filling ashtray.

Carla told me about her heart condition plus her diabetes. I knew she had been diagnosed with bipolar when she first immigrated to Australia. She told me of her frequent hospital visits when her heart began to play up, how her boy would ring the ambulance, then sit with her all night until Milo could catch a plane home. Once she was on track again, Milo would return to work. It was their son's responsibility to make sure she was okay during the night. My heart went out to the boy. At maybe ten years old, no child needed this. Then it all finally clicked into place for me. I was here, albeit not invited by her, to give some sort of respite to this family but admitting it or asking for help was not their way.

It had all been a lie. Larry was the innocent in this. *Did these two people not realise what we had given up coming over here on a maybe?* I was shocked. I realised I was a sticking plaster so her husband could work without constantly worrying about her health. I went to bed that night very confused, very homesick. Cilleen came to mind. I had lived with it all before I knew, without a doubt, I did not want to be part of this. I argued with myself all day; *I'm too old for this*. I no longer accepted anger, bullying or rudeness in my life. I did not have to stay there. I had choices to stay or go, knowing the consequences of my actions would be our future. When Larry rang the next day, he was concerned at my news of her erratic behaviour, but when I said, 'I'm flying home, Larry. I don't want, or have to be here. They both lied. I know why and I don't care. I don't want to be here.' His comment was immediate; 'You can't, you promised me a year. Besides, we don't have any money for a ticket.'

I was disappointed that our first conversation was not about my situation, it was all about the money. He tried his utmost to convince me to stay; 'Please give Ozzie a chance. If I can't make it here then where?' To that question, I had no answers. It seemed no matter what employment Larry tried, nothing worked. Once he became unhappy, then some sort of illness would creep in. I had discussed this concept with our doctor. He'd smiled saying there was a theory out there that agreed with me. Larry had no idea how hurt I was by Carla's actions. I felt insecure, uncomfortable powerless in this house. Logically, this was a new life, not only for Larry but for me, surely there was a silver lining somewhere. It did occur to me that between Carla, Larry and the universe, I was expected to wave some sort of magic wand, then poof, all our problems would be solved.

After weeks of listening to 'made-up nonsense' and watching her weird behaviour, I felt like my own sanity was being tested. There would be happy days when she said, 'Yes, enjoy the pool have a swim, I'll make snacks.' But more often, there were days of darkness, when the pool was locked, the aircon stayed off, blinds were drawn, the house was left in semi darkness. Carla would sleep all day. Their son rarely went to school, he would sit quietly in front of the TV. My leaving was not an option, at least, not until Larry was paid.

I decided to put some happiness into the house, not knowing how much negativity I was dealing with or how it would drain me. I cleaned the house, made healthy meals, cleaned up outside, swept paths, washed windows, did the washing, ironing and vacuuming. Every day I found something to do to keep my body moving, my mind busy. When Carla suggested I pay board of fifty dollars a week, I felt obliged to agree, there was nowhere else to go.

Then the news came that the men were flying home. Larry had been paid his wages, more money than I had seen in a long time. The rental agent in New Zealand had paid us what they owed and we had been paid for the car. Suddenly, the amount in the bank looked healthy.

All that had to happen now was for Larry's contract to be signed, a home to be found, for me to begin my life in Australia. So far it was not looking good. I had unknowingly become Carla's carer, plus I was under pressure to pay for this pleasure. We didn't go out unless it was for milk or bread. A month of unhappy living, knowing I was not welcome, was wearing me down. The migraines had become a constant throb in my temples, taking too many pain killers made my liver ache. I felt that I was on a downward slope with my own mental health. The urgency to leave this house had become paramount.

Two nights before he flew back to Perth, Larry had a twenty-four-hour break. He had gone camping with some other blokes in the bush. I felt jealous when he described the freedom, the waterfalls, the friendships being made. It sounded perfect. I suggested we look for a home in Tom Price. I was told very abruptly, 'That's not happening, you'll hate it up here. There's nothing for you to do.' A conversation we'd had in New Zealand filtered through my mind: 'We can lead separate lives, still be together, it might do us some good.' I was at my wits end with the nonsense going on around me. Carla saw the sadness in my face, asking me what was wrong. I made the mistake of telling her of my request to go up to Tom Price to live. I had at least a half-hour lecture on the benefits of him being up there while I was living in Perth. 'Why can't you just leave him alone, let him get on with it, build your own life. You know you can't stay here for much longer.'

I heard the silent threat, thinking about all the times I had sheltered her. I sat in the room where I slept, reflecting on the Carla I once knew, at times breathless with laughter as we talked about life. I had to smile as one memory trickled in. We were going to the fisherman's ball, the biggest event of the year in Totara North. I had sewn an outfit for myself, plus a top for Carla. Two days before the ball we decided to dye our hair for the occasion, Carla wanted an auburn colour as I did. Once I had applied the dye to her head, as she did with me, both of our heads wrapped up in glad wrap, when the time came to wash it off, the old faucet in the outdoor shed was stuck. The only thing to do was fill buckets of freezing cold water from the well and pour it over each other, both of us shrieking with laughter as it turned into a water fight. What had happened to that loving friendship?

With Carla threatening me, I had two options. The first to grin and bear it, the second was, ask my children or my friends in New Zealand for help, and that was not going to happen. This was the consequence

Jigsaw

of a decision not well thought out. It was not their problem. The next phone call from Larry, we agreed that finding us a home was number one on the priority list. Once he was home it would be time to take a big breath to decide; do we do this together or do I go back to New Zealand? Knowing if I did, it possibly could be the end of our marriage.

CHAPTER 24

I woke with such excitement. Today, Larry was flying into Perth. I was all set to meet him at the airport, when my mobile rang, 'Sorry, love. I'm here for another two weeks. There are three men down in the drilling team, so I've taken the opportunity to stay on to earn more money.' My heart sank. He knew how I felt about my situation, 'Try to stay at their home another two weeks, please.'

There was not a lot I could do. Maybe throw a tantrum, swear , throw something? 'I'll try, Larry, but to be honest with you, I really don't want to face the music from Carla when I ask for another two weeks.' Making two coffees, one heavy with the condensed milk Carla loved, I almost cringed when I asked, 'Do you mind if I stay a little longer? Larry won't be home for two more weeks.' She smirked. Milo had already told her of the crew's plan to stay on.

I had an hour's lecture about it being time to find my own home. I agreed wholeheartedly. This time I answered her, 'You're right, however a car would help! Even for a day so I can get out see some agents.' Her large hand curled around those damned car keys. There was no way she was

Jigsaw

going to loan me her car. She suggested, 'Try a taxi to the shopping centre That's where the rental agents are.' I began my search with bloody-mindedness. I could not taxi it to every open home for rent, with finances on low and no idea where I was, that was not a good idea. There had to be a way. Carla played the *I'm sick* card almost every day. I was her personal unpaid cleaner/carer. She hated cleaning. I had known this from our past together, but sadly, as she slipped between days of friend or angry dislike for me, it became harder for me to settle, our feelings mutual. I did not like her or enjoy her company, so why the hell was I putting up with her crap, simple really, I had given my word to Larry one year in Australia, however I had not expected this sort of treatment.

Carla had never been one to let a good story get in the way of her imagination. The stories grew more preposterous; from a trained Aboriginal counsellor, healer, to home owner of two to three large country homes. I asked what University or high school she had studied with, to show some interest. She said it was all online; it became a blur of just another day with another story. I nodded, repeating over and over, 'That's amazing.' When she ordered me, her fist banging on the table to 'stop cleaning her home.' I was desperate to be busy, however her home, her rules. I discovered a computer under a pile of ironing I was folding, when she saw me pick it up. 'It doesn't work anymore,' she muttered.

Something in her voice did not ring true, so I asked if I could have a play with it. My idea was if I could just get it to start, hopefully I could pop in my thumb drive to continue with the kiddies book I had begun to write in New Zealand. Carla mulled it over while she chain-smoked then agreed. My hands were shaking. I switched it on, it lit up. Carla said, 'You'll need a password, but I've forgotten it.' Time to see if I could make this work. Yes! Whoever had last used it had not shut it down properly. The screen lit up, connecting my thumb drive, my kiddie's story blossomed onto the screen. I was away, only stopping to cook their dinner.

After dinner was over, dishes were washed then put away. Mitch's school lunch was made, whether he went to school or not was none of my business. I carried on writing, suddenly feeling I was achieving something. It must have showed, as she harrumphed her way through her telly program, blew her foul cigarette smoke everywhere, then switched off all lights as she went to bed at eight o'clock.

She did not wish me a good night. The dog and Mitch followed with such hang-dog expressions, I almost laughed out loud. No wonder her son was such a brat; he was not tired, but had nowhere to expend his young energy. Still, I had been told to mind my own business, so I did.

Bed for me was late that night, but I went to bed happy, I was being creative. The next morning, after some personal house cleaning duties, I was ready to continue my children's book, but my thumb drive was missing from the computer table. I searched high and low. I searched through documents, then the bin by the computer and the bin in the kitchen, finding nothing. When she finally did get up at midday, I questioned her, she snapped, 'I have no idea. You sure you're not imagining all of this? I told you the computer didn't work.' Another warning bell went off inside my head. *Why would someone do that?* God please send me a miracle so I can get away from her disillusioned mind. Then logic settled in. I had seen her play this brain game with others, so why was I surprised.

My thumb drive was gone; I don't know why I had not taken it to my room. There was nothing I could do except try to remain sane in a house that breathed insanity. So I waited, looking for every and any opportunity to leave. When the local paper arrived, Carla would demand to read it first. I was usually the last to go to bed, so I would study the papers then, writing down phone numbers and contacts for properties. Long before Carla emerged from her bedroom, I would use my mobile to make contact. Properties were scarce and expensive, I had to join a queue of other applicants to view them.

Jigsaw

On the days she didn't bother getting up at all, except for her smokes or mugs of coffee, I would be informed, 'I'm sick today, don't make any noise,' – which meant no cleaning. I had searched high and low for my thumb drive, but it had disappeared, I had taken to hand-writing stories in my note book. She then informed, 'You can only wash your clothes twice a week, iron once weekly if you must, our electricity is expensive.' My showers were now to be three minutes, not the five or six minutes I had been taking. Some days I packed then repacked my suitcase for something to do. One day while she slept, I quietly took a warm soapy bowl of water into the box room allocated to me, anything to keep busy. Washing the inside of the window and windowsill, then wiping the outside the inside of my suitcase, just for something to do.

To my delight, I found a miniature canvas with tiny tubes of paint tucked away in the outer pocket of my suitcase. *How could I have forgotten these precious items?* I almost cried with joy. The next day as she slept, I spent two or three delicious hours in the shaded area outside, sketching out a beach scene, truly enjoying myself. I went inside to make myself a cup of tea, knowing the heat would dry the paint within the hour. I slipped quietly in and out of the kitchen, but so had their son. He had decided to draw over it with a texta pen. Honestly, I wanted to hit him; I had left my art alone for just minutes.

Of course, she protected him, both of them laughing at my anger. 'Boys will be boys,' she said, adding to the insult, 'Oh, I know your son was a big girl, he would never have done anything like this, keep your hair on!' My reply was immediate, 'My son was bought up to respect other's property.' I had a feeling she was itching for a fight. She may have been able to manipulate me in her home, but leave my kids out of it. I remained mute. I remembered again, the one important rule I had learnt early in my life, that you cannot argue with an empty space. However, while washing my brushes, sparingly as she was watching the usage of water, she tried to bait me. 'Your kids don't respect you, or even like you, by the sound of it.' Carla was being vindictive. Throwing the canvas out, ignoring her spiteful barbs, I stood in her back yard soaking up the sun, tears of disappointment falling freely – that is until the flies found me. Australia and its bloody flies, huge spiders, least of all snakes; I hated this place and truly disliked this person who I had once called my friend.

The one saving grace to this house of emotional horror, was the pool. Milo had given me a key to the pool gate, but the water was not fresh or clean, so I had not been swimming. When the pool man turned up, Carla all sweetness and light while he was there, she even invited me to dive in. It was heaven, the water sloshing up around my body as it closed in around me. The temperatures had been in the high thirties since I'd arrived and I could almost hear my body thanking me. In New Zealand, I had swum nearly every day, this small, now clean oasis, was heaven. I decided I could bear this situation another two weeks, as long as I got some water exercise. I decided early morning and twilight for some peace, healthy body healthy mind this would be perfect.

The next morning, I was up early, excited, ready for a swim. My steps were eager but quiet so as not to wake her, Mitch, or the dog, only to find the padlock had been changed. A huge brass padlock, with a silver chain wrapped around the bars, glinted in the early morning sunshine. Okay, she was playing games again. I walked back inside and had my three-minute allotted shower. This time there had been an egg timer put on the bench. Completing some yoga stretches, I made myself a cup of tea. Mitch was watching TV. This kid never went to school, did no one check up. Maybe things were different here in Australia than when I had my children at school.

Once I rang our eldest in New Zealand. I told her what was happening she tried so hard to make me feel better by calling Carla every name she could think of. Her parting words were, 'Mum, just be warned, she's not your friend believe me. She's insane, please be careful.' She then rang her brother informing him what I was going through. He messaged me. 'Mum, move out! You're not safe where you are. I told him I had made plans for a taxi that afternoon, but I had no idea how much taxis charged or what shopping mall to go to as there where two or three in the area. I had allocated myself fifty dollars a week, however now I was paying that in rent. Having no computer, I could not transfer money to my account, so I had relied on our weekly half hour shopping trips to use the ATM machine. One morning Carla was up early, showered for the first time in a week or more. She had applied makeup, painted her nails, primped and sprayed her hair, put her teeth in informing me Milo was due home that day then took off in the car to pick him up from the airport. Before she left, she took off the chain around the pool fence and placed them away in the shed. 'I suppose you can swim while I have my boy with me,' she said.

Milo's comment as soon as he arrived home was, 'What's happened? The house looks clean.' Carla took it personally, going to their bedroom slamming the door. He followed her, the sarcastic sniping at each other began. I went for another swim, it was hard not to overhear loud voices when I was swimming not ten feet away. 'I don't care if you don't like her living here, you need help. She's here, deal with it.' The truth was out at last. I was here to make life easier for Milo.

CHAPTER 25

I had the jug boiling to make myself a cup of tea, asking Milo if he would like to join me. He began to tell me how good Larry was on the drills. He was already a popular crew member. He asked if I would like to use the car to see if I could find a home. *Would I?* Yes please. The look of venom she gave me could have melted glass. Now I was not only a bloody nuisance, now I was the competition. Their behaviour towards me was what you would expect from teenagers. They could have made it such a welcoming experience with kindness and consideration. I had cleaned up their grimy house, nursed, babysat, washed and cooked. Now they squabbled over if I could use the car for an hour or two. I knew if it were myself or Larry we would have gone out of our way to make them feel at home. Then Carla decided they would drop me off at the largest mall, which had three rental agents, while they visited family for an hour or two

I was so eager to find a rental agent, I don't think I waited for the car to stop. As it slowed down I jumped out, saying 'see you in two hours' almost skipping into the shopping centre. Here was my opportunity to

Jigsaw

find a place of my own to live in Australia. The afternoon went quickly. I found the bank we were with, checking on the amount. It was very healthy, transferring money to my account. I registered with all three rental agents, one asking me to come back in an hour. Excitement rippled through me as she told me she may have something for me. A bookstore had computers on one side of the shop that the public could use, so I paid for an hour. There were so many emails it was pointless trying to answer them all. I scouted for anything urgent, but there was nothing. I renewed my licence to an Australian one, checked my name in for an ABN with the tax department, everything I did went smoothly. I then indulged myself with a haircut and afternoon tea, I felt decadent as I devoured the creamy coffee and chocolate cake when my phone rang. 'Cassie, it's Heather here from Gosnells rentals. Are you available to pop back in for a chat about a villa we have on our books?'

I almost sang, 'I'll be there in two minutes, I'm just around the corner.' My heart began to race. Heather took one look at my flushed face, 'Hey Cassie, sit down, let me get you a glass of water?' For some reason I began to cry; her simple act of kindness sinking into my sad heart. Heather was a woman in her late forties, helpful, full of empathy, not what I had expected I almost broke down when she asked for my address. I babbled I was renting a room from a local family, that we did not see eye to eye, it was proving to be an uncomfortable situation.

My husband was up north as a FIFO worker and I was trying to put a life together here in Perth with little success. 'Well hopefully we can fix that,' she said, 'I have just had a one bedroom and a three-bedroom villa recently placed on my books, let's pop out see them, shall we?' Just like that another person added sunshine to my day. As we drove out into the afternoon traffic, she told me all about the area we were about to visit in a little gated community called Coral Trees in the Armadale district. 'It's a twenty-minute ride to where you are now staying, so I can drop you off on my way home.' Accepting her generosity, I messaged Milo to let him know he didn't need to pick me up at the mall. We drove through the gates of the community, with huge hibiscus trees at the entrance, soft pink bricks glowing in the afternoon sun. Down a wide driveway we turned left, driving into the carport of the brand new one-bedroom Villa. It was stunning. The rental fee was two hundred a week. It was tempting, my intuition began to spark so I asked to see the second villa before I made up my mind.

It was just a two second walk away, one look was all it took. I knew this was to be ours. In the late afternoon, the dozen or so rose bushes in the front yard gave off a heady perfume. The bay window in the lounge took me by surprise. There was a double space carport, the inside smelt of fresh paint. The kitchen, laundry and bathroom were all very modern, with a soft beige carpet in all the rooms, white curtains hung in the lounge. The backyard was bare apart from a small shed that I knew Larry would like. Down the side path, a large wooden gate opened up to a park with a BBQ area, where on a large green lawn sat a cream shade house.

Is it silly to write that I actually felt this Villa's welcome? I knew it was for us. The rental fee was two hundred fifty dollars per week, with everything that needed to be paid, including the bond plus a month's rental in advance, amounting to two thousand dollars. 'Where do I sign?' was my only question. I had found us a home. We had the money, I had the house, the only thing I needed was Larry's signature, plus a security check of past residencies. I was stumped there, I did not have either. I must have looked puzzled, 'You really are on your own aren't you? How about we stop off at my house. I'll help you sort through it all. In the meantime, I've put your name down as the new occupant,' she smiled, giving me a wink. I took the biggest shuddering breath, praying that whatever Gods were watching over me today kept up the good work. 'I would love that Heather. Thank you.'

Jigsaw

Heather lived half an hour away. The traffic was quiet now it was past 5:30 in the afternoon. Her home was beautiful, high on a hill with surrounding apple and avocado orchards. Her husband, Archie, very much an Italian, was most welcoming. 'Come in, come in welcome to our home.' I was wined, dined, and welcomed to Australia, so vastly different from what I had received on my arrival at Carla's. His parents who lived with them joined us. Nona was the chef, the food delicious. Papa worked with Archie in the orchards. These two seniors had faces full of wrinkles, their eyes full of happiness. They laughed together as a family who enjoyed each other's company, showing affection openly for each other. They tried hard to keep the conversation to mostly English, for my sake.

After a tasty dinner of fresh risotto with garden fresh green salad, a gorgeous decadent chocolate desert made with Tia Maria, more wine accompanied with strong coffee, Heather got to work on my behalf. She rang my husband's employer speaking to Mick, the drilling company owner, asking, 'Would he give Larry a reference?' The answer was, 'Yes, certainly. I have a contract for him to sign on his return. He's a good man.' I wondered if Larry knew about the contract – how exciting!

Heather than emailed our last rental company in New Zealand, asking for a reference, I was to provide a bank statement with a month's salary in it. This was tricky, I told her so as we didn't have a wage slip yet. 'No worries Darl, we can sort it once your references come through.' She saw the look on my face. 'We'll make it work Cassie don't stress. Come on I'll drive you back to where you live …' she smiled adding, 'start packing, Cassie.' As I farewelled the family, Nona hugged me tightly. 'Welcome to Australia, Cassie.' I knew I had made good friends who welcomed my friendship.

CHAPTER 26

My news of a new home was greeted by Carla with, 'That rental place has a bad name. It's on the wrong side of the tracks, maybe you're used to that.' I felt my jaw clench. Muttering 'stupid cow,' as I walked into the room allocated to me. Larry was as excited as I was, my two hosts? Suddenly they had become doomsday specialists, when it came to me finding a home for Larry and I. While Milo was home, they went out every day to see family. If Milo invited me to go with them, Carla would stand behind him glaring at me. I declined every time, except once, when he insisted I go to his sister's house for a celebration. I had met them briefly, they seemed like nice, sane people. On the way to the party, Carla informed me that Diane, her sister-in-law was married to a womaniser. 'Be careful,' she warned, 'Rex will have his hands up your skirt quick as look at you.' I knew she would be watching me like a hawk; every move, every smile.

As it happened, their home, like its owner's was classy and modern. I relaxed, had a wine or two and began to enjoy myself. I felt these people actually talked my language; movies, art, books, they had a passion for their work. For the first time in weeks, I was having fun, with lovely food, nice music, dancing. Rex asked me to dance with him, I accepted. Nothing untoward happened, Rex was being polite, simply a host dancing with their guest. Milo also asked me to dance – huge mistake. It was like a red rag to a bull. 'Time we went home,' was announced by Carla, as I was chatting to Diane about her job. Rex wrapped my shawl around my shoulders, inviting me back any time, then kissed my cheek as did Diane. I'd had such a good time I had forgotten about Carla's dire warnings.

Once we arrived home after a very silent drive, I was given another lecture on my affectionate behaviour towards her family. This time I retaliated. 'I'm an adult, Carla. I make my own decisions on who I associate with and how I behave.' I went to my room *as it was called*. A mantra was playing in my head only five more days and Larry would be home.

The morning arrived, I was woken early with a knocking on the door. Milo poked his head around the door, offering me a fresh cup of tea. He spoke one sentence; 'She's not herself. Plus, Larry will be home next week. Can't you wait till then?' Relief flared in Milo's eyes as I agreed, 'Just till Larry's home.' In all, I had been there six weeks. So far, my introduction to Australia was two or three trips to the shops for groceries, two very short swims, a ride to a petrol station for gas, plus housework and gardening. One very successful trip to the mall where I had met Heather, my rental agent. I had spoken to perhaps six people in that entire time. It was very different from my homeland. It also included a woman named Fern. She was attending Carla's wellness clinic, Fern being the only attendee. I was informed that Carla had met Fern through their sons. Fern was having a hard time with her marriage, Carla had offered couples counselling, claiming she was a marriage therapist.

I left them talking, wondering whether to warn Fern that Carla was not a 'marriage counsellor'. The legalities over here were very different to New Zealand, but it was still fraud. *Should I stop this? Do I interfere?*

Wandering out to the kitchen, I began to make myself a cup of tea, offering the same to Carla and Fern. Carla was on her best behaviour, welcoming me to join in? Something was up, my gut did another little warning flip. Carla smirked when she informed Fern she had introduced Larry to me, which was correct, then said she'd been counselling us both for many years. 'Why don't I let Cassie tell you her story?' she said.

I was stunned. It was true, she had introduced us, but counselling? What could I say? This was completely untrue. Saved by my phone ringing, it was Larry's tune, I nearly fell over getting to the phone. He was confirming his flight numbers with me when he heard the hesitancy in my voice; 'What's wrong now?' I knew he was not interested, it was all female stuff to him, I wondered if he even realised the abuse I had accepted so we could begin another life, or would he also label that as female stuff. Was it his faith in my ability to carry on no matter what, or was it knowing I was stuck between a rock and a hard place? He knew unless I left, there was nothing I could have done to change it. At least I now had a beautiful villa to move into.

I slipped Fern my phone number as she left, she rang the next day as Carla slept. We hit it off immediately, discovering we were both New Zealanders from the North Island. We began chatting about our homeland when she invited me out to the movies plus dinner with her that night. I was over the moon of course, I accepted. When I told Carla I was going out with Fern for dinner, Carla began to warn me that Fern's husband was extremely jealous. If I wasn't careful, there could be violent repercussions. Was this true? Was I putting another woman in danger? Or was it all in Carla's mind? In her opinion, Australia crawled with sexual predators, in her opinion anyone I met, male or female, in Australia they were all out to make my life miserable or sexually assault me.

When I look back, I realised that the Carla I had known in New Zealand, was no longer there. Her health was in a horrible state, any relationship we once had did not exist. Carla insisted she had one friend who was the salt of the earth, who was considerate, helpful, always checking up on her. I was convinced it was an imaginary friend, as I had not seen or heard her speak to anyone except Fern or myself.

There were so many big red flags that said *mental illness*. I had been informed it was bipolar, but I believe there was something else going on. I had watched my sister Cilleen struggle all her life with this dreadful disease, losing friends and family as fast as they met her. They were both hugely obese woman with chronic inflammation in their bodies, their minds wandering, one minute in fear jealousy and dislike, the next happy and smiling. I was also concerned for their foster son, Mitch. This child wandered from TV to Carla's side all day every day. Sometimes there was a day at school, but mostly he seemed lost. I had only once broached the subject, to be told to mind my own business, 'You're not welcome here as it is.'

However, in case I felt there may be a smidgin of truth to Carla's warning, I asked Fern if what I had been told was true. She admitted that her husband had a very explosive temper and it was sex that calmed him down. Although embarrassed, she explained that he had an extremely high libido, also adding it had been Carla who suggested the 'more sex the better,' for them it worked. I felt my eyebrows rise up to my hairline. I was surprised at her honesty and I wanted to add, *what about you? How do you feel about sex on tap?* Instead I decided to tell Fern the truth. Fern sat there with her mouth open while I told her a few facts about Carla. "But I've been paying her fifty dollars a session, sometimes twice a month. How can someone be so horrible?' What could I say, except, 'Look, if your marriage is in trouble find a qualified therapist. Carla is not what she says she is. She's not a therapist, her advice could harm not heal.'

We bought takeaways on the way home, the movie long forgotten. She asked me to 'pop in to meet her love' as she called him. I expected an Adonis, tanned, tall full of sex appeal. He answered the door. 'Enjoy the movie, my love?' he boomed at Heather. I looked down from where the voice had come from. Keith was very short, bald, bow-legged man with a very large girth, covered in a matt of black hair, wearing tight black underpants, not at all what my imagination had cooked up. Keith shook my hand offering me a nightcap. I accepted a coffee, trying very hard not to stare, as his lycra underpants which seemed to dominate everywhere I looked. He would say something to me, my eyes were instantly pulled to his groin. I had to remind myself I was an adult 'stop staring!'

We discussed the day's events, as he sat there with his little legs crossed, his large hairy girth expanding over the top of his pants, while he delicately sipped coffee, his little finger raised in the air. *Where was my sane world?* It felt like I'd fallen down a rabbit hole. However, nothing else untoward, I was not a witness to any foul temper displays. Keith was very pleasant; strange but pleasant.

Fern drove me back to Carla's. The house was in darkness when I arrived, all doors and windows locked up, though it was only ten o'clock. I had to bang on her bedroom window for quite a while before I heard her tell Mitch to unlock the door to let me in. She switched on the kitchen lights, lit a smoke then asked me to join her in the kitchen. I wondered if we were going to have another session on how sick she was, what a pain I was, or maybe she had decided I was now drinking too much water. To my surprise, I got the rundown of my night. She told me Fern's husband had rung her. He'd been abusive, ranting about my behaviour in his home, how rude I was taking Fern away from her duties as his wife. Again, I had the feeling I was living in some crazy *other world* where sane people didn't exist.

I stood up, saying I would call Keith tomorrow to apologise. Nothing made sense. I knew this had to be another lie, but why? My head was pounding. Time for some painkillers, hopefully a good night's sleep. The following day was Saturday, one day I still find it hard to forget. I had woken once again with a headache, which I noticed was at the base of the neck. I knew this was stress. I only had painkillers with me, wishing I could rest up with some specific oils rubbed on for tension or a magnesium bath. None of that was possible here.

I had intended to ring Heather, hopefully she had some good news, then Fern to apologise if I had caused any strife between Keith and herself. I took my three-minute shower returning to my room where I found the door was jammed shut. No amount of shoving or pushing would move that door. It was jammed tight from the inside. I immediately woke Carla asking her for her help. She barked an order, the door was released immediately. I shoved my way into the room, whoever was in there had obviously dived out the window, as it now hung open.

I was in shock when I saw how my room had been trashed; my suitcase ripped apart, my personal items strewn everywhere, the mattress, albeit an old kapok one, had big chunks missing out of it, scattered like large puff balls around the room. The bed itself leaned to one side, one wooden leg had been torn off. I was stunned at who could do this? Carla admitted that Mitch had been in my room with his friends. She'd tried to stop them but had gone back to sleep. I was mute with anger. I had not been out of the room five minutes. I knew they both disliked me living there, but this was insane. To do this to someone, even an unwelcome guest, was not normal behaviour. Her explanation, was boys will be boys, I wouldn't worry about it too much. It was the dog's bed, it's not the end of the world. I stood there in shock. I was speechless. How do you reply to that? Nothing made sense. I made myself a hot drink, wishing it were something a lot stronger. At least it explained why the bedding was putrid, I had been sleeping on the dog's bed.

CHAPTER 27

I rang my daughter on my mobile she soon picked up something was amiss. I told her everything. I heard her gasp with shock when I told her about the day's events in my room. 'You're paying rent? Her reaction was, 'Mum, talk about being used. The thieving cow! You're a guest, even if you were a surprise one. It's just not right. Does Larry know? Her description of Carla's behaviour was not exactly the Queen's English, there was definitely no love lost between them. 'I think you should leave before she hurts you physically. Please find another place to stay or come here to Christchurch live with us, your grandson would love it.' I had to agree. I was not wanted or welcome in this house. I had lost all respect for this person who masqueraded as a friend. I phoned Heather to see what was happening with the villa. All we needed was confirmation from the rental agent in New Zealand. *What was taking so long?* When she answered, 'It could take a while,' I broke down in tears. 'I'll be there in ten minutes,' she said, 'can you wait by the front gate?'

True to her word, Heather arrived quickly. Her big bronze car swooped into the driveway like an avenging angel. 'Hop in, we're off for a coffee.'

Jigsaw

When I told her about my morning, she surprised me by saying she had done a police check on me, Larry and I were given the all clear, I laughed out loud when she said, 'Are you sure you don't want something stronger? Pub's around the corner.' I could see it now: both of us off our trolley when we returned, the anger that would be hurled at me. Tempting as it was, I declined. I really liked Heather. She had a fun sense of humour, she even looked fun; long black curly hair, blue eyes with a twinkle, pale freckled skin, her giggle that would set her large pot belly jiggling. Her clothes had a Romani flair to them, the sandalwood perfume was ever-present, along with the jingling of anklets and bracelets.

She asked how Carla and I met. I explained, 'Back home in New Zealand. My group of mates soon discovered she was a habitual liar, but she also had a caring side. That's not the person I see today. This one is deceitful, obviously mentally ill.' I felt very tearful, apologising to Heather. I simply needed a shoulder to bleat on. I was confused and homesick. 'Well put a smile on it, Cassie, the villa is yours.' She dangled the keys at me, 'I received what we needed from New Zealand before I left. When are you moving in?' I literally leapt up, coffee and cake going everywhere to hug her.

Carla was up, my morning was scrutinised, placed under a microscope, taken apart, then put back together. As I had nothing to hide, I was honest about my whereabouts, how much I enjoyed Heather's company, Carla saying, 'I suggest you don't go near her as a friend, she's not liked at all in our community.' Here we go again, dare I ask, *what community?* No one was stopping me from moving out, at last I had a home. 'Well I think she's spot on,' I replied, 'as now I have a villa to move into.' I showed her the keys. Her toothless mouth clamped tight over her cigarette. I told her the address. 'That's a crime-filled neighbourhood, you're going to be sorry,' she said. I was feeling worn out by her constant negativity. I just walked away, there was not much point in having a discussion. I had tried to fix up the room but it still looked like dogs had been let loose in there. *Was this really what I had left my home for?* They had eaten, I was not hungry, so while they were both watched TV, I made myself some tea and toast, ringing Larry to tell him the good news that we had a house. When Larry finally answered, it was, 'Having a few drinks, love, call you tomorrow.' I felt deflated. How I would have loved to ring someone, anyone, to say that I loved Australia, *I'm having a fabulous time here*, sadly that was not the truth.

I rolled up my clothes to fix the holes in the mattress, found some old hardcover books amongst the junk in my room to prop under the bed as I couldn't repair the broken leg. As I lay there on the lumpy, smelly mattress, I recognised my thoughts had become morbid. I began to count my blessings, but they too turned morbid as I thought of how I'd cleaned up after them both. My artwork had been destroyed, my thumb drive with the children's book was missing, I was insulted and treated badly. Trying to talk to Larry, just to vent to get it out of my head, was pointless. He was happy, though he sounded drunk most nights, which until moving over to Australia, was a rarity. Well that was my impression, however it seems it had not been that easy for him either.

Fortunately, I mean fortunately, we had been completely unaware of any problems. We both thought when Larry had been invited to come over, it was much too simple. However, when Milo had suggested Larry to his boss, he knew full well it was unlikely to be permanent. I asked Larry how he'd found out. 'I had a chat to Mick, as nothing felt right. No one seemed to know what to do with me.' As it turned out Larry's past jobs had given him plenty of experience with all types of water pressure. When Larry sent through his banked wages, it was the largest amount we had ever seen for eight weeks work with perks, plus a contract for one year offered and signed.

With the news that Larry would be home in a day or two, life seemed

Jigsaw

brighter. Now with a new home to shop for, here was our chance. The day we moved into our villa, Larry had to go back up north, Carla agreeing to drop him off at the airport early in the morning. Another four weeks of him being away, without a car! but I didn't care as this was going to be my patch of paradise. We had bought only the basics; a bed, a couch, a set of pots and pans plus cutlery. I also hired a small TV for something other than writing to do at night. The double bed we had ordered proved to be a problem as it was flat pack. I had no screwdriver or Allen key to put it together. I was happy with the mattress on the floor for the night, a tin of baked beans was warming up, while I put our meagre possessions away. I found a family photograph and placed it on the mantle, my eyes could not look away. I had wonderful memories of that day. I took in everything, from the colour of our two daughters hair, clothing; our happiness together showing in our eyes. In the photo, they were smiling, both happy. Our grandson was sitting on my knee, his continuous wanting to pat my face or tell me he loved me or play fairy kisses in the palm of my hand, driving the photographer (Larry) insane.

He had taken the photo a good while ago. I could still smell the sweet baby shampoo as I had bathed our grandson that morning while his Mummy got herself ready. Then the grief hit me so hard I sank to my knees in pain. It was my first night totally alone in this strange country. I let the tears flow, holding nothing back, my throat and face ached, my chest was on fire. I honestly felt like I'd been baptised with fire, my plea to the heavens, *please let this be a better life*. I was woken in the early morning by something tapping on the bedroom window. I lay there spent, too tired to find out what it was, but it was insistent. Sitting up about to peer through the blinds I noticed a small red dot of light travelling up and down the open section of the window. In Australia, they have protective screens across doors and windows, so I felt safe enough, but couldn't figure out what the red light was. The tapping became insistent, suddenly it clicked. Someone, not something, was out there, wanting me to open the blinds. And whoever it was had a video camera aimed at me.

I was now fully convinced, I had given up everything to live in a land of weirdos. Wrapping my bed spread around me, I walked around checking all the doors and windows; they were locked tight. If the nutter wanted to tap on my window, fine, I was going back to sleep. I slept till eight in the morning, when the sound of a car pulling up in my driveway woke me. It was Carla, of all people, saying she had dreamt the place was haunted. With that, she pushed her dog inside, handed me a bottle of cold milk, saying 'He will sort it,' she then drove off. I stood there in my nightie, hanging onto the dog's lead, fully convinced I was the one with the mental health problem.

This poor dog had been wary of me ever since I had taken his bed from him. He had a sad look about him, as he was never walked or allowed to run in a park. Under his fur, were small balls of cysts. I had seen Carla giving him milk with dog biscuits, never clean water or meat. One day at Carla's, I had cleaned his dirt-encrusted food bowls, put water in one placing homecooked meat balls in the other. The dog had almost fallen over with joy, he wolfed it all down, then promptly went outside into the small courtyard to empty his bowels. I was told off then, asked to remove the dog's mess as it attracted the flies. I was tired of the arguments and sniping, so I just did as I was ordered to do. It was obvious to me that the poor dog was dehydrated, she however pointed out that her dog was loved: 'He had his own room with a bed, until you appeared.'

So the dog and I had breakfast together. Making myself a cup of tea, a bowl of hot porridge, he also sucked back a huge bowl of water. We sat in the courtyard in the sun and I chatted to him about life in Aussie so far. Going back inside to refill my cup of tea, when the dog froze he would not budge. No matter what I said or did, he wouldn't go back inside the villa for a good half hour. He just stood by my back door growling at

Jigsaw

whatever he could see in the kitchen. He snapped at me when I tried to push him inside. When Carla arrived back wanting her dog back saying, 'It's all fixed now.' The dog happily got back in her car. I had no idea of what had happened. Was I the one who needed medicating? Everyone else seemed to accept things as they were, no questions asked.

An hour later my phone rang. It was Heather, 'I'm coming over for lunch. I'll bring something with me.' Twenty minutes later, I heard the Oldsmobile chugging into the driveway. When she saw the state of my bedroom, with wooden slats everywhere, she made a call to her son-in-law, who just happened to be in the flat pack industry. What a Godsend Heather was. Within half an hour my bed was upright, with fresh clean sheets and pillowcases. I was offered a lift to the local shopping mall. 'I'll pick you up a couple of hours,' said Heather, 'then we can drop off your groceries why don't you come home for dinner with us.' True to her word, Heather picked me up just where she had dropped me off, we took the food back to my villa. Waiting for me at their home was her family, a gorgeous lamb roast meal was about to be served, a cold glass of white wine was placed in my hand. I was finally able to relax. We discussed work, the need for insurances here in Australia. It seemed everything and everyone was considered fair game. Why was I not surprised? This land had not won me over. Not yet.

CHAPTER 28

As Heather drove me back to my villa, I mentioned the previous night's window tapping, the red dot going up down the window. Heather didn't seem concerned, saying, 'Probably some nosey basket case, I bet it's all blown over by now. Make sure you're all locked up. I'll call in tomorrow to see how you are.'

I wasn't so sure; my nerves were like fine wire after living on a tightrope with Carla. Once tucked up inside, my phone rang, it was Larry. He'd had a few drinks again, he was very bonhomie. 'Life is going to be so great from now on. I'm earning good money, plus you now have a little home to put together.' I wanted to be happy for us both, but all I could think was; *great you have work, mates, everything provided for you, where do I fit in?* There was no point in bursting his bubble, so I agreed saying, 'Well, I have agreed to a year, so I had better make the best of it.' which was greeted with, 'Not that chestnut again.' That night I slept well, waking to kookaburras in the trees in the park that surrounded the villas. Wandering outside to enjoy the fresh morning, I noticed the gate to the driveway was open. Perhaps I had forgotten to lock it. I did my small load of washing, thinking of the loads I had once done for my family, the big breakfasts, lunches, dinners, the loads of dishes. Why did I grumble back then? At that moment, I would have given anything to be part of that family scene once more .

My family was all grown up, now living around both countries. Oh, how I wanted to bundle them all up, together again, wanting to say how much I needed them. Then being an adult took over and I knew they had their own lives to live. Two of them had partners and children, while the other two had busy lives with their own businesses that seemed to be very successful. No matter what, I realised that this had been my decision despite their warnings. Grief in all its scenarios is such a weird thing; it can hit you at the strangest of times.

The day I learnt of Cilleen's death, grief squeezed my gut so hard I felt faint. My niece who had once been so loving and chatty, rang. At first I thought, how nice, she's rung to say, '*Hello, Aunty, how's life in Australia?*' instead all she said was, 'Thought you should know, Mum died. She's to be cremated tomorrow. Bye.' The phone went dead. I spent the day trying to write a letter to Cilleen, smiling to myself as I remembered our last time together. *But what do you say to someone who has passed? who will never read or feel your love ever again* I simply faced skywards speaking softly, Travel well, sister. Heal your heart.' Later that afternoon, Heather arrived. I made the tea while she told me of her day. When she informed me of an assistant's position where she worked, I was delighted, agreeing to ring the manager the next day, thinking to myself, *this is it. My chance to make a little money hopefully make some friends.*

When she left, she said, 'Call me tomorrow. If you get an interview I can give you a lift over there.' When Larry rang, I was so happy with my news, however he was not. If I worked, that meant his tax would change, I would no longer be a dependent. He would rather I did not apply. To be honest, I was shocked. When I had not been employed in

New Zealand, he was unhappy, now, he was telling me not to work. I felt trapped; damned if I do damned if I don't.

I informed Heather I was not applying; my reason was that I wanted to get settled first, make my new villa into a comfortable home. Slowly inching my way along in everyday life, with Heather or Fern calling in whenever they could, I still smile now as I remember the joy I felt when I heard their cars pulling into my driveway. I began to make friends. Esther, my next-door neighbour, a lady in her eighties, took me under her wing, advising me with the garden; I had no idea about gardening in this sand pit they called Perth. Another neighbour, Shirley, also took pity on my endless wanderings around the small park in the complex. It must have seemed a little strange to her. When Shirley knocked on my door, offering me a ride to her church craft's centre, I accepted with pure joy. I rediscovered the art of mosaics, soon my own masterpiece was hanging on the fence in the back yard. That was two days of my week taken up. Heather suggested that on Thursdays she would call in early to pick me up, drive me to at the shopping mall where I would buy my weekly groceries. We're both movie buffs so every Saturday, if there was not a family commitment, we would head off to the cinema.

At times Carla would call in and stay for ten or fifteen minutes, then leave. It was more of a duty call, so she could report to Milo that *all was okay with Cassie*. Larry was enjoying his work up north. He did not seem to suffer with homesickness as he not once said he missed me, family or friends.

For the first time in years, he had a bounce to his walk, his voice was happy. I was curious though, in a conversation with Fern one day, I asked if this was normal? 'Did all men in FIFO become indifferent to what was going on back home?' Her answer shocked me. 'It's not a pretty picture, Cassie, it's a real test for marriages. Over thirty percent off FIFO marriages fail. From what I have seen, the FIFO wives that are wise, learn to be independent, they enjoy the time on their own. Those who think they will have a mountain of money to enjoy have no idea of what bringing a family up on your own feels like. Then there are women like you who have lived a certain way for many years who can see the benefit simply by using their brains, not their hearts. I actually wish my old man would become a FIFO worker, it might save a lot of arguments.'

I found it an interesting conversation. Heather and her family had had an open conversation about the FIFO subject one night and they agreed with Ferns opinion; it could make or break a partnership. Once when Carla arrived, I decided to open the same conversation with her. Why was I not surprised by her answer. 'Why don't you stop whinging and begin thinking about the rewards you will have in the future,' having an intelligent conversation with her was not possible, her opinion dulled by the drugs she took daily.

One afternoon as the sun set, I took in all I had around me; a very pretty home, the scent of the roses in the air wafting into the lounge, I had made new friends who were making sure I was comfortable. I could make myself a very rewarding life living in Australia, if that was what I wanted. Larry really enjoyed his life as a FIFO worker. He chatted about his mates, enjoyed his work. Maybe I should do the same, just accept this was now my home. I was also aware we may become two very different, independent people. If this meant our marriage failed because of this, then so be it. At least we could say we had both given it our best shot. When he rang that night, I could hear he was taken aback by my pleasant greeting.

There was no unhappiness or questions; I had my friends and my artwork, I often dined out and I was regularly socialising. Money was not a problem, our little villa was coming along nicely. It all looked and sounded perfect to an onlooker. Except, there was a deep loneliness in my heart that can only be taken away when you can confide in another, when they truly understand. To be honest, I felt I had always been lonely for the love of a like-minded soul to connect with. Both my marriages had been full of trauma and drama in one form or another, all I wanted was a deep mind-body connection.

A connection that went past the physical and emotional. What I now found attractive was stimulating conversation, philosophy, trying new foods and travel. Maybe I was searching for something so rare, or it was just not mine to have. Or maybe I would find it here, in Australia. Whereas Larry he had his dream, work, mates, happy wife and home.

On our nightly phone call, we discussed our days, I was working on my garden plus my next mosaics project. Adding, I had also seen an advert in the local paper that Trinity, a senior school in Perth city, had a number of courses for adults to attend, one of them being creative writing and poetry. The following day, I was catching the train for the first time, to find out what there was to do in the city. Not once did I mention fear or New Zealand. I also did not mention that I was still being annoyed, occasionally by the red light blinking at the bedroom window, the tapping noise now accompanied by whispering.

I had reported it to the Heather, who admitted they'd had a break-in not long before I arrived, but all security screens had been re-installed, locks checked out on all the units including mine. On her suggestion, I had reported it to the police. There was nothing they could do immediately, but I was to call them straight away if it happened again.

I went to bed full of ideas that night, feeling that if I was open to all experiences, everything would fall into place. Heather and I chatted for ages on the phone the next morning making plans to go shopping then possibly to the movies on the weekend, perhaps we would have a manicure or pedicure. I had slept well, a shiver of excitement went through me as I planned to catch the ten o'clock train into Perth City the following day.

Jigsaw

The day whizzed by. I attended my mosaics class, I loved it; a three-hour craft class with women of all backgrounds and ethnicities. Once home, it was time to settle in and make an ideas map of what I wanted to see or do in Perth. I sat up in my bed writing until midnight. Sleep did not come easy as I felt like a three-year-old, I was so happy. Waking at six o'clock, I showered, dressed ate my breakfast, ready to leave by eight o'clock. Then Larry rang. It was unusual as he always rang at night, when he'd finished chatting to his mates plus downed a few drinks.

He wanted to wish me a wonderful day; again, unusual for him. At first I thought something was up, but he was genuinely happy to hear I was busy. I was very early, excitement rolling in my chest as I walked to the rail station, my head full of thoughts of classes that hopefully, I could join up at Trinity.

As I began my walk to the station I stopped in my tracks. The park next door looked different. The green trees and bushes that grew around my villa were picture perfect. I actually felt my chest expand with air my shoulders loosened. Looking up at the huge expanse of brilliant blue sky, I knew everything was as it should be. Feeling hope simmer in the bottom of my heart, I had a knowing that I could actually live my dream of art and writing. It was all here, I could live here in this land of endless sky, sun and sand, I would make a life for myself. It was all about possibilities. I was soon to learn the width breadth of that one wonderful word, 'hope.'

CHAPTER 29

Walking through Hay Street Mall I discovered a small art shop tucked away, making a mental note to call back in on my way home. There was a large red sign in the window that said 'Sale'. I found the smell of paints, crayons, oils and paper intoxicating as I passed the door. It brought the biggest smile to my heart. Here was something that completely gelled with my passion. Heading into Trinity, I had found the office inside the beautiful old church and the manager, Alison. I showed her the certificates I had, leaving an hour later, employed as a tutor for three hours a week in basic creative art therapy. She also invited me to lunch with some ladies in the college café. I soon had invites to join art classes, plus a new group who loved theatre. 'Would you be interested in attending different musical shows in Perth?' *Would I?* I couldn't help the grin that spread across my face.

I wandered back the way I'd come, through small alleyways, finally enjoying this new life that was opening up for me. My phone rang. It was Geoff from the theatre group I'd just joined. Was I available to see a movie next Saturday? The group were meeting at the Crown Casino for

Jigsaw

a drink, then going to the movie. Why not? The art shop was amazing, buying exactly what I needed. It seemed today was a good day, I bought my dinner, a huge salad takeaway, I was agog at the amount of mixed salad I could buy for five dollars. The stall holder, an Asian woman, rubbed a teeny piece of raw garlic then a small slice of ginger around the bamboo tub, added a mass of chopped vegetables, a dash of pink sea salt and ground in some black pepper. It smelt divine.

Once back at my villa, Carla rang and we spoke about my day. When she said, 'I told you Ozzie would be the making of you,' I wanted to say *no thanks to you* but decided it was a magic day nothing was going to spoil it, not if I could help it. Larry rang early that night I told him about my job. I was so excited but all he was concerned about was that it would change his tax rebates. He calmed down when I said, 'Larry, I'm only earning forty dollars a fortnight. Get over it.'

When Heather arrived she said, 'Got your text, you're amazing, look at you go. I'm so proud of you.' A bottle of chilled white wine was produced; I provided the amazing salad, popped in a few warm croutons plus cheese nibbles. We put our feet up, toasting our lives in Perth. She was no stranger to Carla's behaviour or treatment of me. When she made an observation which would stop any conversation, 'Well maybe it was one of the best things she could do for you. Yes, it was extreme, but it got you moving. Just look at you go. As for Larry, he's over the moon happy, you're happy, so what's the problem?'

I could not agree. I shook my head, 'No, Heather, what she did was uncalled for. I will not/cannot accept that even if you suffer with an illness, it does not give you permission to make another's life miserable. Showing little kindness, never hurt anyone.' There was no disagreement, just two adults having a conversation. There were no threats or insults to make each other agree, it felt good. With a second glass of cold white wine, we raised them in the air toasting a new life ahead. When she returned three days later, she was wearing her professional rental agent hat. It was a house inspection, something I had forgotten about and was not used to.

As she wandered around with her clip board, busily taking photos then writing in her report, she congratulated me on keeping the villa perfect. It seems every four months this would happen for a year, then after a year it would reduce to six monthly. I was yet to tackle the gardens, as the weather was too hot to stay outside for longer than half an hour. Heather's advice was, 'Talk to my Nona as she was an expert on growing garden plants.' Note taken, between Esther and Nona I was about to learn about gardening in Western Australia

I could not wait to start a new art piece; it would be for the lounge in our new home, an abstract in mauves adding blue undertones with an iridescent pearl streak running through it. Once I had the easel and canvas up, the colours softly melded as I prepped each pot with loving care. I was once told, 'Treat your art like you would a newborn baby.' I had followed that rule of thumb ever since. I became lost in my new art work. Andrea Bocelli sang a love song to me as I applied each stroke, his voice absolute magic. My day went by quickly, enjoying a casserole I had made for dinner. Cooking for one was something I was still getting used to, however once happy with my art I was into bed by ten o'clock.

I slept lightly, waking once to something or someone scratching at my bedroom window. My heartbeat skyrocketed when I heard the front door being tried. I raced through the small villa flicking on every light possible. My hand was shaking as I dialled the police, only to realise I had dialled the New Zealand police number. Frustrated, I pretended to speak to someone on the phone reporting in a loud voice that I had an intruder in the grounds. Whoever it was, was determined, they circled my home trying the back door, then a few minutes later the laundry door. I pulled a small carving knife from the draw, waiting to defend myself I

Jigsaw

was ready to run. I heard the back gate open then closed quietly. With no more tapping or thumping on the doors, I laid on top of my bed. *Why me?* I lay there for the rest of the night, wide awake until the dawn sun tipped the sky with orange, before finally falling asleep, waking to a furniture truck reversing up the driveway.

The lounge and dining room suite had arrived. I must have looked dreadful, as the two men unpacked, placing the furniture into the rooms I had allocated. The older man chatting away to me; he asked questions, I informed him I was new to the country, my husband was a FIFO worker, life was looking good. My hand shook as I paid them the money for their services. The older man asked me if I was okay. I nearly cried choking back my tears I said, 'I must be coming down with something.' I did not expect them to return ten minutes later with an iced chocolate doughnut plus a takeaway coffee. 'Here you are, Darl, chin up, look after yourself,' they said as they drove off. Then I did cry; big sobs with fat tears. It felt weird to be liked by total strangers, yet here I was being welcomed in so many ways. My life in Australia had truly begun; a life of discovering who I was, my beliefs, my skills, my nature, my spirituality plus so much more. This jigsaw of life I was a part of, was about growth in every aspect. If a seer had shown me what was to occur, I think I would have dug myself a hole so deep that you would never have found me. My life in Australia so far had been bumpy and scary; my beliefs about me dumped into a large jar then shaken up. So, join me while I take you on a journey some would find it hard to believe.

CHAPTER 30

The month of April was here, I had been living on my own for a month or more. Larry was due home on the weekend. The villa was now furnished with essentials, over time we would buy anything extra to truly make it into our home. I had spent two weeks almost non-stop, working on my new art piece, naming it *Mauve Melody*. The blue pearl I had mixed into a fluffy plaster mix of gesso shimmered in the lamplight. My plan was to have one painting in each bedroom, including the lounge. I was so proud of my colour choice; the art went with the light grey walls, pale mauve curtains, a lounge suit of electric blue, plus new TV. It looked classy. I didn't like a busy room filled with knick-knacks. The days when my children ruled the home with their toys were long gone. To be truthful, the kids were really good at putting things away, their Dad being the worst offender of all.

Having no car, I had been relying on public transport or friends for a ride, maybe a weekly taxi to the shopping mall. When Larry arrived home, he would have to take the airport shuttle, a train, then a ten-minute walk to the villa, however Carla had often given Larry a ride when

Jigsaw

she was there to pick up Milo. One night when they had dropped Larry off, I invited the two of them in for a hot drink. Milo took one look at my art, giving a soft whistle, 'That's bloody beautiful, Cass. Did you do that?' Larry was used to my artwork, saying, 'Oh that's nice,' as he began making drinks for us all.

Milo could not stop staring at the art on the easel. 'I can't believe you did that. How long have you been an artist?' Now it was my turn to be surprised, 'I thought you knew Milo, I've always been artistic.' Carla refused to look at it, I could feel my face twitching into a smile. I couldn't help myself, 'Do you like it, Carla?' True to form she couldn't help herself. 'I've seen something like it in the seconds shop on the main road. Did you copy it?'

'No, Carla, I created it myself,' I replied. Suddenly Milo interrupted, 'What would you accept for it if I were to buy it?' Larry was wide-eyed at the way the conversation was headed, 'Do you want to buy this, mate?' Milo stepped back studying the depth of the strokes, the luminous shadows. He was no art critique but something in it was affecting him. 'It's beautiful. What's the asking price? What would you sell it to me for?' Carla's face was pale, her mouth set in a thin line, her brown eyes turning hard; 'Let's sleep on this, before we make a decision.' Once they had left Larry was full of questions 'Okay, lovely, what's the price you're asking?' If there's one thing I knew in my years of selling my artwork, it was to never *ever* undercharge, as it always comes back to bite you. You underate your work, it will be considered cheap

I had a figure in my mind of $2,500, with a $500 discount. I loved it and didn't really want to sell it. If Milo accepted, well, two grand is two grand. I could always paint another. Larry was asleep before his head hit the pillow; I took my time, pondering if Milo would accept my offer. That money would set me up in art gear plus a small potted garden out the back. I woke late the next morning with Larry nowhere to be seen. I thought he'd gone for a walk around the district, two hours later I rang Milo asking if he'd seen Larry. He suggested he was probably at the pub. I was shocked asking him what he meant. He replied, 'He loves his booze, Cassie. Might be best to have a chat with him. It could be his downfall in the mining industry. No one likes a mouthy drunk.' It didn't make sense to me.

Larry liked a drink, yes, but mouthy drunk was a bit harsh. As I had Milo on the phone, I informed him of my price for the painting. He replied; 'What? Two grand for that?' Enough was enough. It was time for me to stand up to this rude couple who called us friends. 'Milo,' I said, 'number one, Larry is not a drunk if I hear that again, its slander. Number two, I would not sell you my art if my life depended on it. Sorry to have troubled you.' I turned around to see Larry drive up into the carport. Now I understood – he'd been car shopping without checking in with me! He honked the horn twice.

'Okay Cassie, I should have asked, but I saw it and bought it. Don't make a thing out of it.' Wrapping his arms around me kissing the back of my neck, he said, 'Let's go for a drive.' This man I had married frustrated me so much, I wanted to kick his bum so hard. But we were now the owners of a nearly-new, dark blue four-seater Apollo It drove like a dream. An hour or two later, over a cold drink at a café in the seaside city of Mandurah, I asked the price, Larry looked sheepish; 'Four thousand with a five-hundred-dollar deposit.' He saw the look on my face. 'Did you not think to ask me my opinion, Larry, did I even want a car?'

The difficult, angry Larry appeared, the one I knew so well. 'First of all, you know a big fat zero about cars, so why would I ask your opinion? Second I thought if you put your money for your painting towards it …' Suddenly, I was back in New Zealand, with him demanding I work like a trained monkey. Well, those days had gone. His question hung between us. It was then I felt that thin cord of affection begin to fray, his eyes slitting when I told him about my conversation with Milo. 'There will be no art sale Larry, in Milo's opinion you're a drunk teetering on the edge of being fired. Fix this, Larry, or I feel you'll be looking for another job very soon.' Any argument was squashed as he knew I was right. Having to have the last word he muttered, 'I may as well work the six weeks through Christmas – not much fun here.' I did not say a word thinking I should be careful what I wished for, as in that moment, it sounded like bliss for both of us.

We spent the next ten days being barely polite to one another. Larry claimed he was lonely, as I continued my hobbies with my new friends. Driving him to airport was a relief. This trip had been full of tension. I called into Fern's on my way home. Keith was warm, welcoming with no signs of being rude or offensive, fully dressed, thank heavens. I sat with them both for an hour enjoying fresh homemade scones with a hot milky cocoa. Keith admired our new car, looking under the bonnet then kicking tyres. He then got on his hands knees, looking under the car. 'You have a small oil leak, otherwise it looks like a great car – enjoy.'

With Larry returning to his life up north, my life was simple. I was responsible for myself only, doing whatever I wanted to, whenever I wanted to do it. It was the most unusual, pleasant feeling, as I was enjoying it. There, I had said it aloud; 'I enjoy being on my own.' If Larry took up the offer of working through the Christmas holidays, it meant I would be free to fly to New Zealand to spend the holidays with family. When had my love for him changed? When had I ever felt this happy with my life?

The Trinity Art Club had an exhibition coming up, I was very happy to be invited to enter my artwork – Mauve Melodies. The opening was a VIP night, which meant we could all dress up to the nines. I had invited both Fern and Heather, as well as Diane and Rex, Carla's in-laws. This was going to be a fun night out.

Kez Wickham St George

The Perth newspaper's photographers would be there. With this night in mind, I had new business cards made-up, designing myself a logo, I felt very much at home in this atmosphere. Myself and my two new friends had decided to taxi it in together, we all looked very glamorous; my two friends in black cocktail dresses with colourful jewellery, their make-up and hair perfect. I also wore a black cocktail dress with a sheer over shirt, richly embroidered in bright colours. I had no jewellery but had spent time on my hair, make-up and shouting myself a relaxing manicure. We all looked wonderful.

When Diane and Rex arrived at the exhibition, I introduced my two friends. We all wandered around talking about the art on display, there were some stunning pieces, red dot sales appearing on quite a few. Diane suddenly gave me a nudge, 'Looks like you have some interest.'

I found it interesting to observe the couple as they discussed my work. I had written the description myself; a simple description of technique, the suggestion of where the creative ideas came from, and the all-important price. It was all in the brochure. The couple interested were in deep discussion, it felt like they needed a nudge. I walked over introducing myself as the artist, answering their questions, offering them one of my business cards.

A blue dot appeared beside my work, which meant 'interest shown.' I was happy with that. The night went beautifully, meeting many people. It had been such a lovely night; warm weather, great people, on the ride home it was interesting to hear my friend's impressions about the art on display. Two days later Diane rang me, 'Can we pop over for a cuppa, Cassie?' I was happy to see them. I made afternoon tea as we chatted about art, plus work or travel we intended in the near future. Diane asked if I had seen Carla recently. I said, 'No, *was she okay?*' We may have grown apart however I did not wish her any harm.

I had a feeling that a friendly chat was not why she was here. Diane stood, 'Okay, Cassie let's get to the point.'

But when Diane said, 'I would like to put an offer in on your artwork at the exhibition, plus I want to purchase two small triptychs,' it took me a while to let it sink in. My heart skipped a beat; this was an enormous amount, over four thousand dollars! Diane explained, 'Cassie, I'm the CEO for an interior designer firm. We are heavily invested in granny flats and tiny houses, as they are called in Western Australia. I'm buying your work to display in one of our new display homes. However, I also have another two homes ready to dress for a client in a month, I want to place some artwork on the walls. Before your unique style is discovered, I want you to work exclusively for me.' I couldn't speak. At last my artwork had been recognised. After a lengthy battle for recognition back home, I had given up trying to sell, entering competitions just for the fun of it. As for selling anything in Australia? I had decided that as I loved creating art on canvas, I would paint for myself. I was having fun, enjoying being creative.

Offering her my hand, I accepted her offer. She could pop over to pick up the artwork that was still at the exhibition the following Sunday, I was given six months to create another six new pieces. Diane offered me a contract to sign – she would bring it with her when they picked up the art piece. She had readily agreed on my asking price of $4,500. A deposit would be transferred to my bank account.

Once she 'd left, I just about fell over myself to ring the girls. Both of them excited for me, I thought of ringing Carla then thought better of it. Larry had not rung for three days; he had always sulked. That was Larry, I was used to it. I invited my two friends out to dinner the following Saturday night. The deposit was enough to buy the half dozen large plants pots I had admired for the garden. I had also seen some pretty garden lights, plus two wicker garden chairs that would look amazing in my tiny backyard. If I was smart, I could buy what I wanted for my little villa, plus have enough cash to buy a return fare to New Zealand.

CHAPTER 31

Waking to a glorious morning, I stretched, feeling the tightness in my lower back; I would need to find a good massage therapist very soon. It was my way of keeping strong. I showered, then made myself breakfast when Carla knocked on the door. 'Just thought I'd pop around to say hello.' I invited her in to have a cup of coffee with me, as she walked in she noticed the artwork was missing. 'Oh, have a sale, did we?' I was honest thinking she would be happy for me, 'Yes, I sold it,' I said explaining about the exhibition. 'Hopefully, I can pop some plants in around the back patio, buy some outdoor furniture.' I dare not add that I had invited her in-laws to the exhibition or that Diana had purchased my work.

I was shocked when she leant forward, 'Well don't forget what you and Larry owe us. How about paying us back first? You still owe us over $800, before you go off on a buying spree.' I had no idea what she was talking about. I had paid her the $50 dollars rent she'd asked for religiously every week. We owed them nothing. I knew reasoning with her or asking for an explanation would not work, so I had to be clever with this one. 'If we owe you that amount, please invoice us. We will need a receipt as well.' She paused, I could feel she desperately wanted a slanging match. Well, not in my home; 'Carla, I'd like you to leave please.' Surprise flared in her eyes, then she did as I asked.

I checked my bank account, excited that the deposit had been transferred overnight – I was so grateful. It was time to get to work doing what I loved, bringing some positive energy flowing through the house, creating art. Two or three hours had slowly melted away, I was happy with what was happening between myself the canvas. It's a feeling only an artist can feel as paint slips from the brush; kissing the canvas it's a whisper of delight, pure magic.

Larry's number blinked on the screen as the phone rang. 'Hello there, you're early today,' my greeting pleasant. 'Cassie, I'm confused,' he said. 'Milo's just paid me a visit. He says you've just been paid thousands for your art. Now they want to be repaid for all they've done for us.' I explained it to Larry. 'I have only just received the deposit a commission for more artwork will arrive soon, it's not thousands Larry. I wish … but it's a wonderful start.' He did not hear the happiness in my voice. 'Milo's just given me an invoice for your living expenses for the eight weeks you lived with them. What the fuck did you buy? The bill is over two thousand dollars!'

I was shocked almost speechless. How can two people be so vindictive when you begin to earn money? 'Rip it up, Larry, it's all lies. Calm down, stop yelling at me.'

I could feel my own voice rising in frustration. I mulled it over for an hour or two, another coffee was made, my artwork forgotten. I saw a shadow slide across my front door, then retreat. Our new car was parked outside. Who was sneaking around now? *For God's sake, this place is insane.* Wrenching the door open, I found an envelope under the window wiper. Inside was a handwritten invoice. Every cup of tea, coffee plus all meals had been itemised. There was a list of $20 for each time I had used the washing machine. There was an amount for electricity, water usage also for petrol for every time I'd been a passenger. The amount was for $1,095. The $50 I'd paid weekly, added up to $600 had been discounted. The amount I apparently owed was $1,500.

Then there was Larry's bill – an airfare of $800 from Auckland to Perth, which as we understood it, had been paid by the drilling company, plus a $50 a week rental fee while he stayed with them. The total amount they claimed we owed was $2,400 to be paid within five days.

Suddenly I saw it for what it was – a power play. Carla had never liked anyone within her circle to be a winner. This was her way of saying, 'You owe me, I'm still in charge.' My shock turned to laughter as I saw just how stupid this really was. Well, they were not getting any money from us. Just to be sure, I rang the drilling company. Luckily Mick, the co-owner, was in the office. I liked Mick, he was all business, no nonsense. I asked him if he could verify that the firm had paid Larry's airfare to Perth. There was a silence, 'What's going on, Cassie?' I said there was some misunderstanding about who owed what. He explained that as Larry was introduced to the firm by Milo, Milo had offered to pay for the fare. Although this was not normal procedure, to bring in a stranger to the drilling sector without interviews or a certain criteria met. However, once Larry had passed all the requirements contracts were signed, they had reimbursed Milo for the airfares in full. I heard Mick ask his secretary to bring it up on screen. 'According to our records, Cassie, Milo was reimbursed six weeks ago.'

I wanted to say that Carla was blackmailing us, in fact, I wanted to cause her some real heartache, but when Mick said, 'Any more enquiries, Cassie?' I thanked him, ending the conversation. This was none of his business. Now to stamp this nonsense on the head. I rang Heather asking her advice. Hopefully she would know a bit more about the law

Jigsaw

here in WA than I did. She could not stop laughing. 'She what? Oh you poor Darl. You had to live with that crap for how long? Man, that's crazy stuff.' There was more laughter which set me off. 'Look, Cassie, ring your local citizens advice, surely they'll be able to help.' I did not bother to ring; I was out the front door sitting in the citizen's advice bureau door within ten minutes.

These fabulous people, provide a free lawyer for half an hour. I was ushered into Mr Walker's office. He looked over the handwritten invoice the first thing he said was, 'Whoever wrote this can't spell. This is rubbish. I'll take photocopy of it to pop into a file. If these invoices keep arriving, contact me then I shall write to her.' I was not happy with that decision, I wanted it put to rest immediately. 'I'd be happier if you would do it straight away, please. It could mean my husband's employment if it goes any further.' Mr Walker stared at me for a good two minutes. I could see his mind ticking over before he said, 'You're right. I'll have it written up. It will be in the post tomorrow.' Before I left, I asked if he would be so kind as to forward me a copy, giving him one of my business cards. I left his office happy with the result. Once I received Mr Walkers letter to Carla, I would forward it to Larry. Driving home, it struck me as ironic that for my eight weeks of abuse, for that amount, I could have stayed in a nice B&B. Although I would not have met Fern, Heather or Diane. I would not have sold my artwork, or been offered a contract. For whatever reason, I had met these welcoming people and in a weird way, it was all to do with Carla. I was grateful I had these opportunities, but what a painful way to do so.

That night when Larry rang, I told him what had happened. All he was really concerned about was his reputation at work. He was due to fly in that weekend; the weekend I had arranged to have a celebration dinner with my friends. Hopefully, he would keep his drinking under control. It would be so nice if we could make friends as couples, enjoy regular outings together. Fingers crossed. Life was busy, with my local creative writing group, my own art contract to fulfill, going to the mosaics workshop, plus the Trinity seniors in Perth. Weekends were movies, or shopping time spent with Fern or Heather – life was good.

Larry arrived back in Perth. He'd been away for six weeks this time and we felt like strangers. *Were we drifting apart?* I tried to arouse him every night with new perfume, sexy nightwear, blatant sexual overtures. He had always enjoyed a massage, I tried cream, potions and lotions. Nothing worked. He was unresponsive, complaining of pain when he urinated. I suggested a doctor, but he was dismissive. 'Nothing wrong with me, I just don't want to be touched.' We went garden shopping together but he showed little interest, 'Whatever makes you happy, it's your money.' His mood swings always kept me on my feet, but this was new.

Saturday night arrived, the night we were all meeting for dinner but Larry opted out, 'I don't feel like meeting new people. They're most likely the arty type you like.' Before I said something I was sorry for, I had a shower, dressed up in a pale grey silk top, blue dress jeans, added my maternal grandmothers crystal drop earrings. I offered to make him dinner before I left, he waved me off, 'Just go. See you when you get home later tonight.' This was not Larry. Larry was opinionated to the point of rudeness, he usually enjoyed meeting new people; he had always enjoyed a meal out.

Dinner was wonderful, however I kept looking at the door hoping Larry would bounce through. At 10:30pm it was time to go home, Rex walked me to my car. I loved driving at night. I liked the feeling of being in a capsule all the street lights twinkling. I was only half hour drive from the villa. As I drove up, I was sure I saw a shadow move from the side gate to the park. A shiver raced down my spine. I was not going to check it out, instead I jammed the key in the lock bolting through the door. Larry was asleep on the couch; I had been away four hours while

Jigsaw

he had skulled a six pack of beer. I cleaned up as he lay there inert to any sound I was making. Finding a rug to put over him, I kissed his forehead climbing into my lonely bed. My one thought: *We had everything we wanted, so why was he unhappy.*

The following day I tried my best to ferret out what the problem was. A brunch was planned and a lazy day ahead potting some plants; a hobby we loved to do together. I reminded him of the one-hundred-year-old rose he had saved, of the many baby ferns he had found entrusting them to me. We put the flat-packed garden furniture together. I offered to shout fish and chips for dinner, wanting a simple meal. I drove him back to the airport two days later. We had not said much to each other the entire time he was home. Larry was content once he had received my forwarded email from Mr Walker, warning both Carla and Milo that *it was an offence to write an invoice with no legal claim to any finances, unless financial gain on their behalf was agreed to by both parties in writing.*

Larry was off once more on a four-week stint in Tom Price. I parked the car in a half-hour bay, walking with Larry to the airport lounge. I knew some of his co-workers, we all greeted one another. Milo was there skulking in the background. I gave him the most withering look I could muster. Larry's plane was ready to board, and I saw him wince as he stood up. I reached out to steady him. 'Leave it, Cassie. I'm okay.' I kissed his cheek. 'Love you. Ring me tonight. Take good care of yourself.' I left the airport knowing something was definitely not right with Larry.

CHAPTER 32

For three of those weeks, I had the weirdest experiences every second or third night. The nocturnal visitor, the local peeping tom, was back. There was tapping and scratching on my bedroom window, the small red light glowing, letting me know he had a camera going. I had rung the police twice now with a complaint. They had visited me, two Police cars in my driveway certainly stirred up the village gossip. They tried to collect fingerprints, finding two cigarette butts outside our car. Then one lonely neighbour decided to get in on the scene. She arrived at my door saying she had proof 'we' had a peeping Tom. She'd seen him two or three times outside my home. The police asked me to remove two large bushes outside my window as he was obviously using them as a screen. I rang Heather, who was most accommodating, coming over to help me cut the bushes to remove them. Although her news was sad, she had sold the villas.

One night, I was asleep in bed and was woken with the smell of cigarette smoke. Sitting up, I groggily watched grey plumes of smoke being puffed through the window. I slammed the window shut immediately,

Jigsaw

ringing the police who arrived almost immediately. However, apart from a cigarette butt and a footprint, there was nothing.

With the police car in my driveway, the neighbour who had claimed to have seen the offender sailed into my home, fully made up with a tight-fitting bodice pushing up her over-abundant breasts. She chose her target; a lone policeman taking photos notes. Both officers looking like possums caught in headlights. While eyeballing the officer trapped between her and the front door. She asked them to visit her home, saying, the peeping Tom had been at her windows as well she was sure had ejaculated on her front door. Both police men's eyebrows shot up, 'Madam, are you sure?' Her eyelashes flickered madly, 'Oh yes, I listened to him grunting as he masturbated.' Now my face was flaming. I felt for the two men in uniform trying to defend themselves from this voluptuous come on. If this was not serious it would have made a great movie.

Whoever was tapping on my windows ramped it up a notch, suddenly deciding to ring my doorbell at 2am. I took the batteries out. He returned, now banging on the back doors windows in the early hours of the morning. The police were completely baffled, as to why they could not catch him. Two burglaries had been reported in the village, so the police installed a detective on night watch, placed a police camera in the lounge. They could do nothing. Whoever it was, seemed to have inside knowledge of where or what the police were doing. When my new landlord rang, he explained everything would be the same, nothing would change, he wished me well.

That day I was off to my local art class, where I met Sandy, a tall good-looking blonde woman, who, knowing I was living on my own for most of the time, decided she would offer me an opportunity to join a very special club. You could only attend their meetings with a personal invitation. It all sounded very mysterious. I invited her to my home after class one day, made hot drinks, put out the cheese, pickles and crackers so we could have a bite to eat. Sandy began our lunch conversation with, 'How do you feel about sexual stimulation?' I did not have time to swallow, choking on my biscuit dip, when she informed me that she thought I was the right fit for her club of three. She explained that she had a fabulous marriage, however her husband was no good in bed, she craved great sex. She must have taken my gurgle of surprise as permission to carry on. 'We meet in the woods past the Gosnells library, seven o'clock tonight, bring your jump starters.' I wasn't sure I had heard right, so I said, 'My what?' 'Your jump starters, Sweetie.' I asked why. Her big blue eyes stared into mine, 'Sweetie, to get the buzz we need, we attach them to our nipples then to the batteries. God, I have the best climax.' My food stuck in my throat, I could not swallow, I couldn't believe what she was suggesting wondering *why me*? One of her pale lashed eyelids closed slowly over one eye. I guess it was supposed to be a seductive wink. She left with, 'See you there, Babe.' Needless to say, I did not go back to that art class, blocking her emails and her phone calls. Why would anyone say such things if it wasn't encouraged? I wracked my brain going through any conversation we'd had. Nothing.

Two days before Larry was due to home, he was still in pain. I could hear it in his voice, slightly breathless, almost staccato, our conversations short. There was no spark, no energy. I begged him to see the medic team. 'You need to see someone Larry. It's not better, its worse. Please see someone.' The day before he was due home, Tesha, a member of the local writing club was having a Christmas in July luncheon; we were all to take a five-dollar gift with a small plate of food. Once I arrived, I was greeted with a very European greeting, a kiss on each cheek. The luncheon was lovely. My gift to another was an art piece on a miniature canvas with an easel. Tesha was the hostess with the mostest she was also the recipient of my gift. She kept looking at it and admiring it. As we were leaving, she asked me to stay on, I was happy to. She asked to see

Jigsaw

my portfolio. I showed her my Artonline website, her husband Ken was also interested. They placed a commission for one large artwork in bright apricots creams with a gold fleck running through the Gesso. I named a price, the same as I had charged Diane; they said, 'Worth every penny.' I asked for approximately six weeks before they would be ready. They agreed, inviting me stay on to have afternoon tea with them.

Tesha and Ken had a beautiful home in Roleystone. Their travels around the world were extensive, shown in the artifacts they had collected on their adventures. The deck was built like the bow of a ship, very Zen, a deep ming blue ceramic pond bought back from Italy showing off the deep golden fish swimming in it. Surrounding the vast deck were lush miniature palms in matching blue ceramic pots. The breeze had turned chilly, so our afternoon tea was in Ken's study where I was invited to sit in an embroidered wing back chair, an heirloom from Germany. I admired it, saying, 'It was the loveliest chair I had seen.' Animals of the forest were embroidered with so much detail, they looked real. It felt wrong to sit in it.

Once home, I decided on a nana nap for this tired, semi-retired artist. Larry was due home the following day, thinking of our early days when we were both new to each other, days of being broke but together. When his arms would go around me as we snuggled up in bed. Today, I had everything, the lifestyle I once dreamt of surrounding me. The nana nap had turned into a deep sleep when my mobile rang. It was the Tom Price medical team. Larry was being flown out to Fremantle hospital, immediately for an emergency procedure. With a calmness I was not feeling, I asked for the details. With shaking hands rang Fern, knowing I was in shock, I should not drive. I asked her for a lift, 'Of course, Cassie, I'll be straight over.' We arrived the same time as the helicopter delivered Larry, my heart aching as I saw my husband being wheeled into ER, the hospital team taking over. Larry looked like a small sleeping child wrapped in a white blanket. Four hours later, after many tubes inserted, all the tests performed, I dreaded hearing those words again, 'He has cancer.' A mass in his urethra was found, it had been surgically removed. We'd been told many years ago that the medication he was given for bowel cancer might have side effects. Sometimes it was an immediate reaction like ulcers in the mouth, sometimes these things sat hidden for years, then reared their ugly heads. Painkillers were given, a urine catheter inserted, he was then sent home under my care. No alcohol, no fizzy drinks, plus a healthy diet was suggested.

It took an awful disease to push us back to where we started as a couple. I spoilt him as he lay either on the bed or on the couch watching videos. His employer sent us flowers, his wages were to be paid regularly. Nothing was too much trouble. My two friends and their husbands finally got to meet this mystery man I talked about. They all got on. Best of all, we talked, my stories of our flirtatious neighbour making him laugh, 'Stop, Cassie, I can't breathe.' We held hands, we laughed together, he would watch me as I painted. 'I love watching you work, Cassie, you become so intent.' Four weeks went too soon. Larry was feeling like a new man, catheter free, with no pain. Milo had rung Larry while he was recouping, I could hear the tension as they spoke. It was 'sort of' an apology from them both. Larry smiling when he repeated part of the conversation. We think Cassie took this too far – there was no need to involve a lawyer.' Larry's reply was, 'Cassie has the right to make up her own mind. If she thought it was necessary, then I agree.' Wow! Larry had backed me all the way.

While he was home, the nocturnal visits from the local nuisance seemed to have stopped for a while. I was first up one morning, the radio playing quietly. I could see the park from the kitchen window. The early morning sun gilding the treetops with gold and pinks, everything looked peaceful. I began making breakfast for us both, when I realised

Jigsaw

our outdoor furniture was missing. How strange! Unlocking the back door, I called Larry. We both stood there for a moment, a little bemused. 'What the hell?' Larry exploded. Our two chairs and small table had been unscrewed, it now lay flat on the concrete in very tidy piles, the bolts with screws lay in a small mounds, beside them, a bouquet of dried flowers was placed to the side. The police were informed, they paid us a quick visit, but there was no harm or vandalism done. Nothing to report really, although, along with the peeping tom incidents, they admitted it was worrying. Larry was due to return to the mines the following day. There was no doubt we both enjoyed the money Larry earnt, he was a respected member of the drilling team, otherwise 'the firm' as they were called, would not have made sure he was okay. Yet, this time I found it hard to say goodbye.

We both wanted to travel, Larry had spoken to Mick while he was off work. Mick had encouraged Larry to apply for a drilling position with a Mining convoy heading east. If the application was successful, it meant leaving everything I had built up here to live in a caravan, as the convoy would be visiting many distant mine sites. One slight problem – we would need a caravan. So, when Larry suggested looking at caravans before he flew back, my heart was torn. I had grown to love it here so much. I was involved in many clubs, had success with art sales and had begun making notes for a coffee table book of my artwork. I had made progress in talking to a publisher, but with Larry unwell I had not gone any further with it. We both adored travel, that had been part of the deal when we agreed to live in Australia; travel as much as possible. I decided to leave it until he was next back home so we could plan together.

CHAPTER 33

You know that saying when opportunity knocks, well this was one of those times. Both of us recognising an opportunity we did not want to miss. We headed for the main road to the suburb of Cannington. Along the road were caravan sales of every sort, we visited every one of them. My heart was stolen by a 12ft canvas pop-top. I knew once I entered this tiny little tub on two wheels, it was mine. Larry could tyre kick as much as he wanted to. The salesman, Brian and Larry could barter between themselves, I just knew. Mentally counting up my savings I spoke to Brian, who said he would accept a deposit of two thousand. My dream of going home to visit the family in New Zealand happily slipped away. Larry's mouth snapped shut. I took hold of his hand; 'This is the one.' Larry wanted all the bells and whistles, this little caravan had none of them. The price of $7,000 not negotiable. I figured that the $5,000 owed by my two clients would pay for the rest of the amount owing. Larry squeezed my hand, 'You one hundred percent sure?' I was so sure; this little van was mine. 'Okay, mate, looks like my wife is smitten. Where do we sign and when do we pick her up?' We spent the next two days

Jigsaw

planning our very first holiday, maps lay all over the lounge room floor. The last thing Larry said to me as he boarded the plane, his eyes dancing with excitement, 'We're now caravan owners, start planning a trip.'

I was still excited about planning a trip. I was parking the car when the sound of a gun being fired filled the air. I froze, waiting to feel the pain of it ploughing into my body, my one thought: 'No! Just as it felt as if everything was coming right.' I felt dizzy sick, my feet frozen to the concrete drive, then relieved when I realised I had not bolted the wooden side gate; the wind had slammed it shut. Feeling very stupid, I let myself in the front door, heading for the kitchen, to prepare a cup of tea before a good night's sleep. Every time the wind blew something around or I heard a sudden bang or thump I wanted to cry. Being on my own for the first time in a long time was nerve-wracking. I had felt safe while Larry was home.

I slept late, missing mosaics class, taking my breakfast back to bed, settling down with a book. When the phone rang it woke me, the time had just gone 9:30am. Tesha was ringing to find out how her artwork was going. I said two more days to dry, it should be good to go. We arranged for her to pop in to collect it in three days, making it Wednesday morning. She offered to make something delicious for morning tea and I was happy with that. I decided to send her an invoice for the amount owing.

Once I was up, with a load of washing drying, I then cleaned my home. Every mundane job was done until my house sparkled. I had been meaning to clean the outside of the windows for a while, so, 'No time like the present.' It was while I was washing the laundry windows, I noticed the side gate latch was broken, making mental note to report the damage to the landlord. I found some garden string, tying the gate firmly closed. I was busy tweaking some of my artwork for Diane when my neighbour, Sheila, popped in with an invite. 'Would I like to accompany her to the local theatre?' A new play was on, she had a spare ticket as she did not like going out alone. Agreeing, I said I would pick her up at six o'clock. She lived directly opposite me, the local theatre was only a half hour drive away.

We had a lovely night. Sheila was my senior by a good twenty years, yet she still enjoyed life to the full. Dropping her off at her door, I turned into our driveway and saw the side gate was once again open, swinging in the wind. Knowing I had tied it securely, I had the eerie feeling I was being watched. I felt I had two options: stay in the car and see what would happen; or drive away, find a safe place to park and ring the police? As it was, Sheila, could see my car lights were still on, as our villas faced each other. She rang my mobile, 'Are you alright, Cassie?' I replied, 'That peeping Tom is around here somewhere. I think he's in my backyard waiting for me.' I wanted to scream with fear. 'Why not drive over here dear, park your car in my driveway, I'll be waiting for you.' With a sigh of relief, I did as she suggested. Once safely in her lounge, I rang Larry. 'Get the cops over there immediately, do not go inside until they're by your side.' Again I did as I was asked. The Police arrived and apparently I wasn't the only complaint about strange activities in the neighbourhood that night. I lead them to my front door. One of them walked through my home checking doors windows; 'No one inside, Ma'am,' his voice coming to a stop as the older police officer and I stood gawping at the carnage on the back patio. Everything Larry and I had planted was uprooted. Every pot smashed. Every hanging plant torn off and trashed. The artwork I had put outside to dry was slashed to pieces. The outdoor furniture was torn to matchsticks. I had no words, the senior police officer saying, 'Do you have somewhere else to go? You can't stay here tonight. I believe this is a warning. He will be back.'

Sheila offered me a bed, the police saying, 'No, too close to home. She needs to get as far away as possible, tonight.' I rang Fern who was full of empathy once I explained, 'Of course, Cassie, come over now.' I did not

Jigsaw

sleep, I just kept asking, *why*. My phone rang at six o'clock Larry was full of questions that I couldn't answer. Fern arranged for a day off to stay with me, Larry trying to make arrangements to come home. The phone was constantly ringing. My brain froze as Fern answered the next call. It was Detective Sergeant Cooper wanting to meet me at ten o'clock at the villa. He made sure I understood *I was not to be on my own OR to enter the property without him or armed police by my side.*

My mouth agreed but my mind had frozen. Cop Cooper, as he was known, was very much a detective. He walked with me to the villa went in first, flipping his coat back, clicking a little button on the leather holster. It was the first time I had ever seen a gun ready to be drawn. The inside had not been touched but the laundry door had been jimmied open, my bras and panties displayed on top of the washing machine. 'Sorry, love, this is one sick bastard. He's certainly after you. You can't stay in Armadale until we sort this. Do you have another place to go?' I had stayed the night at Ferns by now, Fern had rung Heather.

She was onto a place for me to stay immediately; a bed and breakfast in the city. Larry had even worse news. He couldn't fly home at the end of the week as he was about to go on convoy to another mine site in the Pilbara. I asked if I could join him. 'Sorry, love, you would hate it here. I'm camping in a caravan with three other blokes.'

Every time I closed my eyes, I saw the back patio of my villa. In my wildest dreams, I had never thought this would be me; bed surfing at friends, afraid to go to sleep, jumping at every shadow or sound. I was so tired, my body crying out for a rest but my mind re-examining every detail of what I had seen. My brain was still asking why? At 1am I had an epiphany: *I was the owner of a caravan. Let's road test that little sucker , I could live in it.* I even knew where I wanted to go – my favourite seaside village, Rockingham. Once dawn hit the sky, I was up, time to put my thoughts into action.

I had kept the phone number of the removalist who had shown such kindness to me when I had moved in to the villa. I told his receptionist who I was, that I needed his help urgently. I rang my landlord about the break in, telling him I couldn't live there again. He tried to bluff: 'I'm sure it's not that serious. I'll have the door fixed. You can move back in, can't you?' He had been a good landlord I didn't want to upset him in anyway, but I knew I couldn't stay there. 'No, I can't. My life is in danger, the police have asked me to stay away unless I have protection.' My next call was the caravan sales office, asking to speak to Brian My question was, 'When can I pick our van up?' 'On full payment,' he replied.

'I'll be there this afternoon to pay in full. Is cash okay?' He was delighted. My next call was to find a caravan park in Rockingham, a small seaside town in Perth we had visited and I had loved. I rang the Palms Springs Park booking in for two weeks. The removalist rang, I explained what I needed, plus storage, he agreed to arrange it all for a minimum fee. Following police instructions. Once he arrived, I could return to the villa. It was all arranged. I then rang 'the firm' asking to speak to Mick. Informing him of my situation, police warning me to leave Armadale immediately. I asked if he had any sort of transport that could pick up the caravan to tow it to the Palms Caravan Park for me. He was most helpful, agreeing to meet me at the caravan sales office. He was more than happy to help, the complete rearranging of my life had taken two hours; it felt right.

Meeting the removalist, I helped them pack, he had found some cheap storage for me. His offer halved when he saw what had happened to the plants. Making a phone call to his wife, who loved plants, he was willing to take them all, including the broken pots. I accepted immediately. I wanted nothing from the chaos. As we sorted through the plants, the neighbour at the back of my villa popped his head over the fence, 'Moving out, are we?' I had met him when we first moved in, occasionally greeting each other if we were outside. I knew he was a prison guard and a grandfather. I also knew he was looking for a bigger place to rent. He knew very little about me, he had complained once about my music being too loud. This neighbour jumped over the fence, with such ease something clicked. I did not have the time to mull it over as he asked if he could have a particular plant. I agreed, he went directly to the plant he wanted, yet the yard was a mess

When he left he did so via the side gate, something, again, it did not feel right. He had jumped over the fence so easily, yet he couldn't jump back again. The removalist also cottoned on to what I was thinking, 'Don't go there, love, its mucky enough as it is,' he said. Maybe he was right.

While we were loading furniture into the truck, the property owner drove up, screwing a sheet of plywood over the smashed laundry door. We shook hands, he was sorry I had to leave.. Then it was time to meet Mick at the caravan sales yard. Stopping off at the ATM, withdrawing out the cash I needed. My senses were on high alert, wondering if I was being watched or followed. I was so anxious, I stumbled. A hand reached out to steady me, I screamed. The poor man whose face I was screaming into, let go of my elbow. 'Lady, stop, you're okay.' Mumbling an apology I hastily backed the car out. Mick was there to greet me, he had bought his wife along for morale support. What a lovely couple. Marie had packed a large box of groceries for me. They hitched the caravan up to the ute, I paid Brian the remaining money I owed, papers were signed, keys handed over, everything was ready. My signature shaky as my nerves were a mess. Within the hour, I was watching Mick back my new home onto site number 21, Palm Springs caravan park. He made sure it was steady as a rock, putting the caravan feet down, hooking me up to power and water, turning on the gas, then checking all was working. Marie had thought of everything, she had even packed a sleeping bag, and a pillow. Thanking them both profusely, I waved them off. All I wanted was to get into the van, lock the door and lie down before I fell down, I felt drained. I had two more phone calls to make: one to Fern assuring her I was fine where I was now living. She would inform Heather. Then, I tried to call Larry, who was not available. I left a message that I was safe. I lost the meaning of time; my mind was working on rote .

The late afternoon sun was shining directly onto my little van. I was wrapped in warm bubble as the fear began to shift, logic began to filter through my thoughts. This was a 'gated' holiday park, it had a feeling of space about it. I took a deep, calming breath for the first time in two days. In the box of groceries, was a large bottle of water, a plate of meat with a fresh salad for my dinner. I felt blessed. Larry was working for such caring people. I showered in the ablution block at dusk, ate my meal then lay down on the very comfy bed, looking around at our new home. It was all tan inside, with curtains of deep green, the tiny sofa, also covered in green. This little life saver was all I needed until I could sort things out. *Where did I want to go? what did I want to do?* Did I want to go back home or live in this tiny caravan where everything was so basic and simple. I could stretch out here. No one knew me, I felt safe. While I slept, my brain had been busy sorting, placing things in order. When I woke with the kookaburras chortling in the tree next to my van, I knew without a doubt, that Stuart my ex-neighbour was the peeping Tom. I had no proof, I just knew. The Armadale Police had asked me to check in to let them know I was safe, they would let the Rockingham Police know of my whereabouts and to keep an eye out. My friends promised a weekend visit if I was up to it.

When Larry rang, I was calmer than I'd been for days. I felt like I was on holiday … and I was in a way. He kept saying, 'I can't believe you've done all that on your own, Cassie, I'm so proud of you.' I told him my feelings about Stuart. 'Don't be hasty, Honey, you have no proof.'

Jigsaw

I agreed. It was not up to me. However, when we did eventfully return the spare villa keys, I called in to let Sheila know I was okay. Larry had walked me to her door, knowing I was nervous about being back there. She admitted, 'I think you're right, Cassie, he's not pleasant man.'

We still had no proof. It was just a gut feeling, I still had many questions. Why had there been just one small plant left? How could he leap over the fence from his side, yet could not do so when returning to his yard? I knew the truth feeling angry, then incredibly sad. All of the carnage and fear, for what? The want of a three-bedroom villa? Carla and Stuart would make good company for each other. Time to rest and repair to begin a new way of life in Rockingham.

CHAPTER 34

Larry loved being in the caravan with me. We both decided it wasn't a bad way of life. All around us holiday makers were chatting to each other about where they had been or where they were heading. I knew this was what I wanted for my life; travel, meeting new people, finding the fun, enjoying life. When it was time for Larry to return to the Pilbara, he held me so tightly at the airport, whispering his love for me as we said our goodbyes; he had never *ever* done that before. Perhaps our caravan life was working for us. In the early morning I drove home with a smile on my face, bypassing the road we normally took from the airport to Armadale as I was no longer part of that community. I called into a local haberdashery shop, buying pillows, sheets, plus a doona. All the household gear I needed was stored somewhere in Rockingham. I did not need any of yet, as this wee caravan took ten minutes to clean, if that.

My life in Rockingham was to be kept simple and calm as possible. If there was to be a simple time in my life, it was now. Every night, once I'd locked up, I would make myself a cup of hot herbal tea, then journal about how I felt that day. Larry would ring about seven o'clock, sober and caring. I think he was aware at how close I was to losing the plot, that would mean he would have to come home. It could mean his job, which he loved. Together, we were a team. Suddenly, I felt he actually got it. Standing together we were strong, on our own we were divided. As the first week became a month, I informed Larry I wanted to stay in Rockingham. I loved the atmosphere, plus we could come and go in our van whenever we liked.

The camp managers were very welcoming when I asked to become a permanent resident, for $120 per week, which included power, water, plus weekly garbage collection. I had a site allotted to me. The camp manager, Ross, walked me over to two empty sites. One had a generous-sized willow tree gracefully hanging its branches over the site, the other was close to the ablution blocks. I fell in love with the willow tree, the number 27 painted on the concrete lab, this was my favourite number. I knew this would be home for some time. I absolutely loved it there. A three-minute drive to the beach, close to a small shopping centre, the people were friendly and welcoming. Larry was due home in two weeks, the time had flown by. We loved every minute of being together. We had many decisions to make; what to do with our gear in storage was number one. We decided to sell it all. We found the storage address, both of us in shock when we saw the state of our furniture, the rubbished jumble of boxes which once contained our things. It had been rifled through, most of the little treasures we had collected while living in the villa had been stolen. What we had left was two couches, a dining room table, and the double bed without the mattress.

The shed was not a secure storage space so to speak, it was used for storing gardening gear where staff could walk in pillaging our belongings. Larry approached the owner of the shed. 'Nothing to do with me, mate. All I did was a favour for a friend, stored this stuff out of the weather.

When are you taking it away? If you want, I can buy that stuff off you. My daughter is moving out and needs furniture.' He offered $400 for the lot. All three of us knew it was a super bargain he was getting, I nodded in agreement. We sorted through finding two box's with our clothes in, another with our photographs, plus one very old antique box given to me by my mother. Packing the few boxes in the boot, we were paid. I expected sadness and regret, instead we both felt free of any encumbrances.

I rang Dianne asking if we could drop over, 'Yes, I'd love to see you, come over for a coffee.' It was time I explained what had happened to her artwork. She was shocked I had been through so much, she was happy to give me an extra three months to find somewhere in Rockingham where I could complete my contract. While at Diane's, her brother Milo rang. She told him we were visiting, he immediately asked to see us both. I held Larry's hand so tightly as we stepped into Carla and Milo's kitchen. The smell that hit us was rank; rubbish from the bin had spread onto the floor, the bench covered in dirty dishes, fly's crawling everywhere. Carla sat at the kitchen table, billowing cigarette smoke. She seemed to have grown even bigger since we last saw one another.

Milo offered us tea or coffee, but we declined. A long time ago, this had been a beautiful home, its bones were nice, what remained of a large forgotten garden was still pretty. It had been a lovely family home with the added attraction of a pool. Milo's news was that they were selling up, moving to a smaller home, so Carla could manage the house better. Three months previously, we would have jumped at the opportunity to buy it, the asking price insanely cheap. 'Did we want to get first opportunity to buy it?' asked Milo. 'Give us a day or two to think about it, please. We'll let you know our decision.' It was certainly tempting; we could be home-owners once more.

As we drove back to Rockingham, we discussed it. If we bought, I would have my own studio at last. It was out of Armadale, so out of danger and I would be able to swim whenever I wanted to have pool parties. In my mind, I had already replanted the garden. I saw palms around the pool. I would re-curtain and re-carpet, give the house a good clean and interior paint. My art would sit on freshly painted walls of soft green. I would replace the flooring in the kitchen and the main bedroom would be stripped of everything you could put your hands to. I saw soft apricot on the walls with a grey colour in the furniture. I saw a chance to redecorate, to begin again. It was just on dusk as we drove into the camping ground. I saw our little caravan under the willow tree. The simplicity of what we had dawned on us.

We placed two camping chairs outside in the warm breeze, when Larry asked, 'What are your thoughts, Sweetheart?' The picture changed in my mind. I now saw Larry working long hours to give me the beautiful home I craved. I saw us growing apart once more. I saw all the hard work we had already done back home. We had built a family home many times over, so our children would be happy and comfortable, their happiness of the utmost importance to us.

It was time to wipe the slate clean. 'You know what Larry, we already have all we need. I don't need anything else!' Larry rang Milo telling him our answer, 'Sorry, mate, it's a no, we're both enjoying what we have.'

It was now August, where had the weeks gone? As I dropped Larry off at the airport, I recognised that our relationship had become relaxed, both caring what each other thought. The ease of caravan life agreed with us both. Before we had driven to the airport, I had pinned a note to the camp notice board looking for a small cabin to rent. The reason being I was looking for a studio close by. On my return, the camp park manager asked to see me. He had seen my note, offering me a small cabin to work in. It was not the cleanest or the nicest place I had been in, the light was shocking. It was a small, run-down wood cabin with a stained, rotting bench and its floor, green grass grew though in one corner, however it had a tap with cold running water and electricity. The offer was for three months at fifty dollars a week. I asked for six months as I still had Tesha's and Diane's artwork to complete. Ross thought about it then held out his hand saying, 'Meet me in the office in an hour, I'll have the papers made out.' Just like that, I was back in business.

I began to shop for what I needed to update the cabin, a local hardware shop became my favourite haunt. Recently my journalling had become serious and I knew there was a book in me somewhere. I knew I needed some guidance. Working on the laptop at night, I searched the internet for a creative writing course. I found an online travel-writing course with a Tasmanian university and sent an email making enquiries. I soon had a routine going, waking at seven o'clock, walking around the caravan park for exercise. After breakfast, a shower, a quick tidy of my little home, I would go to work in the old cabin where my artwork was coming along beautifully. First and foremost, cleaning this cabin until it shone. This was my workplace, so my rules applied. In the two months I had been living in the camp, I had befriended the cleaning couple, Addy and Charlie, Addy very willing to help me clean up the tiny cabin.

The first job we tackled was the floor. An old piece of thick cardboard was found then tacked over the top, Addy warning me, 'We live by a fresh water lake, Cassie. There are plenty of tiger snakes roaming the campground. We also have redback spiders a plenty, so keep all the holes blocked up.' Charlie took over mending the bench, plus he soon had the window opening and closing with ease. Addy and I scrubbed the place clean. She placed an old watering can full of freshly planted geraniums by the door. The day I moved in, my arms were full of easels, brushes, paint and canvases. As I set myself up, these two arrived with a thermos of tea, tin mugs, milk, sugar, paper plates with freshly made blueberry

Jigsaw

muffins. As we enjoyed morning tea together, I remembered my Mum saying, 'Don't forget to celebrate everything you do, Cassie, life goes by too fast.' She was right.

CHAPTER 35

Addy became smitten with my art technique as I placed a loaded brush onto canvas. She was always ready with questions of colour mix, plus application. These two had taken me under their wing, helping me to clean and patch this cabin. I now wanted some space, however I had the feeling that Addy wanted to move in. One day I had a brilliant idea, 'Addy, how would you like to paint my cabin door?' Her eyes shone, her head nodding, I added, 'Perhaps the window-sill could do with a fresh lick of paint too.' We drove to the paint shop; they knew me by name now. I showed Addy paint swatches and we both loved the cerulean blue. As I worked inside, Addy painted the door and window frames, the geraniums had already sprouted bright red flowers. I had become quite attached to it. It smelt clean, the smell of gesso and paint intoxicating.

I was buzzing with creativity. To thank her, I shouted her for morning tea at the café at the local pub. Charlie was already ensconced with his buddies at the bar, although he greeted her, Addy ignored him completely. I realised there might be a problem there. I invited her to come second-hand shopping with me. I was after some containers to hold my brushes. Finding what I wanted, I looked up to see Addy holding a small, rusty door knocker. It was very old, a green patina bloomed over it. Her blue eyes looked into mine, 'Can you afford this? it would look lovely on the cabin door.' Within two hours, she had screwed the door knocker on, while I painted across the door 'Cassie's Cabin', a padlock now added to keep it secure. It was now watertight, clean, filled with art gear. Addie was there every day as I opened up, maybe she was lonely. Perhaps her life was not what she wanted.

Every day when I was in the cabin, I would hear her approach, her footsteps now familiar. I had noticed she was occasionally adding little homely touches; a little hanging pot plant outside, a tiny pot of pansies on the windowsill. Soon her story tumbling out, they were pensioners, they had immigrated from England made unwelcome by family with Charlie's addiction to gambling. They had little money, the cleaning they did in the camp paid for their rent. Their caravan was as small as mine, although Charlie had added two or three extensions. It was a mish mash of plastic, carboard and tin. I felt sad when I overheard them referred to as 'trailer trash.'

Saturday was my day to shop, have a relaxing coffee. If Fern or Heather were available they would join me for the morning. Fern was once again having marital problems. I would listen as friends do, advice was for the professionals. Sadly, Heather's Nona was unwell and she now spent a lot of time with her, we hardly saw each other. I understood this as they were a close family. Sunday was the day I cleaned up the art gear. I would take a bucket of sudsy hot water to the cabin, clean its windows, sweep floors, clean up brushes, plus any other art utensils, ready for the beginning of a working week. Once home, I would then study the travel-writer's course. Larry had been given a different shift he was now 'two weeks on, two weeks off.' He had been made a permanent at Tom Price. We still spoke every night. Now and again I could hear from his voice that he had been drinking, but nothing as serious as before. Life took on a steady beat. I loved the simplicity of it all.

The time in my art cabin was nearly up; Diane's art had been delivered and paid for. I rang Tesha to say her artwork would be ready to hang in a week. They agreed for me to deliver it to their house. They invited me to stay the weekend, so I agreed. As soon as I unwrapped it, they adored it, paying me immediately. Ken made a very tasty Italian dinner, a white chocolate sponge desert with coffee and homemade dark chocolates. It was perfect. I had always found conversation with these two stimulating. They did not know the nuances of art, as I did not know about their professions. Tesha had a doctorate in physiology, while Ken held many diplomas in medical physiotherapy. We watched a documentary on a new museum being built in Cairo, the displaying of the treasures of Tutankhamen's tomb and how some of the art had never seen the light of day until the making of the documentary; it was fascinating.

Tisha offered me a beautifully weaved cashmere wrap as the night turned chilly. It was a stunning, midnight blue with a silver thread running through it; 'From the Casablanca markets,' she murmured. The texture was amazing. It settled against my legs like a second skin. Around nine o'clock, Ken decided he needed a stiff drink. I declined. While he was preparing that, Tesha disappeared for a while, saying she was making up the spare bed. When all was ready, she took my hand, leading me into what was to be my bedroom for the night. Many candles flickered in the soft breeze as we entered, the light soft and the heady aroma of bergamot was in the air.

The queen bed was covered in blood-red rose petals, made all the more dramatic by the pure white lace bedspread. Adding to the luxury in this room, stood a bath of enormous proportions; one of white marble with gilded gold claw hammer feet that glinted in the soft candle light. The petals continued across the floor into the steaming water. I had never felt so spoilt. Folded on a stool beside the bath was a white fluffy towel, beside that a large bamboo basket full of lotions and potions at my disposal. 'I'll let you slip into the bath, see you in a little while.' She kissed my cheek. It was nothing unusual for her, she was always very affectionate. I lay back in the sudsy bath water, feeling my body relax into the warmth. The bath was so deep, the water was up to my chin. I was in heaven. I heard the door click open. 'Everything okay, Sweetie?' I held my thumb up. It was all so perfect until I felt her sinking into the water with me, her hand rubbing my leg, her fingers sliding up into my crotch. 'Whoa, what the?' I croaked.

'Honey, all in together? Ken wants to know if he can come in. He likes to watch as we dry ourselves.' She looked coyly at me, 'You don't mind, do you?' It took a minute for it to sink in, 'He wants to what?' She saw the surprise on my face. 'What? You didn't know? Sweetie, we invited you over for the night, surely you picked that up?' I have never gotten out of a bath so quickly in my life! *Why is clothing so hard to pull on when you're wet?* About to bolt out the door, Ken stood with the drinks tray in one hand. He was nude, his erection like a giant pink finger pointing at me. Tesha called out, 'Cassie, don't be silly,' but somehow I made it past him, and his genitals, grabbed my bag, dived into my car. My heart was in my throat, as I turned the key, backed out of the driveway, driving home as fast as possible.

Once I was back in our caravan, I rang Larry. 'Hey there, thought you were away for the weekend at your mate's place.' I told him what happened, he burst out laughing. 'Larry, stop, this is serious. What am I going to do? Why would they think I'm a player?' His chuckles became infectious. It was hard to be seriously offended when your husband can't stop laughing. 'Cassie, the affection that woman showed you, showering you with gifts for no reason, even I felt jealous. Surely you clicked she wanted more than friendship?' No, I didn't get it. She was a tad overwhelming in her friendship, I agree, but I'd never seen it as sexual. We said our good nights, Larry still chuckling at my horror of a night. As I settled down to go to sleep, memories of her gifts flickered through my mind.

One time, Tesha and I had been shopping for some material, for new cushions for her two lounge suites. While in the shop I had admired a beautiful ceramic tureen, the price an eye-popping amount of money. Two days later, it had been delivered to my door. Then there was the time a huge bouquet of cut flowers were delivered. Larry had been home that time, the bouquet dwarfing his head when he carried it inside. The card was wishing me a happy birthday, which was months away. Or, just before the villa had been trashed, she had asked me to be home one afternoon. She had something for me; it was the beautifully embroidered chair I had admired. I knew this was Ken's favourite chair from his office. Tesha lugged it into the villa, saying his office was being re-modelled, 'Could you look after it for a while?' I saw no harm in it, however Ken did, he was over the next day demanding his chair back. Why did I not pick up on these things? Everyone else seemed to. I had not thought anything more of it, until now.

CHAPTER 36

I rebooked my art cabin for another six weeks. So far it had kept me safe, dry and happy. Diane had ordered another large canvas, this time as a gift for her company's secretary who was about to go on pregnancy leave. Her words were 'gentle colours for the babies room.' I purchased a pale turquoise with butter yellow, my thoughts were to tint them with white if they weren't pale enough. However, Addy was horrified I would choose such bright colours. I almost informed her, 'Your opinion doesn't matter,' but then remembered how I felt when I had my opinion knocked flat. Addy began to advise me on what to paint, when? did she decide she was an artist? I admit I had encouraged her to be creative, however today I found her constant interruptions annoying, so I said, 'Addy, I have a time limit. I don't have time to spend with you at the moment. I will call out when I've finished?'

One very angry woman stormed out, slamming the door behind her. I spent the morning prepping the canvas, deciding on abstract, colour and context, happy with the beginning of my piece. I headed home, looking forward to a salad sandwich, when our camp manager, Ross, called me into the office. It was time to pay for the extra six weeks. I happily swiped my card collecting the receipt. Then Ross leaned across the counter, 'You know whose put an offer in on your art cabin?' I shook my head. Ross inclined his head towards Addy's site. 'Them two want it, she claims she's an artist.' I was stunned. 'It is mine for another six weeks though?' He nodded, '… then it belongs to those two.' I shrugged, 'If it means that much to them they're welcome to it.'

I worked four to five hours every day, every now and then I would notice something missing. The tin of red geraniums now sat outside Addy's front door. The hanging pot plant she had lovingly made for me disappeared. The old door knocker she had found, that I had paid for, also disappeared. I knew this was their way. A little bit of petty theft here and there; they were known for it. I had been warned. Wrapping the finished canvas in a soft blanket, I was very pleased with the outcome. I rang Dianem, I was delighted when she said, 'I'm out your way, Cassie. I'll call in to pick it up.' We had such a nice catch up. I offered her morning tea, the willow tree shading us from the afternoon sun. When I told her this was my last artwork for a while she was very understanding. 'When you're ready hon, my clients love your work.' We were discussing the sale of Carla and Milo's house; it had been snapped up, completely gutted, repaired, then resold quickly for an amazing amount of money. 'I bet you're sorry you didn't buy it now. You would have made quite a bit of extra cash.' I looked around me, at what I had, I agreed with her. 'You're right, but here today, right now Diana, I'm happy,' I replied.

My life had changed and continued to do so; owning houses worth many thousands was not in the plan. We both stood inside my caravan washing, drying our cups, when a clunking noise outside alerted us that someone was there. I peeped outside. Someone had put a wheelbarrow full of my art gear outside the van door. I only just told her the story of the cleaners who had bought my little art cabin. Both of us were stunned

Jigsaw

as the cabin glided past us. It sat tied to a trailer, Addy driving the tractor with Charlie and his mates following on foot, making sure it did not tip off. Normally they would stop and chat or would smile and wave, but today it was like watching two grim reapers.

It puzzled me why they would move it, however if a small broken timber cabin meant that much to them and friendship did not, so be it. Diane giving me a cuddle, 'You certainly have a lot of ups and down, don't you?' I wanted to cry. I didn't have a problem if they wanted the cabin or not. I had finished with it, it was the childish way they went about it. I walked my friend to her car. Hugging each other goodbye, she said keep in touch but I felt incredibly sad; people confused me. We both jumped at the huge crash, it shook the ground. I heard cursing then people were running everywhere. I looked at Diane, our eyes huge; *what the hell was happening?* When the dust cleared, there lay the hut, on its side, almost flat. It had not taken the move well, its window was broken, the blue door laying on the road. It looked like someone had let all the air out of it. It had become a big pile of broken wood. Diane got into her car. 'Now that's what I call instant karma,' she said, smiling as she drove away.

I walked back to my safe haven, my thoughts trying to figure out why I attracted such weird people into my life. My first hosts in Australia had been a shock to the system, then being stalked, my home trashed, Sandy who urged me to join her battery power group. The weird behaviour of Tesha and Ken, I had no words for their behaviour, now the two in the camping grounds. Either I was naïve like Larry said, making friends with anyone walking by, or these people were just not meant for me. The question remained; *why was I attracting them into my life?*

The day was ruined for shopping or cleaning, so I decided tomorrow would be better. Before bed, I popped all my art gear under the caravan. As I had no storage, it was the only place for my two small canvas plus the odd assortment of paints. The brushes were expensive, so I brought them inside with me. Over the next four weeks or so something small would disappear from under the van. Then the two canvases went. They had been my cheap experimental ones, so not worth a lot of money, whoever it was, they were welcome to them. My bank account looked healthy, and Larry was due home for a month as it was Christmas time. We were planning a trip to Kalgoorlie, winding our way through many unusual places to the seaside city of Albany. It would be about three weeks on the road, places we had not seen before, it was all very exciting. My online journalling studies were going well and I was getting high scores. I had set my art aside for a while. I saw that Addy now had her paintings exhibited in the camp office. I cringed at her basic squiggles or spots on stripes of bright colour, with an asking price that made my eyes water.

I had called into the local visitor's bureau for brochures on the places we both wanted to visit, it was fun planning our first holiday in a while. On the outside of the travel bureau was a public notice board. I read about a local business women's advert, inviting women to join a network group for a Christmas dinner 'meet and greet' to be held locally. It sounded interesting and hopefully I would meet other creatives. I collected the travel brochures and headed for a café, deciding to ring the networking number while I was sitting by the beach. Rockingham had certainly stolen my heart; it was a beautiful place to live. Pressing the number in, I was soon talking to a Mandy who owned a nail bar in the mall. 'Yes, please join us for the meet and greet. May I ask what your business is?' I replied that I was a professional artist. The reply was a curt, 'Oh, I think we have one of those already. Sorry, we only include one of each type of business.' The phone went dead – it was not my week.

There wasn't much I could do about the abrupt phone call I'd just had. The café was filling up fast, the noise of people, the clatter of dishes becoming too noisy. Deciding a walk along the shoreline would be

Jigsaw

perfect. The tide was in, taking my shoes off I wandered into the tepid water. It brought back memories of New Zealand, when as a family, we often wandered home, licking ice-creams, enjoying the beach, picking up shells, watching the waves catch the sunlight. How lucky we were living in such beautiful places with no fear of war or famine. I was grateful for Fern, Heather and Diane's friendship, the old saying about 'birds of a feather' was very true. I thought of my friends and family, expecting a rush of homesickness, a little ache still remained. I thought of our youngest daughter, her only calls were to her father requesting money. There was no rush of sadness more like a an acceptance. Was this contentment? Finally.

I was itching to get on the road; everything else seemed boring. I decided to wash the car, giving it a good clean inside then outside. By six o'clock it was done; I was tired, but it was a good tiredness. Larry rang, we had an hour's conversation; 'Not long now, love, we will be on the road in no time.' He asked me to have the car checked over, fill it with gas, plus have the oil checked. This was new to me – I had not done this before. I booked the car into a local garage 'Doug's Mechanics.' Yes, he would take the car first thing in the morning, he would do it all.

He was so nice when I arrived. It was a small family business; Doug was Dad and his two sons were training as mechanics. 'Would I like a lift back to my home?' They would deliver the car when it was ready, before closing for the day. True to his word, our car was delivered, his invoice on the dashboard. Doug's handwritten invoice reported tyres changes, oil checked, transmission checked, all electrical points ticked off, the list was long, they had done their work well, everything was perfect.

Waking to another beautiful day, warm with a light sea breeze, feeling relaxed, I pulled out my journalling material. I began to read what I'd written about life in Perth. Feeling a little frustrated because I just knew that there was a book here, but how and where did I begin? when my phone rang. It was Mandy from the nail bar. Apparently, she had made a mistake, 'We would love to have you attend. The meeting is on tomorrow night. You can pay at the door. See you there.' Chatting to Fern the following day, I mentioned I would be attending a networking Christmas dinner, she asked me who was running it. 'Someone called Mandy,' I said, 'she's a nail technician.' There was a silence. Fern had become very protective of me since the break-in at the villa. I had seen her handle a bullying situation where her son was concerned, when in protective mode, my sweet kind friend changed instantly to a female version of Dracula. She asked me if I would like her to attend with me. We agreed on the time she would pick me up, me calling Mandy back asking if I could bring a friend. Her greeting and tone very different from the first time we first spoke, 'Of course, the more the merrier.' I dressed casually. I had no choice really, as clothing was limited in my little caravan. I wore brown dress slacks, navy blue T-shirt with navy jacket. I added my pearls to jazz it up a bit. Fern, as always, dressed beautifully. She laughed when she saw me, 'Guess you don't have a huge wardrobe now, but you still look smashing.'

The meet and greet had already begun, as we arrived Mandy met us at the door. 'You're Cassie, right?' her handshake felt like a limp fish. I paid for our Christmas dinner drinks at the bar, finding two spare seats. It was the weirdest networking I had ever attended. Fifteen women were in the room, and the speaker, a stout blond woman by the name of Cissy, claimed she was the program's leader. Cissy wanted the doors to be locked so no late entries could walk in, she wasn't happy when the restaurant manager explained that it was not possible due to health and safety laws. I waited for the welcome to country speech honouring the land of the Indigenous people, however it began with Cissy asking us to stand to introduce ourselves to the group.

When it came to my turn, I introduced myself, adding that I was new

Jigsaw

to the area. Cissy called out, 'I said your name and occupation only,' I quickly sat down, my face flaming. Fern stood as she was next in line, but Cissy yelled, 'You're not a local, sit down.' Cissy more or less told the group we were all idiots, to follow her on Facebook, then described her embarrassing body hair? Then abruptly announced, 'Your meals are being served in the next room.' I expected a Christmas celebration, maybe a tasty roast meal.

But no, it was Chinese, with sticky rice, a choice of duck or fish with mushrooms. We stood in line, each holding a small white China bowl. Once the bowl was filled, we were offered a spoon and fork wrapped in a napkin, then returned to our seats. There were no tables, it wasn't easy to stand, eat and mingle with others while balancing a bowl of food. What I did notice, was the ladies attending were very obedient, 'Yes Cissy, no Cissy."

We held our bowls on our laps as this person, who obviously thought she was all powerful, told us some very personal stories about her life. I had the feeling she thought she was entertaining us. Fern and I looked at each other, together we stood up. Cissy's large bosom expanded, 'Excuse me, ladies, I haven't finished.' I gave our apologies giving an excuse about another appointment. Her mouth hung open, 'I'm sorry, did you say you were busy? Well, do forgive me for taking up your precious time.' Fern dropped me off at the caravan park, wishing me a good night, 'You know how to pick them, don't you?' both of us in disbelief that this self-opinionated obnoxious person had a local following. I could not believe these ladies paid to be insulted. I was feeling tired, happy to brush my teeth, have a quick wash then jump into my bed. Checking my phone before I switched the lights off, Larry had left a goodnight message, hoping I enjoyed my networking 'Christmas' dinner. One more day he would be home. We had the company Christmas party to attend and then we were off on a holiday. With nothing to pack away I was ready to get on the road. How simple life could be.

I spent the following day, addressing Christmas cards to family and friends in New Zealand. Instead of buying gifts, I decided to transfer money to family bank accounts. Our youngest had not spoken to us for some while, though we knew through the grapevine she was in Tasmania in a serious relationship. My eldest daughter, I had no idea about, I felt it was healthy to admit we did not like each other or enjoy each other's company. My friends in Perth? I had sent Carla and family a card knowing I would see them at the company Christmas party. Fern, Heather and Diane received pop-up Christmas cards that I'd purchased in an art shop in Perth many months ago.

It was dusk when a cab pulled up outside our van, its headlights lighting up the darkening surrounds. Larry got out, paid the taxi then held his arms out to me. 'Going to wish your old man a welcome home?" I was speechless, he was not due home until the following night. 'Ready to take off?' he asked. 'What about the company Christmas party?' I queried. 'Not for me, Cassie, I see them every day. If we leave now, we can be in Southern Cross by nine o'clock. You don't mind, do you?' Mind? I had been waiting for this for so long. While he hitched up our little caravan, I made sure everything inside our home was locked down or tucked away. Just like that, our first adventure in Australia had begun.

CHAPTER 37

True to his word we arrived at the village of Southern Cross at 8:30pm. We both had this magic feeling that we were running away to new places, new adventures. Larry had rung ahead, booking us into the caravan park overnight. We were given a site number with a code to enter the gated campground. We didn't unhitch the van, as we intended to leave for Kalgoorlie the next day. We both slept well, as I made us a hot breakfast the next morning, Larry checked all the things you check when towing. I heard a yelp from the back of the van then laughing, 'Cassie, come out here, we have a friend.' Curious as to who it was, I did as he asked, only to find the biggest emu standing a short distance away, with Larry's sunglasses in her beak.

Larry had put them in his back pocket while checking the rear end of the van. It certainly wasn't scared of us, giving us warning signs not to come closer. This was done by standing up to its full height, over two metres tall, and spreading its huge wings, another three metres across at least, then stepping quickly towards us. The camp manager appeared, pressing on an air horn to chase it off. 'Sorry, folks, we try to keep them out for this reason. Bloody nuisance. You won't get your sunnies back mate, they'll be pecked at till they are wrecked. You both okay?'

We were fine, just a tad overwhelmed by the size of the bird. As Larry and I both headed off to the showers, it was nine o'clock already and becoming hot. Those who knew we were heading north for the Christmas break had told us we were 'mad' – and they were right. By the time I left the shower block, the heat plus zillions of flies were fierce. That was another warning; 'Wear a fly net – you'll need it,' they'd said. they were right, the flies came in swarms to settle on my damp skin. I had never experienced anything like it before, it seemed this was quite normal for the outback.

I made our morning coffee with a sticky bun each, so we wouldn't have to stop for lunch. As I opened the door to call Larry, the Emu's head snaked passed me, gulping back both buns, then trotted off. I'm sure it had a smirk on its face. 'That's the outback, Cassie. It's not all cafes and pretty people,' was Larry's comment. 'Best get used to it. There's so much out here that will bite, sting, or want to kill ya. Just be careful, you're not used to the outback yet.'

Kalgoorlie here we come! We booked into another caravan park, this one with a pool. I had not experience forty-five degree heat before, so I was not feeling 100%. Visiting the famous hole in the ground that was still producing gold, we did a gold miners tour, joined in a camp Christmas party, sang and danced until midnight. We visited the well-known 'stables,' where in their heyday, the miners would spend vast amounts of money on a good time with the ladies of the night.

We enjoyed a high tea with the madam of the stables, who was an amazing storyteller. The temperatures remained in the forties, despite regular dips in the pool, the heat was getting to me. When it was time to leave Kalgoorlie, it was my turn to drive plus tow. Another new experience, and one I wasn't sure of at all.

Jigsaw

Larry had decided he wanted to have a night camping in the bush. We didn't have a toilet in the caravan, so that meant digging a hole. I was envious that all he had to do was stand by a tree then aim. I drove slowly and that pushed Larry's buttons. He could not understand that I was not competent at towing, watching for traffic behind us plus oncoming traffic, while keeping an eye out for skippies (kangaroos), wild cattle plus the feather dusters (emus). Watching the dials, bells and whistles was stressful in the dehydrating heat, finally, Larry realised I was struggling with the heat and towing. 'Pull the hell over, woman,' he erupted. 'You're going to cause an accident, I'll drive.' I was not going to argue. I got out of the car to move to the passenger seat, the flies once more landed on me in mass. Yuck! Unfortunately, Larry's temper was now in full throttle, fully aimed in my direction; 'You're so useless, how the hell did you get a license? We don't have all day you know; I think you need some driving lessons!' The insults were hurled at me for a good half hour. I waited for him to finish, then quietly asked where the next town was. 'Why?' he snarled, 'Going to ring a friend? tell her "Nasty Larry's being mean to me"?'

This was not what I'd foreseen for our first real holiday together in a long time. In my mind, we were a happy couple touring around, not this, not being abused. I could feel my temper rise. My answer to his insults was out of my mouth before I even thought about it. 'No, Larry, I'm going to find out if there is a bus back to Perth. I don't intend to sit here for another three weeks to put up with you or your insults. I don't want to travel anywhere with you if you cannot control your mouth.' 'Fine,' he growled, 'no need to find a ride, I'll turn around. I'm going back to work.'

And just like that, we were on our way back to Rockingham. The silence so loud, I had spoken my thoughts. Larry had done his normal angry knee jerk. I thought how sad it was that two people who had spent close to thirty years together were still arguing. Suddenly, New

Zealand looked inviting. Normally I would reach over, make comforting comments, but this time the comfort tank was empty. I'd had enough of people being rude, mean, crude and dishonest. If it meant I'd spend the rest of my life on my own, then so be it. A strange feeling of relief settled around me. I had made a choice that involved no one else but me and my life.

Larry drove through the night, stopping only once. I bought bottles of water, two muesli bars at the gas station while he fuelled up. Watching him through the window, I saw him share a joke then laugh with the male attendant. But once back in the car, the Larry I was travelling with returned, refusing anything I had bought. He drove with anger, his jaw thrust forward, the speed dictated on the road, ignored. At 3am we turned into our caravan park back in Rockingham. He backed the caravan into the site, let down the jack wheel, put on the brake, parked the car, picked up his bag then walked out. Not a goodbye, nothing. He had disappeared into the darkness of a new dawn. I realised it was only a few days until New Year's Eve. What a way to start a new year!

I went to bed, as it was too early to start thinking about attaching the hoses or cables that provided the amenities. I waited for the tears of remorse and guilt, always thinking I could have done more. Instead, a small inner voice said, *you have already done that, if he's not learnt to have an adult conversation by now, he's not going to.*

This was not the first time he had walked out on me though, however it was going to be the last time. The following day, I would begin to make plans for my return to New Zealand. I can't say my sleep was refreshing, as there were so many thoughts racing through my head. On waking, I wandered around the van attaching water hoses, drain hoses and power cables. I wound down the feet of the caravan which made it sturdy to walk inside, I was home again.

What a whirlwind holiday! Now it was time to take stock, make some

Jigsaw

phone calls, finally settle the small nagging thought I'd had about Larry that had been in my head since I'd arrived in Australia. Making myself a strong pot of tea, rummaging around for some biscuits in the cupboard. I pulled out my journal writing down the pros and cons of staying here in the van with Larry coming home every two weeks. It all came down to the fact that he needed to grow up. No one, including me, likes a sixty-four-year-old child who still has tantrums. Admitting to myself, I had not been perfect; my behaviour had been turned and twisted when I had attended a counsellor, though I felt I had created a 'better me.' I had certainly been through a lot since arriving in Australia. I'd stayed on through abuse and violence just to please Larry.

On the flip side, I had made two very good friends and I absolutely loved where I lived now. Slowly a plan formed. I go back to New Zealand spend some time with family, leaving the van and car here, and return in a couple of weeks with a decision to sell up or stay.

Once I wrote the words in black and white on paper, my world stopped, I had just given myself permission to be Cassie. The feeling of this decision was like a wash of relief over my body; no more restrictions, no more stupid rules and arguments, no more finger pointing or accusations. I acknowledged we had been in love with each other once, a very long time ago. What we had now was a close friendship. The big question was, was I prepared to carry on being Larry's closest friend and confidant, or did I want more? Was this how married life ended? A petering out of closeness? Losing that feeling that you are the only one who matters in their life? Maybe it was for the best if we both moved on. I could see us ending up as disappointed old couple who didn't even like each other, but lived together because there was nowhere else to go. That one thought tweaked my disappointed heart, released the tears that needed to fall, knowing I had done my very best to be a good person, mum, wife, aunty, sister and friend. Not caring if anyone heard my sobs when they passed my tiny home on wheels.

Self-belief in myself was like window wipers going on. Suddenly, the view became clearer with every swipe of the blades. If he could walk out, so could I. I rang our eldest daughter in the South Island, 'Want a visitor for a week?' The yelp of pleasure reassured me I was welcome. I rang the travel agent in the mall and booked my return flight, leaving in three days. I Informed the caravan park office I would be away for fifteen days. They were surprised to see me; 'Thought you were of up North for three weeks, heat too much for you, eh?' It was none of their business. 'Something like that,' I mumbled. 'I'll pay for another month? I'm off to New Zealand.' Again I could feel them wanting to know more. Well, they would not hear it from me. I spent the afternoon ringing my friends to let them know I was going home for two, maybe three weeks. They were all surprised at my quick return, Fern asking, 'Family unwell?' Heather then Dianne asking if I was okay, I assured them both I was fine, but I wanted to visit my family, it was long overdue.

The night before I left Rockingham, I emailed Larry a letter in case he returned to the caravan while I was away. It was not a goodbye letter, it said I would be back on the 20th of February, my flight number with the ETA. I was canny enough to know that if Larry had even a whiff that maybe I had gone for good, he would sell up while I was in New Zealand, pocket the money and then I would have to badger and beg for my share. He had done this before, and it had not been any different when we sold up to move to Australia. Hopefully, I was not only older but wiser now. I had not heard from him since our sudden return to Rockingham, which was nothing unusual. He often sulked when we argued. Sadly, this was his way of punishing me, which I now knew was a form of bullying. The taxi was ordered for Wednesday morning at ten o'clock, my flight leaving Perth at one o'clock. I had just one day to go before I would be

Jigsaw

on my way, excitement filled my heart, longing to see my grandson and daughter. It had been close to two years since I had said goodbye to the 'land of the long white cloud.'

CHAPTER 38

Waking to a beautiful, warm sunny morning, I showered, checked over my baggage, then completed my journal before the taxi arrived at the camp park gates. The feeling of freedom engulfed me. No one was giving orders, there were no questions or demands, a feeling of confidence was fizzing through my veins. If only life felt like that all the time. At the airport I checked in ,watching as my bag disappeared on the luggage carousel. As my flight was called, I almost expected Larry to bound into the airport full of apologies asking me to cancel. Too late! I was on the plane, ready for take-off and in seven hours I would be in Christchurch.

The journey went quickly as I snoozed most of the way, waking to be told to 'buckle up' as we were landing within the half-hour. After a smooth landing, I waited in my seat until the rush to get out was over. Going through to customs a pretty Maori lass read my passport saying, 'Welcome home, Cassie.' God, it felt so good, everything felt familiar, down to the Maori tiki carvings on the wall. The exit doors swished open, I didn't have a chance to scan the crowd as my grandson cannoned into

Jigsaw

me. 'My nana's home,' he called out, telling everyone in earshot who I was. His seven-year-old arms circled my waist, 'I'm not letting you get away again.' My heart ballooned with love. I had missed him so much. Looking up for my daughter, she was there with open arms; 'Mum! I've missed you,' she said. I had walked back into where I seemed to fit best, a warped piece of jigsaw was back in its place once more.

The week flew by. I was sleeping in my grandson's bed, while he had a mattress on the floor beside me. Every night I would go to sleep, his eyes staring at me. Every morning, he would wake me, 'Nana, I can't believe you're here with us.' Every day he was by my side. This little man I had helped to raise was just what I needed, a confirmation that my life was not wasted. He would be the one to carry my DNA onto another generation. My daughter asked if I would like to visit Kaikoura, a seaside town on the outskirts of Christchurch. Of course, I agreed. We bundled everything we needed into her car, a wonderful three-day holiday began.

It was so much fun; the radio on, wind in our hair, with many stops for pictures and snacks. I knew she couldn't really afford it. She was on a solo Mum's pension, while studying for her master's in communication at Christchurch University. I offered to pay for the accommodation finding a lovely B&B next to the seaside. We spent our days swimming, laughing, eating, talking. My grandson played in the shallows of the rolling waves collecting seashells. The south Pacific Ocean had never been warm however I was encouraged to take a dip, rushed out again, screeching because it was so cold. My grandson thought it was the funniest thing he'd ever seen. At dusk, we went for long walks along the beach, while I told my daughter about my life in Rockingham. On the last night in Kaikoura, after I'd tucked my grandson into bed, I made my daughter and I a hot drink. Sitting on the door step we watched the sun go down, its brilliant mauve fingers tinging the deep blue waves as they swelled then crashed onto shore.

'Okay, Mum, I've heard all about your life in Perth, so how's Dad getting on?' I took my time to answer as I didn't want her involved in my decision-making. 'You haven't mentioned Dad very much, is everything okay?' I shook my head. 'Honey, I don't want to ruin what we have now, can we just enjoy our time together? It's not been easy.' She was not silly, none of my kids were, 'Is he giving you a hard time again? He's certainly given us the flick. We've tried so many times to connect with FaceTime, emails, or phone calls all I get is a big fat nothing. What's his problem?' This was news to me, Larry had claimed he hadn't heard from the family at all. I felt for her, deciding to be honest. I put my arm around her, just like when she was little, she cuddled into me; her words, 'You've always smelt like flowers, Mum.' I felt I belonged. I explained we, her parents, pretty much led separate lives. He preferred to be up in the mines with the blokes, I preferred to live on my own. When he came home for two weeks … we managed.

She exploded with anger, 'Mum, for fuck's sake, be honest with me. I'm not a little girl any more. I think what he's asked you to put up with so he can be employed is disgusting.' I pulled back, 'What do you mean?' 'Oh come on, don't be coy. All your news was about that bitch Carla, her wanky old man, Milo. Then the abuse. Mum, Larry let you go through that because he wanted to please everyone, except his wife. Then you move into a beautiful home. Mum, the photos you sent. It was stunning what you did to that little place. Some prick trashes it, where is Larry? 'Oh sorry I'm on convoy, look after yourself. Now you live in a caravan park amongst trailer trash, and I'm not allowed to say anything? I don't think so Mum. You deserve so much better than what you have accepted as your lot in life.' Her body was shuddering as she took a big breath, 'Come home, Mum, join the living again.' Wow! she had never spoken to me like that – ever. *And when did she start calling her Dad Larry?* She didn't know I had been a little light on the honesty, she only knew half

Jigsaw

of what had happened.

'Mum, you taught us all, if you're not appreciated for who and what you are, then what is the point? Time you took your own advice.' There was a pregnant pause, I whispered, 'Point taken, sweetheart, I want you to know though that your Dad did not plan any of what you have just said. Yes, he did let me cope with it all, but there was nothing he could do, he was a four-hour flight away. Next and most importantly, he considers me adult enough to manage on my own. It was a culture shock, I have to admit, having no one to call on was awful, but I chose that, not him, I chose to move to Australia, I could have said 'no.' Last of all, you owe your Dad a little more respect. I was the one who said camping was the life for me, I bought the caravan. I don't live with 'trailer trash,' I'm part of a community that loves the freedom of that lifestyle.

I could have a home with all the bells and whistles if I wanted to, but I've had all of that. I wanted to experience something different. Now, I'm off to bed, we have an early start tomorrow.' Our daughter did not like being reprimanded, our goodbyes a little stiff when I flew out to Auckland city the next day. My niece met me at the airport. The last time I had seen this young lady was just after our holiday to Fiji. She had changed, now married, divorced and remarried with three children, and a husband who adored her. It was obvious she loved her family, her husband, not so much. He was berated for any opinion, told to shut up so many times, I felt sorry for him. *Mind your business, Cassie* was the warning running through my head. Not for the first time, she reminded me of her mother, my sister Cilleen.

I stayed for the weekend, though they had such a busy lifestyle, I hardly saw them as they taxied their kids all over Auckland for different sports clubs. Saturday night was going to be our family night, however her man too tipsy at the footy club, he had fallen asleep on the couch, while she was in such a flap about some Mum who had wrecked the dance recital. The three young ones were slumped all over the furniture. She yelled at her husband to help her clean up, I offered to cook meatballs with spaghetti for our family meal. No one was all that interested, so I cleaned up the kitchen benches, packing my case for my bus trip the following morning. My alarm woke me at 6:30am, my niece was already up, announcing I needed to take a cab to the bus depot because she was ultra-busy. I was only too happy to oblige. Knowing my welcome was over, I left knowing I would not be back, not if I could help it.

The coach ride to Whangarie was lovely, so comfortable, they even had a small bathroom on board the bus. I remembered the old bone shaker bus we used to take, this was pure luxury. In three hours, I was standing in my girlfriend's kitchen. To my surprise, she now had a partner. I wished she had told me! They had been together for a year, still very much in love. He offered to drive me to a motel after dinner. Okay – the welcome mat had been pulled out from under my feet, What now? The welcome I had imagined, with friends I had once called family, was non-existent. It was obvious I was in the way. The message was loud , "It's lovely to see you Cassie, now let's find you a motel to stay in.'

As I settled down to sleep at the Cherry Blossom Motel, it was blatantly obvious, I knew where I belonged – in my little caravan at Rockingham by the beach. I gave thanks I had not been hasty selling it all before I left. I wanted to fly home as soon as possible. There was one more person to see, my old neighbour Margi. It was a good half-hour walk and I needed the exercise. It was an humid, overcast day, I had forgotten how humid New Zealand could be. By the time I reached her home I was puffed. A young man, I presumed in his thirties, opened the front door. 'Can I help you, lady?' I asked for Margi. He paled, stammering, 'Grandma died a year ago.' I explained I was her neighbour once, giving my condolences, I turned to leave when came face to face with my old villa. It was unsettling, the grounds had been left to go to weed, the paint was peeling off the window sills, no one lived there, the

Jigsaw

grass was knee high. It looked old, sad and lonely, was this how I would have ended up if I had not gone to Australia – old, sad and on my own?

Back at the motel there was one more thing I had to do, find my eldest nephew's phone number to see if we could catch up for a day, I knew very little about him. I knew he was married, with two children, he had once lived in this city. I rang reception asking for a local phone book, searching for an hour under the letter H. Nothing, ringing his sister in Auckland, asking 'Did she have his phone number?' Per usual, she was impatient until I said his name. 'I thought you knew aunty, he suicided last year. I honestly thought you knew, I'm so sorry.' I disconnected the call, why had no one told me? We had been close for many years, until he married. I knew his marriage was demanding, I had no answers. My phone trilled, my niece asking if I was okay, then she told me the story she had heard. An unhappy marriage ending in a divorce, he remarried and moved to Australia. They had invested in a sugar cane plantation, things did not go as planned. He became depressed putting a hose into the muffler of their car, turned the motor on, ending his life.

His wife refused to chat with any of his family. She sent via email a copy of his death certificate and his will. Also an after note included of no contact with her at all. I could hear the tears in her voice, we said our goodbyes. I sat there for quite some time remembering his beautiful brown eyes, his laugh, how he always bought a smile to my face. This wee man was my first love, why did he not ask for help? I wanted to cry, I wanted to hug him one more time. All I could do was hug my pillow, let the tears fall praying he was safe and loved where ever he was.

Sitting on the bed, dazed with the recent news I checked my phone, Larry had left two voice messages. I rang him. He hadn't been back to Perth so he didn't have a clue where I was. There was a pause when I told him. A question hung between us, 'So, are you coming back to Perth?' he asked. I told him I'd be there in a couple days. There was something he was not saying, curiosity got the better of me. 'Okay, what's up?' 'Cassie, if you want to stay there I'm happy to pick up our van and travel. I'll admit I'm a grouchy bugger and have made many wrong choices that have been devastating to you and our the girls, you all just seem to just get on with life. I'm ready to admit my behaviour on our Christmas break was not the best, but I'm so used to the blokes I work with, jumping in the cab and driving.' *Was this Larry I was talking to*? He rarely apologised. 'So if you want to stay in New Zealand I'm okay with it, and if you want a separation it's yours.' I hadn't spoken. 'You still there, Cassie?' I stammered a reply as he continued, 'I love my work, Cassie. I don't intend to return to New Zealand, there's nothing there for me. I'm staying here doing what I love, where I have a say, my input is respected.' It sounded like he was reading a statement to me; this was not the Larry I knew.

'I'm happy for you, Larry.' However I was so uncomfortable with his honesty, he had rarely been this direct in entire married life, so what was going on? 'Cassie, I need to see you face to face, if you come back here, even if it's just for a week, I simply can't tell you over the phone. Let me know your arrival time I'll pick you up at the airport. Do you need any money?' That one question stopped me in my tracks. He had never, ever offered me money, not even when the girls and I were desperate for a little bit of extra cash. Nothing made sense, had he met another woman or got the job he'd been considering applying for in Dubai? It felt like Larry was saying goodbye. Was there another woman, my mind went into all sorts of scenarios. It was time to find a travel agent, at the motel reception. I asked if they had a number for a taxi, 'No need, ma'am, our airport car can drop you to the city mall.' It felt familiar sitting in the mall, making plans to move on. I'm sure the piped music was the same two years ago, as was the décor. I had no one else to see or make contact with. I suddenly felt like a stranger in my own country. No one was saying hello as they used to, there were no friendly faces to say, 'Hi,

Jigsaw

Cassie, how are you?' The travel agent booking my original departure date. Leaving Whangarie at midday the following day, transferring to a connecting five o'clock international flight to Melbourne, then to a midnight flight to Perth, arriving at one o'clock.

I had the next fifteen hours to play with, purchasing new clothes for the plane then found a beautician in the mall. I had the works, facial, manicure, pedicure, waxing, a mini massage of the lower back, her fingers finding the sore spots. It took a chunk out of the afternoon by five o'clock I felt fabulous, ready for an early dinner, the local hotel just a ten-minute walk away. It was an icon from the seafaring rough tumble days and inside the decor was early 1900s grandeur, a small restaurant inside overlooked the fishing wharves.

I remembered once they served fabulous roast meals here, I ordered for one and sat myself in the ladies snug bar. This was a blast from the past. In my younger days, my girlfriends and I used to meet here regularly. *Why not indulge myself?* I had this feeling in the pit of my stomach my world was going to change, I could feel it starting to tilt. Sitting in the fading dusk, a hot steaming roast in front of me, I texted Larry my arrival times. I had no clue what was going to happen when I arrived. I decided not to speculate. I rang Val, hoping she could find time away from her man to spend some time with me. 'I'm leaving for Australia midday tomorrow, any chance of meeting me tonight?' She arrived within the half-hour, looking like a blushing bride, being in love suited her beautiful face. Without her partner around, we could talk freely. 'I wanted to ask you the other evening, why are you back here without Larry?' she asked. 'We're having some time apart.' Val could read me like a book. 'Okay, what's life with Larry doing now?' I shrugged as I did not know for sure. 'Larry has to realise I have boundaries to what I will and will not accept. And, my friend, I would be putting some boundaries with your new man as well. I arrived here especially to see you, so why would you let him say to one of your closest mates, "No room for you here, go to a motel"?' It was out of my mouth before I could stop it. She put her arms around me, 'I knew you were hurt, Cassie, I saw it in your eyes, you're right, he should have known his place, I'm so sorry.' Val left me at midnight, the witching hour as she called it. I certainly didn't expect her leaving advice to hit me so hard, but it was true: 'There is nothing for you in New Zealand, Cassie. Stop looking for what is right under your nose, everything you have done has led you to your desire. It's up to you to recognise the universe has some weird and wonderful ways of manifesting your prayers, go with the flow, Cassie.'

We both knew we would not see each other again. She was not one for the digital world, my friend was a hands-on, deeply spiritual woman who cared with all her heart. Through all the ups and downs we had always been there for each other. I had wiped away her tears as she had mine. We had shared the grief of our folks' passing, our divorces. We had laughed, argued, minded each other's kids and looked out for each other in so many ways. I already missed her laughter, her beautiful all-knowing brown eyes. No one wants to admit they will never see each other again, it felt like a small empty space in my heart. We held each other tight as I whispered, 'Thank you for our wonderful sistership over the many years. I will treasure our love always.'

CHAPTER 39

The air bus began announcing its arrival into Perth. This time I had booked business class, the comfort was worth the extra dollars. Once I was through customs, Larry was waiting for me, his arms wide open, his eyes smiling. I did a quick scan around him for his new lady love, 'Let's find your bags and get you home,' he said, putting his arm around my waist, something he had always done when we were younger. 'Mm, you smell good, you look bloody good too, new hairdo? Or new skirt?' He was flirting with me.

I pointed my bag out as it rolled around the carousel. This was no place to ask questions, obviously he was going to break the news when we were alone. In the car heading back towards Rockingham, Larry was animated with so many questions about our grandson and daughter, about my niece, what she was like now. He asked about Val and whether I'd visited my folks memorial. My voice choking up when I told him about my eldest nephew suiciding. He seemed to fill up the hours' drive with questions. When we arrived at the caravan park, our caravan looked a little forlorn. Dried leaves had mounted up against the wheels and it looked dusty, uncared for. Opening the van up, it smelt musty, I raised the pop top, opened the windows and turned on the amenities. We let the camp manager know we were home, buying fresh milk and bread from the office. It took maybe a half-hour, Larry and I had still not spoken with any intent on what we were doing. I finally had the kettle boiling making a large pot of tea, then settling myself on the two-seater couch, shedding my boots, waiting. It had been hard enough to say goodbye to Val, now I was facing the perhaps hardest one of all – Larry telling me there was another woman.

I waited patiently, pouring tea, buttering slices of bread. Larry sat on the bed, his eyes serious. It was his eyes I had fallen in love with. I stared into them as I sat quietly, watching his emotions flicker across his face, 'Cassie, I've just been offered the most amazing opportunity in my lifetime. I have three weeks to say "yes," or it will be offered to someone else.' This wasn't what I was expecting. I leant forward, 'So, tell me. That's why I'm here Larry, so we can make decisions about what to do next.' He picked up his mug of tea, gulping it down. 'Okay, here it is. We have been offered a life on the road for a year, perhaps two. It depends on the length of the contract.' I put my tea cup down with a clatter, this was not making sense. 'Larry, stop,' I interrupted, 'just tell me the truth please, no more white lies or excuses. Is there another woman? Why are you telling me all about travel when we should be addressing the main problem?'

He gave me the strangest look. 'What problem? What woman? One woman is enough for any man, why would I want two?' He could be so infuriating at times, I wanted to slap that grin off his face. 'Did you think I was mucking about, Cassie?' He began to chuckle. 'You, my darling wife, are a handful; you're a feminist with a strong determined streak, but it's you I love. I asked you to return so we could decide on a nomadic life or a home in the burbs.' He reached over for my hand. 'I would be an idiot to even think of playing around. Can you imagine

Jigsaw

what would happen to me or my job if I mucked about? Cassie, come here.' He reached out for me, I went into his arms. Believe me when I say making love in a small pop-top caravan is not for the fainthearted.

I was ready to go to sleep with all the emotional highs lows going on, the pre-dawn light was creeping through our windows when Larry uncurled himself from me. 'Feel like another cuppa? We still have to discuss my news. Nomadic lifestyle or a home in the suburbs? What are your thoughts?' Larry was insistent. 'Come on, sleepy, this is important.' He had spread out the map of Australia on the small table. I could see red texter circling the different states. It piqued my interest. I sat at the table while he explained. 'Okay, woman, I'm about to blow your socks off, I'm so bloody excited about this,' his finger pointing at Bunbury. 'Here we pick up our motorhome, here we pick up some spare parts for the rig,' he said jabbing his finger at Esperance, '… here we begin our adventure.' His finger finally resting on the Western Australian /South Australian border.

Larry was excited but I still didn't fully understand, buying a motorhome surely meant selling the car and the van. 'Cassie, you don't get it yet, do you? See the big red ring around Australia?' I nodded yes. 'Well that's where we're going. The deal is I travel with the rig to all these places.' He again stabbed excitedly at the map. 'I'll be gone for maybe eighteen months. If you're happy to come with me it's all yours babe. Or we can rent here in Rockingham where you're happy, I do another stint of fly-in fly-out.' As it slowly sank in, Val's words were in my head: 'Stop looking for what is right under your nose. Everything you have done has led you to your desire.' Well, here it was. Excitement curled in my stomach. The enriching nomadic life I had yearned for was right in front of me. Names like Woolloomooloo, Cairns, Birdsville, Alice springs, Darwin and Mt Isa were popping out at me. I looked up at Larry, he could see the wonder in my face. "A modern motorhome? I don't have to dig a dunny hole or tow anything?' His roar of laughter spilled through the windows into the night air. 'Cassie, it's all there for the taking, you just have to say yes.' My 'yes' came out with a huge sigh, 'Yes please.' The following day, Larry went to the office to sign the contract. The secretary rang to ask if I wanted a four berth motorhome with ensuite – of course I did!

I put a small notice on the office notice board that our caravan was up for sale, the manager saying it would go for top dollar. I put $10,000 on it, then added the car for an extra five grand. My phone ran hot for the week, while I packed, gave away or tossed away. One night as I was walking down toward the camp rubbish skip, I watched as Addy and Charlie went through the rubbish. My heart ached for them; what a way to live life, going through the scraps of another's existence. I decided to let them know we were moving on to offer them some sheets, towels, whatever I was not taking with me . They didn't look up until I greeted them. "Hey guys, thought I'd let you know we're selling up. I'm getting rid of some stuff, maybe you'd like it." Suddenly I had two best friends, they followed me back to our van. Larry glowered at them at first, then softened, he knew their story. I unpacked some old sheets, towels, pillowslips, bed cushions, an eiderdown and bed cushions. Addy was over the moon, cooing her thanks, her fingers lightly roving over the satin lace on the bed pillows. Charlie was also grateful. Larry offered him a cold beer to take home with him. My heart felt good. Addy offered me a hug with her blessing. 'Safe journeys,' she said.

We were living with bare necessities. Larry was itching to take off, the motorhome was verified and first drill site was confirmed in Norseman. We had two weeks before we left, all I had to do was sell up. Larry, having signed the contract, was now due in Norseman, he was becoming impatient. 'Sorry, love, I might have to start out on my own, the company will have to pay fines if I'm not there on time.' I wasn't stressing, I knew this was meant for me. A buyer would appear.

Jigsaw

At six o'clock one overcast morning, Larry woke up grumpy, fed up with being stuck in one place. He decided to buy our breakfast at the local bakery. As soon as he left, I received a phone call. A very young female voice spoke, 'Can we come by to look at the caravan and car today please?' I just knew this was our buyer. They arrived at nine o'clock, both in their twenties with a gorgeous little girl cuddled up into Mum's chest. I showed them through one at a time, as four adult people in our van was a tad overcrowded. They introduced themselves as Vince and Summer, their little girl Macey, who quietly sucked her thumb while her mother went through the caravan with me.

Vince took the car for a test drive with Larry as passenger. Within the hour we had agreed if we dropped the price by two thousand, they could afford it. I wanted to offer them a drink, but I had nothing to offer them, not even a chair. They could transfer the money immediately, however, it would take them a few days before they could pick up the van and car to take off on their tour around Australia. I stepped in. I'd learnt from my folks at a very early age that sometimes to receive what you want you have to sacrifice a little. If you can transfer the money through today, I will stay with the van till you can pick it up in, say, three days? Does that suit everyone? They were overjoyed but I could see Larry wasn't happy with my suggestion. So be it. 'It's three days, Larry, not the end of the world. You do what you have to, then come back here to pick me up. I'll be waiting with bells on.'

Those three days dragged by so slowly, still I had given my word. The young couple arrived to collect the van and car an hour before Larry did with the motorhome, Summer asking me, 'Do you have a name for the caravan?' I did. In the days I'd been waiting for their return I had painted her name on her brown rear end. I wondered about all the places she must have seen. She had been my safety blanket in good times and bad, she had cocooned me through a Rockingham typhoon, twice, as well as thunderous hail storms – I had called her Metal Mermaid. Summer ran her finger along the lettering. 'It's perfect. I won't change it, I promise.' Larry helped Vince hitch the caravan up to the car. They had arrived by cab, with all sorts of household gear bundled up inside. As they drove off, I didn't see Vince and Summer sitting where we once had, I saw a much younger Larry and Cassie begin life on their terms, not dictated to by a society that said get a mortgage, get a career, have children plus work hard. I would never know their story, it was theirs to tell, not mine.

Now it was our turn. Larry had parked up the motorhome in the camp parking area, it had attracted many people full of questions. The men wanted to know about motor capacity, while the women oohed about how roomy it was, loving the colour of grey, cream and apricot, 'Time to go,' Larry shouted as he pulled out a pile of paper maps, the GPS was right in front of me. 'Okay, Mrs Navigator, belt up. We're heading off to Leonora, then Merredin, then across the border to Cowra. Lock in the details with Siri, let's get on the road. We have three days to get to our first pit stop, the rig's already there waiting for us.' It seemed there had been a small change in plans. There was now a driller travelling with us, who would be loading the rig and driving it to the sites. He was a young Maori boy by the name of Warrick. Larry drove out of the camp gates, blaring on the air horn as men do. I looked up to see the Metal Mermaid going in the opposite direction. My emotions were mixed. I was excited to be on a new adventure, a working holiday, but I was also sad to see my little bubble of safety leave for a different destination.

CHAPTER 40

I soon fell in love with the lifestyle; it was simple basic. Larry and Warrick went off to work onsite and I did the housework. A quick sweep, a clean of the ensuite, make the double bed, then attend to any laundry. I would often use a large bush to spread out the washing to dry, then I would prepare a lunch for us all. Both men had soon become mates, and I must admit, I really liked Warrick as well. Nothing was too much trouble for him when it came to helping me in any way. He was the same way with Larry. The site they were drilling was a twenty-minute walk from where the motorhome was parked. We had not booked into a caravan park this time, we had everything we needed in our motorhome. We were surrounded by nothing but dry land. The red colour got into every nook and cranny, even tingeing our clothes pink! The sunrise and sunsets are truly amazing in the outback, I was amazed at the colours that danced across the sky. The good news was, I was still studying the online journalism course, so I was writing every day. Larry had offered to erect a beaten-up old sun umbrella he had found in the bush, when I wanted to paint. The not so good news was my first try at writing a short story had been returned by email with a big fat pink strikes through every page. *Declined! Needs more work.* There was no mention of 'please resend when edited' … just declined. At first I was disappointed then saw it as my chance to rewrite, reformat, use the tools I had learnt through my English literature education in New Zealand.

The heat and flies were atrocious, a very unwelcome distraction. There was no break from the heat. It was March, supposedly the end of summer, so surely there would be a cold day soon. If I left the protection of the motorhome, the flies would land on you 'en-mass' – it was relentless. We had not been on the road for long, I already found myself missing face-to-face connections, especially my female friends. I pondered what I could do to remedy this lack of female company. We were soon on the move once more, across the border, where customs went through every cupboard and drawer. The fridge was opened then emptied of any vegetables or fruit. I knew this would happen, so we had eaten the majority of it. They waved us through, we drove into Ceduna for a week in a caravan park. Both men were busy every day taking the drill apart, greasing nuts and bolts, making sure everything was in good condition for the next job. While they were busy, I cleaned the inside of the motorhome from top to bottom, finding the Indian ocean sea breeze more comfortable than the desert heat. Then the outside of the motorhome came under scrutiny. I borrowed the camp hose plus a large-bristled broom going to work. It felt good to stretch my muscles. I named the motorhome *The Bus*.

All the washing had been through the washing machine, including the bedding. It now hung on a proper clothesline that lazily twirled in the soft breeze. The next day, I drove the motorhome for the first time into the small township of Ceduna, finding a park quite a way out of the CBD, as I was not used to parking motorhome in a busy town. Buying groceries for the three of us, I put everything away, getting rid of the plastic packaging rubbish before I left the car park. I had the whole day to myself, so enjoyed a lovely lunch then a browse in the town library. I knew I couldn't join as I was not a resident, I love libraries so it was my pleasure.

I enjoyed the cool calmness of the library and purchased a couple of $1 books from the used-book table. The librarian asked me where I was from and why I was travelling. She was so friendly, I was craving female company, so we got chatting. She pointed me to the CWA (Country Women's Association). 'These ladies are just about in every town,' she said, 'Why not join them? When you travel to somewhere new, you can reach out to make new friends everywhere you go.' What a great idea. As I headed back to the caravan park, I was just in time to see two weary men walking back, time to make hearty dinner. Once I had discovered that Warrick had nowhere to sleep except a sleeping bag on the ground! No one-man tent to curl up in. I knew this wasn't good; there are all sorts of insects or snakes that would love a warm sleeping bag for the night, I'm sure he would be uncomfortable. It was not my place, but I did point out to Larry that it was the company's duty of care to make sure this young man was cared for. After dinner, I went online to join the Ceduna CWA, paying the yearly fee. Twenty minutes later, I received a phone call welcoming me to the district. The leader's name was Jill, she immediately invited me to the next meeting in two days. I informed her it might be difficult as I was driving a large motorhome. 'No worries, Cassie, I'll pop in to meet you after our meeting. What site number are you on?' Problem solved. There wasn't much to see or do in Ceduna I felt my shoulders begin to relax, unwind, spending my days writing, walking the beach. This time collecting shells from the Indian Ocean, vastly different to the South-Pacific shells. I enjoyed looking after the men, making them healthy meals. Watching Warrick's face light up when I offered ice cream for desert, something we hadn't been able to enjoy in the Pilbara. It seemed that my conversations with Larry about his offsider Warrick, not having any decent accommodation, had finally sunk in. When I signed for a parcel delivered to our motorhome by a courier, it was a swag for Warrick. I felt a lot happier about this situation.

From our conversations, it seemed this polite young man had no one who cared for him. Adopted at birth to Pakeha (white) folks, he had been allowed no contact with his Maori tribe. In and out of trouble as a wild child, in jail in his early teens, meant his adopted folks became sick of his hijinks so they sent him on a way one ticket to Melbourne to find himself, with $100 dollars in his wallet. He had wandered around doing all sorts of menial jobs, when he saw an advert for a drillers offsider, working off shore. He had applied, finding himself in Perth for an interview. It had seemed to go well, but he'd heard nothing. After a few weeks, he saw an advert for the position he now had with Larry, because he was footloose and fancy free he was hired.

Warrick was such a nice bloke, helpful in every way, as far as Larry and I were concerned. Warrick wore long dreads, had a nose ring and tattoos covered his arms and chest, his smile a mile wide with perfect white teeth, his personality? Giant gentle teddy bear. Life had knocked him around and he admitted he had his moments of feeling down. Who could blame him? I made sure he felt welcome, he could to stay with us as long as he wanted to.

No sooner had I shut the door on the courier, there was another tapping on the door. 'Hello, Cassie, I'm Jill. Welcome to Ceduna. I hope you don't mind, I've invited a couple of ladies to meet you.' Mind? I was delighted.

Soon there was six of us sitting in a circle. Each of the ladies had brought a camp chair. As we sat in a circle under the shade of the motorhome awning, small, coloured balls of wool began to bob around on the grass, the ladies knitting beanies or scarfs for a charity. They had all offered to accompany Jill to make me feel welcome. I felt embarrassed

Jigsaw

offering hot drinks in paper cups, as that was all that was in the cupboard, serving what was left of the chocolate biscuits. 'No need to feed us love, we came prepared,' one of them said, as a picnic basket was produced, another got out a small camp table. Soon, scones, jam, cream with a sponge cake appeared. 'Do you knit, love?' I was asked. I did but hadn't bought any knitting gear with me. 'Oh, soon fixed,' she said handing me knitting needles with a small ball of wool. What a fabulous afternoon, chatting about everything from work, grandkids, running a home and hints on how to make travelling easier. It surprised me to hear there were many seasoned senior nomads in this small group. Before they left, I was given the name of the CWA to ring once I was settled in Port Lincoln, our next stop. Two large slices of delicious sponge cake were left behind, 'for the menfolk.'

I liked Ceduna; the people were friendly, the weather warm. Warrick was happy that he now had a home of his own, which he set up outside the motorhome. Being a Friday, it was fish and chips night, and at this camp you put your order in at the office, picking it up within the hour. This camp had a lovely tradition on Friday nights, of getting everyone together in the camp BBQ area, regardless of whether you were passing through or a permanent resident. We picked up our order, joining everyone in the communal meal, the camp supplying plates of buttered bread, as well as fresh barbequed sausages.

It was a party atmosphere, until they saw Warrick. A few people had already judged him on his appearance, they were making not so subtle comments. I was shocked. One set of folks pulled their two little girls closer to their sides. I became cross I was ready to leave, so was Larry who was already standing, but Warrick put his hand on my arm. 'Hang on a minute, guys.' He approached a man who had a guitar, a conversation began. Warrick began to play and sing, his voice melodious. He was obviously very talented and soon, those two little girls were dancing to the 1960s music he was playing. Warrick was joined by two other guitarists. The music was wonderful; what they say about music soothing a wild beast is very true, I was most surprised when Larry offered me his hand. 'Come on, love, let's have a twirl.' We had lots of fun, then saying our goodnights, went to sleep with sweet music playing in the distance.

In the morning, I was woken by Larry yelling, 'You never said there was cake in the fridge. Oi! Warrick, get your arse up mate, we're off in a minute, want some cream cake for brekkie.' Larry kissed me goodbye. 'See you tonight, Cassie,' he called, as I peeked through the venetians at these two blokes on the way to work, both stuffing their mouths with leftover sponge cake, sharing orange juice from a large bottle. My heart was happy, so sure I had done the right thing by saying 'yes' to this adventure. The following day, we moved on to Port Lincoln.

CHAPTER 41

Port Lincoln had the reputation of being a rough seaman's port, but I found it to be a bright hub of activity. Arriving here took some time due to the heat. The motorhome seemed to be sucking in the hot air on the main road, Larry cursing the slowness of the bus. No matter what gear or how hard he pressed the accelerator, we chugged along between 80 and 100 kilometres an hour. Larry wanted to go faster. Behind us, Warrick was driving the truck with the water drill on its trailer. As I watched the deepening colour in Larry's face, I knew I'd be better off travelling with Warrick. This was his first sign of anger in any stressful situation and Larry was ready to erupt.

I was glad when we rounded the bend into Port Lincoln, finding the caravan park we were booked into. It was school holidays, so the place was full of young families; my husband's nemesis in the nomad life. The noise of kids yelling as they biked past, or screaming as they plunged into the pool set him off. We settled onto our site opposite the pool, I must admit it was very noisy. Hopefully all it would take was a visit to reception to sort out another site for the bus, away from the pool. Larry had taken off with Warrick to deliver the drill to the drill site, telling me to 'friggin' sort it.'

So I did. We were given another site right at the back of the park amongst trees. It was cool, peaceful and quiet, with a small babbling stream at the back of us. The manager walking me to the site first, warning that the ground was a little marshy in places.

Although nervous about backing the bus in, I drove the bus to the site, the manager reversed the bus in for me. Problem solved, or so I thought, until my phone rang. It was Larry yelling at me again, to come over to pick them up from the drill site as it was miles from the camp site. An hour later, I pulled into where they were waiting for me, Larry's face purple with anger. I had seen this before, more times than I cared to count, however, Warrick had not. I could see he was shocked at Larry's 'the rigg boss' childish behaviour. This was when leadership was called for, not the stamping, yelling antics of a sixty-year-old man. I drove them both back to our campsite, Larry was surprised I had moved us to a nicer spot, until he got out of the bus, then all hell erupted. 'Are you stupid? The marshy spots are dangerous. We're way too close to the creek , there's nowhere for Warrick to put up his bed roll. 'We could get stuck in this bog, its full of mosquitoes,' the list went on. While Larry ranted, Warrick had let out the awning on the bus, set up his swag and made us all a hot drink. In his calm way, he said to Larry, 'I would calm down if I were you, nobody died, we're all good. I like the site. As for getting bogged, if we put the max tracks underneath the wheels we should be fine.' Larry exploded, pointing his index finger in Warrick's face, 'You don't tell me what to do I.' I wanted to say something, but what? This had now turned into an argument between the two men.

'So, my opinion's not worth it then, Boss? Larry's answer was, 'I'm the drill boss, mate.' Warrick's reply was, 'Fine, you can stick your job right up your arse. I don't need it.' He picked up his bag and walked off, turning to look at me, 'You going to be okay?' For some reason I wanted to cheer Warrick's actions; I nearly asked to go with him. But I had made my decision to travel with Larry with a deep hope in my heart that this nomadic lifestyle, albeit a working one, would be some sort of panacea. It seemed that I was wrong. Now Larry urgently needed an offsider for the job to be finished. It didn't take long for the firm to ring, asking what was going on? Warrick had handed in his notice immediately, claiming he was offered work overseas. Thankfully, he had not said anything about Larry's behaviour. As I cooked dinner, I overheard the conversation between Mike and Larry. I heard a different person rather than the enraged drill rigger who'd lost the plot, his calm voice full of respect. I saw him through different eyes. Not for the first time I admitted to myself Larry needed some emotional counselling – he only saw life as winning or losing. There wasn't a lot I could do to convince him. It takes a big mind shift to see things in a positive light when you've always been negative, unless you have a twenty-four-hour cheerleader. I had once taken on that job, exhausting myself emotionally.

Over a curried chicken dinner, he blamed Warrick. He claimed he'd been annoying him all day, with stupid questions, irritating Larry so much he ended up yelling at me. Now the firm was on his back to either return to Perth or find a way to finish the job then move on to Adelaide. If we returned to Perth, there would be a week's unpaid break before getting back on track. Larry finished the job on his own. Every night, one exhausted man would climb into the bus, shower, then be sound asleep after dinner. Until his next five o'clock start, where I would drop him off at the drill site then drive the bus back to the campgrounds. I dare not drive anywhere in case I was called on to pick him up early. I spent my time in the pool, writing, or researching for a publisher that would give me a chance to prove myself as an author.

The day finally came when Larry rang Mike, he had finally finished this job. The firm and farmer were happy. We were informed there would be a driver for the drill rig flown in. We were to continue to Adelaide, have a break for a week until a new offsider was hired. Larry began to fret, he knew company policy was that if an employee was not called back after the break time, it meant his contract was either over or he'd been dismissed. Larry was like a cat on hot bricks, so sure he had been fired. I decided if we were going to have a break, then why not enjoy it? I booked for the two of us to go to Bali for five days.

Larry drove into Adelaide with a scowl, so sure he was on the firing line. Finding a camp to park the bus was easy. School holidays were over, we soon found a huge camp ground, more like a park, full of tall green elm trees. Adelaide is such a pretty city, we had a day to explore. I loved everything about Adelaide. We caught public transport around the City, catching a show in the late afternoon at the famous Cirque Du Solei. I laughed then gasped with every other spectator at the performance, but Larry was grim and sarcastic. 'Nothing special. What a waste of money. Anyone can do those acts with a bit of training.' *God give me strength*! Did nothing make this silly man relax? What was done was done. There was nothing he could do to change the fact that he had insulted Warrick, who had disappeared off the radar.

Booking the bus in for the week, we were shown a parking bay we could use, we packed our bags, locked the bus up, catching a night flight to Bali. In four hours I was immersed in another culture, which I fell in love with. 'I could live here,' I said one warm night, as we sat on the moonlit balcony of our hotel room. 'You may have to if I'm fired,' said Larry. 'There'll be no money left after you've finished splashing it around.' Not even his sarcasm could affect me here. I was in heaven; the people and the customs suited me. We had just finished our dinner when his phone rang, his hand shot out to answer it, knocking my glass of juice to the floor. Larry's face was beaming as he announced we were back on the road again; we were to head across the country to Sydney. Once again confidence shone from his face.

I had two more days in Bali to relax, frequent the massage salon, tour, take it all in. Bali fascinated me. Though I wished my constant shadow would stay in the hotel room watching TV or find something else to do. He insisted on escorting me everywhere, then would haggle the price so low until it was almost free. One shopkeeper took offence asking us to leave his shop, flapping his hands in the air, 'Shoo, go away.' In another shop, I had bought us a beautiful doona cover. *Did I really need it?* Larry made sure I knew it was 'a waste of money.'

Our flight back to Adelaide was non-eventful. As we left, I promised Bali I would be back one day. For now, I was looking forward to driving across to Sydney. Once back in Adelaide, Larry checked over the bus; it was all as it should be. It was time to put our heads down, get a good sleep before we began another adventure.

We stopped in the small village of Lameroo where we refuelled ourselves and the bus. The village relied on tourism everything had a major dollar price on it, so I decided to wait to fill up the fridge plus the pantry. By mid-afternoon we had stopped in a layby where skippies and emus wandered freely, not too fussed about tourists. The next village was Houston, time for a stretch, Larry was to take over the driving. I was grateful. I had a nagging throb behind my eyes. Larry parked in another layby, saying, 'You lie down. I'll make you a cuppa where are your painkillers?' He even went as far as massaging my feet, which knocks me out every time. In fact, it was a family joke – 'Don't touch her feet or she'll keel over.'

When I woke it was dusk, Larry had made himself the single man's standby of scrambled eggs for dinner. I was still nauseous, all I wanted was a hot cup of tea and a sweet biscuit or two, Larry providing both. He'd been studying the map. 'We may have to find a camping spot for a day or two until the new offsider meets us with the water drill,' he said. 'The GPS says there's a campground an hour away in a village named Hay. Shall we park up there for a couple of days?' I nodded. If we had to camp up for a while, then it should be somewhere with good amenities. Larry sent a message to the firm to let them know where we would be stopping for two or three days until the offsider caught up with us. Hay was brilliant, the camp very welcoming. With my headache easing off, it was time to clean out the bus, deal with a huge mound of washing that had begun to accumulate. I soon had two washing machines in the camp laundry going, lovely hot soapy water sloshing everywhere.

While I was waiting, I aired the bedding, pulling out the mattress, laying it in the sun. The back of the van had two large doors, which I opened to let the sun stream in. Completing the kitchen clean up, I began to wash down the cupboards in each side of our bed – there is nothing nicer than the smell of cleanliness. Suddenly, I heard the weirdest sound; a hiss then a crackle like someone treading on sticks as they sneaked up on you. Thinking it was my imagination I carried on, but the sound got louder, especially the hissing noise.

'Larry, if you're playing silly buggers, you can stop right now,' I said as I peered out the open back doors to be eyeballed by the biggest monitor lizard I had ever seen. I froze. Larry, who was now behind me, also froze. 'Geez, that's huge,' he whispered. I was wondering where its mate might be, I was more than thankful we had a bathroom inside the bus. There was no way I'd be venturing out in the dark for a night time toilet run. Our agreement to use the camp facilities while here was immediately null and void. I wasn't going out, not with that monster wandering around the camp.

CHAPTER 42

There is no mistaking the sound of a large truck coming towards you. The heavy rigs rumble like thunder when on the move, I watched the orange rig we had left parked in Ceduna turn the corner of the campground heading to a large vacant sandy area. Larry raced off to welcome the new offsider with lots of back slapping and handshaking. He was a man we already knew; Eddy had always been the cheeky one. I could just imagine the trouble these two were planning. My shoulders instantly became tight as I remembered how much Eddy loved his alcohol. It barely took a minute, before these two drillers were holding two cold beers, Larry laughing loudly as Eddy described his road trip. He greeted me with a kiss on the cheek, 'Nice to see you, Mrs.' For the rest of the night I was spoken to in monosyllables.

When I served dinner, Eddy's included, 'Thanks, Darl.' When I offered dessert, 'Not for me, Mrs,' as he held up his beer can. The drinking continued, empty tins littering the outside of the van.

Around midnight I heard them wish each other a goodnight. Larry staggered in, took one look at my face slurring, 'Don't start,' before falling onto the bed then throwing up. The stench was unbelievable, the vomit sinking into my new doona from Bali. It invaded every nook and cranny and I had nowhere to turn, but outside. Spending the night wrapped in two towels perched in a deck chair, I was terrified that every noise I heard was the huge lizard creeping my way. This was not my idea of a considerate loving marriage. The fear of meeting up with the monitor lizard plus the driving cold finally forced me inside, the smell making me want to vomit myself. I curled up on the two-seater couch. How could Larry do this, when he knew how I felt about drinking? A glass or two was fine, guzzling because you can, was not.

He woke me by stumbling into the small bathroom. It was just on 5am, time he went to find the drill site with his new offsider. His sheepish look at the mess he'd made, 'Sorry, love,' did not cut it. Thankfully, it was another sunny, windy day. Once more the washing machines in the laundry were full of our gear. The mattress was badly stained, which meant we would have to replace it, it stunk. It sat in the sunshine while I lathered the stain with hot water and hair shampoo. After cleaning up the empty tins outside, I settled myself down with a hot milo, the thought of food made my stomach flip over. Opening my laptop to see an email from a WA publisher offering to look at my manuscript. This was what was termed as a vanity publisher, but who knows where it might lead. I sent a copy, warning them it had not been edited or proofed. Then it was off to the camp shop to buy groceries. The entire time I was busy, my gut churned knowing when Larry returned home, it would be ultimatum time once again: 'One drink – that's it.' He knew the work rules were to limit the booze, rigs can be dangerous machines to be around.

Early afternoon both men arrived back, happy with the drill site. The rig was up in place; they would need a ride back out to the site. Larry reached into the fridge for a beer as Eddy's hand reached out to accept it. I was determined not to have a repeat of last night. 'One beer tonight,

Jigsaw

boys,' Eddy gave me a dirty look, I added, 'I suggest we look at another mode of transport to the rig. I'm not a taxi.' Anyone would have thought I'd announced they had ten minutes to live from the looks on their faces. 'You're not my mother or the boss,' said Eddy, 'I'll drink as much as I want.' Larry looked unsure for a moment but stepped in with, 'She's right, mate. We're here to work, not for a holiday piss up. As for the ride, Cassie, it's your responsibility to get us to the job.' 'Really? Who decided that? Shall we ring Mick, the boss, see what's expected of me. I'm not on the payroll, am I?' My hand shook as I pressed the company number. 'Mick speaking. Hey, Cassie, enjoying the nomadic lifestyle? How's the Twerp doing?' (Twerp being Larry's nickname.) 'How can I help?' I put Mick on speaker chose every word carefully. 'Hi, Mick, we're doing well! I'm just making enquiries about the motorhome. Just wanted to know if I'm responsible for feeding the crew plus taxiing them to and from the drill site every day?'

'No, not at all,' he replied. 'Both drillers get a transport allowance for getting to site, some buy a bike for this reason, as for feeding them? Well, Warrick certainly had no complaints, so it's up to you, Cassie, as long as Eddy pays his way. Is there a problem?' Straight from the horse's mouth, so to speak! 'No, Mick, just clearing up a conversation I had with the guys – I'm not responsible for the offsider's meals or any transport, correct?' I was about to say thanks hang up, when he added, 'Cassie, If you were responsible for either, you'd be on our payroll.'

Eddy went bright red, stomping off. He needed to understand that I was Larry's wife, not part of the crew. Larry was also annoyed with me. I'd embarrassed him in front of Eddy, but he knew I was serious. 'Your drunken behaviour was foul. If that's going to continue I'm more than happy to return to Perth to live in a rental. I was happy with you being a FIFO worker, I'll be happy to do that again.' *When will you understand that I did not marry you or agree to this way of life so I would be unhappy?*

'You either pull your head out of your arse, or this dream we have been offered is over.' I stormed into the bus and threw two towels out at his feet. 'You can feel what it feels like to be disrespected,' I said this as I slammed the door shut and locked it. I have no idea if he slept outside or not. I woke at dawn, made myself a cup of tea, unlocked the door going back to bed.

There was no movement outside, the chair was empty, the towels folded up neatly. I checked my phone; two messages from friends in Perth, one voice message from my husband. 'Apologies for the other night, Cassie. I feel it's best if we work our way through to Sydney then you can fly back to Perth. I'm staying with Eddie at the drill site until the job's complete.' Okay, so my marriage was over? I had spoken my truth and this was his answer. So be it.

My decision was to drive to Sydney to return the mobile home, then fly back to Perth. I went to the office to pay for the four days we had been parked here, where I was asked to remind the young man with the rig to return, as he had not paid for his site for two nights. I decided it wasn't my problem, asking them to ring the company. I turned the motor on, turning right as I left the park, soon meeting up with the Western Highway heading to Cowra. The little villages were so enticing, now I did not have a time limit, I was able to visit the touristy places I'd read so much about. I spent the night at a place called Rankin Springs; no caravan park here, just a local council paddock that cost five dollars a night. Other campers were dotted all around me, an ice cream van showed up, the grey nomads swamping it. I had just bought myself a chocolate ice cream when my phone rang.

'Hi, Cassie, Mick here. I just had a phone call from Eddy, apparently you've deserted your post. Look love, your personal life is none of my business, but Larry's contract says he is accompanied by his spouse. The motorhome is also under contract, you're not registered as a driver. You're not on any of the insurance forms, so you're on the road illegally. If you're not returning to the drill site, can you park it in the nearest town, leave the keys with the police please. If you're not continuing as the spouse, we will consider cancelling the contract. Will you advise the office when you have made that decision please?' I apologised; he was right.

It took a minute for it to sink in that I was uninsured and driving illegally. I rang the campground I had left two days ago to confirm I could return to the site. Turning left onto the highway, I began driving back to Hay. It felt like defeat. Larry rang asking when I would be returning, he needed a change of clothes. I knew I would pass the drill site on my way back to the campgrounds. I saw it busy working, Larry saw the bus. He waved, as I drove into the site. Sorting out some clean clothes for him, I left them on a deck chair, realising that he had taken Warrick's swag.

It was set up in the shade of trees nearby. I guessed Eddy had been sleeping in the cab of the drill rig. Both drillers were both busy with the drill, I saw no reason to stay. I returned to the park reclaiming my spot, walking to the office to pay for another three days. I knew we were due to be in Cowra soon. At the office, I noticed a spiritual festival advertised, to be in the same campgrounds where I was staying. Feeling my return was meant to be, already bright flags, pendants were being hung, tents erected. It had a carnival atmosphere, where my spirits lifted, as I had always enjoyed a festival. I saw an advertisement for a women's circle, writing down the phone number, keen to join. It would be just what I needed, to be amongst caring, intuitive women who knew the value of self-belief and positivity.

Ringing the number, I was welcomed by Veronica, I felt the sunshine in her voice as we spoke. Paying the fee of twenty dollars per day, I was delighted by the thought of the upcoming festival. Early in the afternoon Larry arrived. He had borrowed an old rattler two-wheeler bike from the farmer, I expected a confrontation. 'Hello, Cassie. Good to see you. Got anything to eat?' My husband greeted me like an old friend, I almost expected a handshake.

I put together some cheese, onion and tomato sandwiches, stacking them onto a plate. He was ravenous, wolfing them back. He wiped his mouth with the back of his very grimy hand asking, 'We got anything for Eddy?' I felt my shoulders go up, 'No, I do not.' He was about to argue, but stopped when he saw my look. 'Still upset, huh?' Why could he not understand that being upset goes away with an apology, but disappointment stays in your heart for a very long time. 'Larry, I'm here as your spouse until we get to Sydney, then it may be another story. I believe you have an offsider to look after?' Not so subtly telling him it was time to leave.

He climbed back on the bike. 'What time is dinner? Oh … by the way, Eddy will be having dinner with us.' *Had he just demanded I cook a meal for him and Eddy*? I could face this with anger or childish behaviour, like making sure there was enough cayenne pepper in the meal to cause damage to someone's eyeballs. There was another way though, they say you can win a man heart through his stomach. First, I emptied the fridge of any alcohol, then I made a meatless, healthy stir-fry, emptying a tin of chick peas, red kidney bins, a bunch of fresh Kale, with lush thick noodles, lots of yummy ingredients to make it tasty.

They showered in the ablution blocks, as I set the camp table for two. I would be sitting inside away from the flies and sullen faces. Larry had never been a fan of my creative meat free cooking, but always ate what I served. Eddy, though, was a big meat eater. It was no surprise, when he excused himself complaining of tiredness leaving his plate still full. When Eddy biked past on the old claptrap bike, munching on a pie bought from the camp office, Larry's comment was, 'Well, I guess you showed him.' It was an empty win.

CHAPTER 43

As Larry helped me clear up the dishes, a lonely feeling settled around us. He pointed out it was a long walk to the drill site so he would spend the night in the motorhome. If I preferred, he would sleep on the deck chairs outside. I felt I was being churlish, so I showered, giving him time to slip into bed. We slept back to back, he was gone when I woke at dawn. The only thing to say he had been there, was a small pile of dirty clothes on the floor. As I journaled that day, I wrote in all honesty. I needed some help on how to fix a chipped and broken marriage, or should I say a marriage with so many huge cracks in it? Was it worth salvaging? The one positive thought was the Japanese kintsugi proverb: Fix a broken pot with gold and it will be stronger. To be honest I was past salvaging, I felt it was the same for Larry, so why continue making each other unhappy? Why hold onto something that was no longer valued?

We had both given it our best shot. I felt I had run out of any of glue or gold, or whatever was needed to fix the cracks. I felt Sydney would be my last port of call with the man I married. I had agreed with such happiness in my heart, to be a grey nomad crossing this wide open country. However, the majority of this adventure had been crisscrossed with anger or insults. I was no innocent party. I had been fed up and grumpy too, with the heat, flies, plus the expectations of my driving skills. It was for the best that we parted as friends. Closing my laptop down with a heavy feeling sitting in my heart, it was time to join the women's group at the festival.

I could hear the music, tambourines and drums playing and women of all ethnicities were hand joined in a circle, swaying and laughing. I could feel the energy of womanhood, it was wonderful. I was greeted with, 'Ladies, this is Cassie.' In one swoop, I was greeted, included, becoming one with the circle. I, like many others, let down my guard, letting the tears flow, while others smiled with joy. It felt as if I had come home. There was no judgement, jealousy, anger, spite or insults, far away from the male dominated world I lived in.

I left the circle to find some tissues, finding shade under a tree, I sat next to a large, black woman. When she smiled, it lit up her face. I knew without asking this was Veronika. 'Welcome, Cassie, we are glad to see you enjoying yourself.' I looked round for the 'we' as there were only two of us there. Again, that large white toothy smile emerged. 'Our feminine ancestors are here celebrating with us.' I felt a shiver down my spine, knowing if my ancestors were with me, they would be arguing. Around us were many stalls selling all sorts of wares, from kites, jewellery, tarot, mineral make-up, to bright saris. The air was full with enticing smells from the food stalls. There were large to small tents everywhere; some so dark inside they looked mystical, others were big and airy, as massage or workshops of all sorts took place.

I opted for a foot massage, as I do, I slumbered through it. Normally I would feel recharged, today I was running on empty, I decided to head back to the bus. As I passed one of the smaller tents, erected in wigwam

Jigsaw

fashion, a hand shot out, its palm open; 'Pass my palm with silver, I will foresee your future.' She reminded me of my childhood days when Mum would read tea leaves and palms. Why not? A woman of undetermined age quickly took my handful of coins and led me to a carved wooden chair, she sat on large leather poof in front of me. Dusting my hand lightly with talcum powder, then flicking it off with a soft brush, her finger began to trace the lines on my hand.

While she peered at my right hand, it gave me a chance to look around her shelter. I don't know what I expected, perhaps dried skulls tied to poles, herbs and feathers bound together, candles with huge amounts of wax crested around them, snakes weaving in and out of empty eye sockets in carved idols, a crystal ball or two. Or maybe I'd just been watching too many *Pirates of the Caribbean* movies. All I could see in the dim light was a small oil infuser, the aroma of roses filling the air. To the side was a tall stick with carvings and symbols burned into it. A pack of old dog-eared tarot cards and the small pot of talcum with the brush she had just used across my hand. Apart from the high-backed wooden chair I was sitting on, there was nothing particularly magical or hocus pocus.

At first, I thought she had fallen asleep when the muttering stopped, her head remained bowed over my hand, my heart melting with empathy for this elderly wise woman. I gently began to pull my hand away, but she held on tightly. I gently tugged again as I didn't want her to topple off her seat if she was asleep. But when she said, 'You're an impatient one, aren't you? The guides haven't finished with you yet,' I felt reprimanded, so I sat there for another few minutes. Finally, she let go of my hand. 'You've been through so much. Your heart line is strong, but your spirit is tired, as is your physical energy. Your highest hope is about to be achieved. You have only just begun on your journey. There are many roads to travel yet, stay the course, your rewards are close.' I thanked her and left the tent hurrying back to the bus, feeling completely drained of all energy.

I slept for two hours until it was dusk, which was unusual for me. After two cups of tea with a slice of cake, I decided to return to the circle of women. The festival had continued into the night. I settled into a tent with the storyteller perched on a tall stool, at least another thirty or so other women were packed in with me. The speaker, Veronika, was very popular with her stories of myths and legends, the coolness of the night defeated by the heat coming from the many women inside the tent. I loved every word and every story. It had been a long time since I'd been enthralled with passion or grief, as her stories spilled from her mouth to our hearts. I knew there was a connection, I could not see where or why, I just knew it was there. Back at the bus I was more than tired, my limbs feeling like marshmallow, and I fell asleep immediately.

When I woke, it was early morning, Larry had been back, as the pile of grubby work clothes announced. All the bread, butter, cheese, instant coffee and milk had also disappeared. I found a packet of muesli bars then wandered back to the festival, knowing intuitively there was something there for me I had not yet found. Veronika was under the tree where we'd first met. She asked me where I'd been 'last night' as she'd missed me at the closing ceremony. I told her about being overcome with tiredness. She smiled then giggled. 'Did you check the massage oils they used?' I admitted I had not. 'Oh, they use a lot of natural remedies, marijuana oil being one of them.' I was shocked as I had never had any experience with marijuana, ever. 'How do you feel?' she asked. I had to admit I felt great, my mind and body relaxed.

Larry rang me with a list of instructions. 'We move to Cowra tomorrow. Please have my work clothing washed and dried, everything in the bus put away. You may need to buy milk and bread, I took what we had back to my camp.'

Soon it would be on how to dress and act in his company. This had to stop. To save any arguments, I did as he said, spending half the day putting the washing on, packing away loose utensils, emptying the toilet cartridge, sweeping out the bus.

The other half of the day, I spent at the festival. Like a beacon, I was drawn to the stall that advertised productive positive thinking. The woman there knew exactly who she was, what she had to offer, she did not suffer fools. Uri was of Nordic ancestry, her silver hair hung in one long braid down her back, bright blue tattoos on her wrist and throat. When she looked at you, it was with a piercing glare. Her books on emotional productivity were published through a UK publisher. She welcomed me for her three o'clock wisdom session. Unsure of what to expect but intrigued, I accepted her offer. Was she a seer? A prophet? A teacher? As she spoke, I felt myself begin to agree with her, her words on healing emotionally causing the hair to stand up on the back of my neck.

She was describing me, my life with Larry. When it came to an end it was twilight, a beautiful mauve creeping into the sky. It was time to leave, but she knew I had a question. She saw the rest of the ladies out, wishing them a fond farewell when I hung back she said, 'Come, sit with me.' It poured out of me in one sentence: 'I'm lost, my relationship with my husband is now one of mutual dislike most days, and friendship on others.'

Her advice went deep. 'Perhaps the love you once shared is over, there is no shame in that. Once a love dies it is gone forever. To stay in a loveless union is detrimental to your physical and emotional health. Why not plan some time on your own? Get away for a little while and see what the single life feels like. If you feel you can return to this partner in all honesty, then do so, if not stay on the path of knowing your choice was made with an honest clarity.'

I bought her two books. The first had the title *The Lost Power of All Women* the second *The Power of Manifesting Your Dreams,* which was accompanied by an audio tape. I wanted to feel in my bones the confidence she had shared that day with us. I remembered her closing words, that women all over the world believed the lies we had been told by our peers and that women could not comprehend the power we held, whether it was physical, emotional, spoken or written. Her prologue made me smile; 'Had the male of the species forgotten women were the original Spell Makers, Herbalists, Midwives and Elders? No matter the religious dogma written about Adam amd Eve, we as women birthed leaders, diplomats, kings, queens, rich and poor. We, as a collective are stronger than the earthly law of mankind.' My heart beat with a knowing that I was part of the wakeup call happening all around the globe.

It was late at night when Larry arrived back at the bus, checking it over with 'boss-like' precision. Eddy sat in the cab of the truck, sucking on a cold beer. 'Eddy's sleeping inside the bus tonight, Cassie. We have a really early start. He's packed all his gear, it's best we put him up for the night, it will save a lot of time.' As Larry made up the single bed, I wanted to object, yet I hadn't made a fuss when we'd done the same with Warrick; we had always enjoyed his company. The problem was, Eddy rubbed me the wrong way. Even when he looked my way, he gave me the creeps.

Eddy made it obvious he had no time for me. I made dinner for three, baked beans on toast with an egg on top. It was eaten in silence. Larry and Eddy fell fast asleep as soon as their heads hit the pillows, but I stayed awake thinking of all I wanted to do, my next step. Waking to both men making hot drinks at three o'clock in the morning, I was not ready to get up, Larry shook me. 'Come on, Cassie, time to get up. We're heading to Cowra. I'm riding with Eddy, you're driving the bus.' The drilling truck chugged into life, all I had time for was dressing, a hot tea, my seat belt on, we drove off in convoy.

We drove through the small townships I'd recently visited, the drill truck not stopping, so that meant I did not stop either. Cowra township came into view. Larry had booked at a camping ground, my job was to

Jigsaw

find it, then us set up. Their job was to find the drill site to make contact with the owner. I had noticed that the old rusty bike was now attached to the back of the drill. At least I wouldn't be expected to taxi Larry back and forth to the drill site.

I had been looking forward to Cowra. My one dilemma was the bus, as it was much too large for small trips into town. My brain switched on, I rang the CWA. I was welcomed with open arms. I soon found nothing was too much trouble with this lovely group of ladies. There were ten of them, ready to swoop in to show me a wonderful Cowra welcome. Every day, I was invited to a see a tourist spot, a sightseeing tour or a knitting bee. I willingly joined in when the camera club took me out for the day. A seat in one of their cars was always available. Some ladies drove four-wheel drives, others, smaller, older cars. It didn't matter who drove what, they believed in unity, not class. We visited the small villages of Griffith, Hay, Forbes and Young.

We went to the movies in the city of Orange, and visited Bathurst, driving on and around the track, all the ladies beaming with excitement. Larry had wanted to attend a Bathurst race ever since I'd known him, but this day, the pleasure was all mine. Larry was home at 6pm. He ate, showered and slept, then left for work early the next morning. I only knew he'd been around because of dirty dishes and clothing he left behind. We never chatted about our day.

When the time came to leave Cowra, I felt like I was leaving lifelong friends. A farewell afternoon tea was held for me, everyone had baked something yummy. They arrived at the caravan park with their deckchairs and plates of food. It was still very warm, all I had to do was sit, listen, laugh, eat and drink. When it was time to leave, everyone hugged me goodbye. 'Come back any time, we loved your company.' I felt honoured. In two weeks, I had met so many lovely people, visited so many small country towns. This was what I had wanted when I'd agreed to being a grey nomad; the fun the adventure of meeting new people, seeing new things.

Larry was still holding onto his grudge, Eddy sneered as Larry dumped their dirty clothes onto a deck chair. 'These'll need a good wash before we take off.' I opened my mouth to say something, but out of the corner of my eye, I saw Eddy nudge Larry as he passed him. These two were out to make me miserable, give up and go home; wherever that was. Once we were in Sydney, I would be having a very good talk to Mick. I may be the 'spouse' on a piece of paper but there was no reason for the disrespect these two were showing towards me.

I cooked a dinner of bacon, eggs and sausages, with homemade chips and a pepper/mushroom gravy for the three of us. As they began to eat, I knew exactly what to say. 'I've had such a lovely time here, best of all driving on the Bathurst track.' I saw Larry's eyes pop. 'What? When?' I smiled sweetly, 'Oh I've had such a great time here. Everyone's so friendly. Bathurst? Two days ago, or was that the day I went to the movies? Gosh I've been so busy the days are a bit blurred.' Larry's jaw tightened. Eddy walked away, sourness engraved on his face. I could not hide the smile that emerged. Childish? Maybe, but it felt good.

CHAPTER 44

For a week or so, we did one-day drilling jobs only. I cleaned the van, cooked meals and wrote. We stayed in Lithgow, then went on to Yass, Goulburn then the outskirts of Canberra. My days consisted of park the bus, unpack, cook, clean, wash clothing, then pack up again before quickly moving on. There was no tourism here or CWA. This was purely farming country.

On the last day in Goulburn, I had received an email from a UK eBook publishing company; they had accepted my book and a contract was offered. I had to read it twice to make sure I was reading it correctly. I had called the book *Tumbleweed*. They had created a cover and all I had to do was tick the box, agree on the structural edit of a few chapters and they would publish. I shook with excitement and had to tell someone. I rang my two mates in Perth. Heather and Fern who were just as excited as I was. 'When can we read it? When is it out?' I took a big breath wanting to confide in another woman that Larry and I were about to go our own ways. I had them both on a Zoom call, she noticed my tiredness first. 'What's up, kiddo? Boss getting on your nerves? Too much living cheek to cheek?' She certainly had a way with words.

I told them about Larry's rudeness, my anger, then added Eddy to the mix. Both silent as I described his behaviour. Fern spoke up. 'He needs his bum kicked. Don't tell me you're putting up with it. Cassie, how come you're allowing this to happen? I'd be having a talk to the boss's wife if I were you.' She had read my mind. One more night at Balgoo, their dismissive attitude made me feel it like I was at school, once more being bullied by immature boys. Sydney was not too far off. Larry had instructions to leave the drill rig at Katoomba, drive the bus back to the airport to hand it over for a four-week break, before hopefully another contract would be issued.

Katoomba is a very pretty town but we had no time to explore. What I did see of it was picturesque; pot plants full of ferns and flowers down the main street. If we had had the time I would have contacted the well-known author Mary Moody who wrote *Last Tango in Toulouse*. Eddy was issued a bus ticket from Katoomba back to Canberra to sort out some fresh drilling contracts. He was considered a hard worker by the company, but they did not know what a crass ugly person he was to women. Or was it just because I stood up for myself? Whatever it was, I seemed to bring out the worst I him. Larry and I headed off to Sydney, spending a night in a caravan park where we washed, cleaned, and polished what had been our home for the past four months. When we returned the bus, it was given a big tick of approval, we were free to go. I booked two nights in a motel close to the airport. It's such a funny feeling, when your body is so used to travel the constant moving, to walk into a small quiet room without the noise of motors or the road. Larry had a shower, I made us both a hot drink, when he came out freshly shaven, we just looked at each other. 'What now, Cassie?' he asked. Larry had a bruised look about his eyes. 'What do you mean?' I asked, 'We head back to Perth I guess, yes?'

'We need to sort us out, love. We're not happy together. It kills me to even think of us parting as friends, but I just can't see my way out of it. I apologise for Eddy. When I was feeling upset, he would fuel the fire, demeaning all females, not just you. If he had his way, I'd have dumped you, be in Canberra with him doing a pub crawl.'

I winced when he said *dumped*; I was not a piece of rubbish. He was right, I did not like who he was becoming. I had not liked my husband for a while. I was happy to part, so his next words took me by surprise. 'I've been thinking, how would you feel about a cruise? The ship goes around Australia and we have four weeks to make it back to Perth. Let's do it in style.' I asked if I could think about it overnight. It certainly thrilled me to think of a cruise around Australia, but I also knew it would not heal what we had become to each other, a couple whose bright love now left with embers.

Larry was taken aback. I explained I needed time to think as I'd already made plans for a holiday by myself. I wanted to explore more of Sydney, catch up with family while I had a good phone signal. Our eldest daughter knew I was on the road, we had both missed our regular chats with each other. My son in Melbourne had been in regular contact, asking me to visit when I was free. Larry's face was unhappy as he nodded in agreement. Also contact my UK publisher, find out about costs and royalties. Larry was on the phone to Eddy when I finished with my shower. Eddy was full of news about the new contract he had with the firm. He was now the driller, not an offsider, I could see the concern in Larry's face, as he had not yet been offered a new contract.

Larry was sleeping deeply when I rang Mick early the following morning. First I apologised for the early call, asking to speak to his wife, her voice sleepy when she greeted me. She remained silent until I had finished, saying once, 'He what?' when I informed her about Eddy's behaviour towards me. 'Well, we can't have that, though I'm surprised Larry didn't ring us with a formal complaint?'

Suddenly I felt like I was the one telling tales when she asked, 'Are you sure we're talking about Eddy?' I was not backing down, 'He's a rude, ignorant forty-year-old brat, full of his own importance.' Her quiet voice silenced me, 'And Larry's not? We hear all sorts of gossip, Cassie. All Mick is concerned about is if the job is done or not. I suggest you revisit why you're travelling with the rig. Perhaps a more stable situation might suit you better than having to listen to men beat their chests every night. I will talk to Mick about this sort of behaviour. I agree it's not appropriate, but you are living in a man's world when you travel with a rig. Believe me if I could change it, I would.'

Well that was an eye-opener – one I had to think more deeply about, as it seemed abuse or bullying was ripe and accepted between men and women in the mining industry. I was left with a feeling of anger and frustration; was no one going to say anything? So what was next? Become the compliant little spouse, living quietly in suburbia with a dog, a cat and a canary, eagerly anticipating her husband's return. No! I had learnt too much about self-respect and self-love, to agree to that. To allow bullying in any form was beyond my comprehension. I had been lied about, humiliated, put down plus sneered at, and in its worse form in my early years, my body and spirit violated. Two of my daughters had thought it clever to collaborate against me with gossip and lies. When confronted, both screaming abuse at me. I had worried myself sick thinking I was in the wrong. Now I saw it for what it was: pure disrespect and bullying. Enough.

Now I had a purpose. I knew exactly what my next book would present. The position women were put into because we were seen as the inferior, weaker sex, was no excuse. Though to be fair I had seen some marriages where women bullied men and other women. *What was the world coming to?* I had seen it with Cissy at her networking group in Rockingham. When I was asked what I had thought of this so-called networking, I was honest; I did not care for her. When Cissy had decided

Jigsaw

to send me insulting angry messages, I strongly objected. She threatened to blackmail me. She was blocked. I'd had to succumb to bullying when I stayed with Carla and Milo. I had put up with bullying most of my young life, each experience building up into a tumult of words, aching to spread itself onto paper. Now was my time. Now, I had grown up, I was determined to have my words make some sort of impact on the world. Bullying in any form is not okay. The warm juices of re-purposing my book ran through my veins. Yes, I would publish, but first I intended to re-write a few chapters. I wasn't beating around the bush anymore, I wanted this book to make an impact. To tell others bullying, being unkind, using your words as a weapon, threats and abuse was not smart and it's not okay.

Larry woke when I slid back into a warm bed, his arm snaking around my waist, pulling me close. He began to hum Rod Stewart's signature tune, *Sailing*. 'Want to go sailing with me?' he asked. *Why not?* I wanted to see, to experience as much as I could. I knew there was no great love between us, we had become strangers to each other in many ways, yet when I was with him a tiny glow remained. Maybe this was how marriage was supposed to end up, in a deep friendship. Maybe the passion of anger could be reversed into a passion for each other. I wondered how he felt about me, and living the rest of our lives as best friends. How would he feel when he read my book? It was all about us growing into different people, accepting each other as mature adults, warts and all.

His eyebrows shot up when I told him I had been offered a publishing contract – I could hardly believe it myself: I was being published. I couldn't rest, wrapping a dressing gown around me, I sat in the cold morning air on the tiniest balcony in the universe to ring our daughter. I told her of my travels, of Bathurst, the movies in Orange with the CWA. We laughed about our grandson's escapades and boy scouts. She agreed travel seemed to be my thing. I told her of the cruise her Dad had suggested. There was a pregnant pause, 'You're not coming back home, are you, Mum?' I admitted it was not on my priority list. I could tell she was hurt. 'When will we see you again?' she asked. 'In the very near future, hun,' I said two words I wish I had never said as the next time we spoke would be in sorrow, 'I promise.'

The day was full of seeing the hotspots of Sydney. It's a massive city with much to see and we took a double decker bus tour with twenty other fresh-faced tourists. As we stopped at different places, Larry was busy on the phone, his smile a mile wide when he showed me the bank balance. 'I've been paid a very large bonus, plus I have a new contract, Cassie. They want me back, I start back in four weeks' time. Let's find us a travel agent, and book that cruise.' There was one four blocks down from our hotel, we both staggered through the agents door full of joy, like excited teenagers. Ten minutes later, Larry had paid for the cruise in one swipe; five thousand dollars for ten days around Australia.

We were to leave Sydney Harbour at five o'clock in three days' time. I studied the itinerary, and took one look at our clothing; every item was old and faded. It was going to be a shopping day tomorrow. I preferred op-shopping, I had heard that Sydney had some fabulous laneway boutiques, I just had to find them. I mentioned it to the receptionist once I was back at the hotel; *did she know of any second's boutiques*? 'Madam,' she said, 'do I have the person for you!'

Enter Mel into my life. Funny, sassy Mel with short vibrant red hair, tattoos in every space available, piercings in ears, lips and nose, the most beautiful British accent, her eyes deepest of blue. At a very slim six foot tall, she was formidable. She was known as Sydney's Boudica, which I soon discovered when the receptionist rang to say my travel guide was in the foyer. The lift pinged softly as the elevator door opened, I was greeted loudly with, 'Hello, gorgeous,' as she strode towards me, mischievous fun written all over her. After a quick introduction to Larry, it was obvious

Jigsaw

he did not care for her. She was a bit too boisterous, he liked his women quiet and subservient, everything Mel was not. He had opted for a roam in the city, looking for bloke's stuff for the cruise. I was out all day, each boutique had a gem or two of clothing that I liked. By noon, it was lunch in the old Sydney-siders pub, by now, I had an inkling that Mel was male. We discussed my book, Mel asking, 'Oh, darling, I hope I'm in it.' We discussed what bullying meant to her, although I saw her eyes flicker with a sudden sadness, all she would say was, 'It's hard being a cock in a frock, sweetie.' I nearly choked with the laughter that bubbled out of me. Mel had another date at two o'clock. She embraced me to say her goodbye, it was like being hugged with happiness. Mel was joy incarnate; I will never forget her laughter booming through the alleyways as she guided me on one of the best shopping days I had ever experienced. As we hugged, she said, 'Can't wait to read your book, Cassie,' which endeared her to me even more.

Once back in our hotel room, I showered and unpacked. Suddenly I had a wardrobe bigger than when I left my home in Armadale. Once I laid everything out on the bed, it seemed I had made great choices, thanks to Mel. Not only had I purchased a black cocktail dress with a bolero of red lace, but I had also mixed or matched most of the clothing beautifully. Again, thanks to Mel, who certainly had an eye for colour and style. I now had a day-to-day wardrobe, plus an ensemble for each night. Thankfully Mel rang her favourite hairdresser while we had lunch. I was booked in for the following day, Mel saying, 'She's with me, Darl, treat her right.' Larry had left a message: *Italian tonight? I'm across the road.* I looked out the window; he was looking up at me waving. We both loved Italian. Larry had brought two large suitcases, one each; the one thing I had forgotten to do – luggage. We discussed our day both agreeing Sydney was bigger than we had ever thought, saying, 'I'm ready for bed,' at the same time.

The next day, Larry was to sign new contracts. He was busy on the phone making pick-up/drop-off arrangements for the drill. For me, the transcript of my book was burning a hole in my thoughts. I had signed the contract. I was to make amendments adding what I wanted to say about becoming Cassie. The publisher had offered an editor as an added option. *Why not?* I could afford it now. My main problem, after the cruise, was accommodation. If I was to leave the convoy of drill rigs, I would prefer to live in Rockingham.

It was a popular seaside village and I decided to call Heather to see if she had a contact or two in that area. I had just begun to dial when Larry stopped me. 'Cassie, I have a huge favour to ask you.' I put my phone down. He looked so dire – maybe the cruise had been cancelled? Or the contract was cancelled? Larry sat beside me taking one of my hands in his. This was bad news, I knew the signs.

'Hun, the new contract calls for a couple.' I groaned, 'Not again,' when Larry continued I will have an offsider, you will be signed on as my spouse. It also means being back in a mobile home again. It will be three months on the road, we will visit Uluru, Coober Pedy then six months living in a combined camp at place called Cloncurry in outback Northern Queensland. In all, it will be just over a year away from Perth. No pressure Cassie, I've asked that Mick speak to us this afternoon before we get on the cruise. If we say no, it will mean a dip in wages, I will become FIFO worker once more, you can find us a home in Perth, or go back to New Zealand for a while. Your choice.'

This was huge. My heart leapt at hearing we were being offered more travel, to places I had never been to or dreamed of going to. 'What time is he calling? I have a hairdresser's appointment in an hour. I'll be back by 2:30pm.' The fact that I was even willing to discuss another drilling contract was an obvious relief from the look on Larry's face. His arms went around me, 'I promise, Cassie, I'll be on my best behaviour.' I had

Jigsaw

heard this all before; each time empty broken promises. It was time to have a good ponder about what I expected from the nomad lifestyle that had been offered to me and I had willingly accepted, at times it was harsh uncomfortable work and other times wonderful.

I could count on my fingers and toes what annoyed me about Larry, maybe he could do the same about me. Number one, I disliked the word spouse. I did not enjoy Larry's attitude when he was with other men. He had allowed Eddy, his last offsider to be rude towards me, to me that was giving his permission. What if we were given an offsider with the same base nature as Eddy who believed women were to be bullied into submission, stepped on, ruled over with sarcasm and dishonesty. There was much to consider.

CHAPTER 45

What is it about a hairdresser that you want to confide in them? I had formed a close bond with my hairstylist in Rockingham. She knew more about my life than some of my good friends. This one was no different. She asked how my day was going, like an exploding egg, I told her all about Larry and Eddy, how much I disliked them both when they were together, how I wanted to travel. I explained how I had run away, then been hauled into line by the big boss. How I was disappointed in his wife. While the stylist snipped then combed, she looked like she understood every grievance I uttered. Even when she snapped the cape off from around my shoulders, held up the mirror and brushed me down, she had a look on her face that said, 'I understand.' I paid the bill, walked out, knowing she had hardly heard a word, yet somehow I had come to a decision. Perhaps talking it out was like a mini therapy; someone had listened without judgement. Deciding to walk back to the hotel, I passing the Eatery alleyway; every small shop down this cobbled laneway was a café of some description.

An abundance of plants grew everywhere, not one small space was wasted, buckets of multicoloured daisies or geraniums bloomed in many bright colours. Ferns grew from large or small pots, an ivy had found its home there, winding up the walls, and across wires to support it. It had a sense of calm about it, even though there were many people at tables, everything was muted. It was lovely to sit in the cool, calm green shadows, order a pot of English breakfast tea with a warm fruit scone with cream. I asked for a pen, it was bought with my order. I wrote my pros and cons on a napkin. First was a conversation with Mick; if he wanted me to drive the motorhome plus feed the offsider I expected some sort of compensation, not the old adage, 'What's one more spud in the pot?' If I was expected to taxi these men around, my name should be on all insurance forms connected to the motorhome.

When it came to the offsider, I preferred a family man. If he was rude and crude in any way, I wanted his permission to ring and report any sort of bad behaviour, instead of being informed to, 'Stay home – you're in a man's world now.' That stupid comment still irked me. With the accommodation, I would choose the motorhome, suggest transport (bikes) to be provided for the drillers to get back to our base for a meal. However, I would not share my accommodation with the offsider again. I preferred a swag to be provided for them or a camping ground with a cabin provided for them, where they could use the ablution blocks.

Next on the list, was Larry. If I agreed to accompany him, I would expect him to show me respect at all times. We would openly discuss our travelling together for the year. With an open honesty we could discuss our relationship. When Larry had money in his pocket he was always happy. While he had a job he enjoyed; he was happy. If any of that dwindled, he sulked, becoming moody, sarcastic and rude. What he did not know was the more time I had on my own, the more I loved it. The more I travelled meeting other women, the more independent I became. Could he handle who I was growing into? I was no longer the Cassie who clapped with excitement at good news, who indulged her family no matter how they behaved towards her, or allowed others to bully her, to swallow their opinions just to keep the peace or my employment. That Cassie had died. In her place, was a woman of sixty plus who loved herself and her life more than anything or anyone. Could he accept that? If not, I had no place in his life or his in mine. I truly believed emotional growth and communication was imperative to us being together as a couple.

It was two o'clock when I tucked my list of pros and cons into my pocket. Walking into the hotel room, Larry had his phone on speaker, Mick chatted with Larry for a while then he asked to address me. I drew out the serviette and neatly placed it on the table, then greeted Mick. I thanked him for the amazing opportunity. Larry's face was beaming, until I calmly read what I wanted if I was to agree to travel in convoy. Larry's face registered horror, as I made each word count. Mick listened to my requests, without interrupting. When I stopped speaking, he politely asked if I had any more suggestions. His reply was calm, business-like. 'I feel we can agree on those requests, Cassie. I apologise for any misconduct from the recent offsider. May I speak with Larry please?' No demands, no anger, no consequences; this was business and I appreciated Mick's candid reply.

On the other hand, Larry's reactions was not calm. 'How dare you compromise my job with your silly demands? Who do you think you are?' I looked at the time; we had two hours to board the ship, we should leave now. With his hands on his hips, he glared at me demanding an answer. It felt like a parent reprimanding a child. 'Grow up, Larry,' I said. 'It's not about your contracts, it's all about your recent behaviour. Your actions had consequences which you should be made responsible for. I've had to put it to the CEO of the firm for assurances that this immature conduct will not happen again.'

His face paled. I knew he had not thought of it in those terms; that his spouse had felt it necessary to ask his boss for protection. 'Now I'm off to have some fun on a cruise, whether you like it or not.' I picked up my case, smiled at this man I called husband, 'Are you coming or staying? We can carry on with this conversation on board, or you can stay here, find your own way back to Perth.' Larry grabbed his suitcase, pulled mine out of my hands, mumbling to himself as he marched towards the elevator.

Oh my, the cruise ship was long, white, elegant and in full party mode. A calypso band played singing to the crowd as we walked through customs, our boat pass, then cabin pass plus cabin number allocated to us. Finding my way along a long corridor of soft beige carpet past many cabins, I slid our key card into the entry as the door clicked open into a small room, muted with soft light, a king-size bed, many pillows, with a small ensuite. The cabin fridge was stocked with all sorts of nibbles. There was a small TV plus a wardrobe. I could hear the ship motors humming. Over the intercom came the Captain's voice: 'Ladies and gentlemen, welcome aboard. We will be leaving Sydney Harbour on the hour. Please join us on deck for a farewell party. Welcome to your holiday of a lifetime.' I could not miss this, it was the beginning of a dream for me. Larry followed me to the deck. It was covered in streamers, the calypso band was on board, the Sydney skyline was darkening, everyone was dancing, singing, having fun.

I felt the wonderful feeling of being stress-free. I could feel my feet tapping in time as a waiter asked if I would like a drink. I nodded, but then with a cheeky smile he added, 'Or would Madam like to dance?' I was whisked away to the dance floor. This was fun. I had not cha-cha'd or tangoed in ages. To my surprise Larry was also on the dance floor with a young lady; he was not a dancer, but he was smiling, doing his best. The horn blasted our farewell to Sydney, my whole being alive. The ship was now well under way slicing through black water, what a fabulous night. We were asked if we would we like to join the formal dining room for dinner or remain on deck to join the cruise barbeque.

I opted for the barbeque, when Larry said he was going back to the cabin, his face had turned a slight tinge of green. There he stayed, in bed for two days, until he got used to the movement of the ship. I would get up in the morning, attend everything I could. Making a circle of friends who I sat with at dinner, going to the night deck movies or the nightly cabaret shows, which I adored. I was rarely back in the cabin until after midnight. Larry did his best to be with me, but every time he took his head off the pillow he complained of vertigo and nausea. I had been to the on-board chemist, asking if it was normal; perhaps he should see a doctor. The chemist replied saying, More normal than you'd think, Ma'am.'

I glowed with happiness; every day was a new adventure. I fell in love with cruising.

Every morning at the breakfast buffet I would have my breakfast, then take Larry some dry crackers, some fruit, with two or three bottles of water. In two days, we arrived at the first port, Bunbury. This small town was a delight, I did the bus tour. Larry was now feeling well, he did the museum tour. We met back on board for a late lunch. I had a nana nap while Larry attended a talk on tall ships. He came back to the cabin laughing, 'Poor speaker got seasick … he threw up onstage.' The afternoon went quickly as we scanned the ships daily newsletter for what to do and see in our next port of Fremantle.

It seemed a tad weird, as not so long ago we had lived not an hour away from this city. Still I opted for the art trail, Larry put his name down for the brewery tour. Agreeing to meet up at the cabin later in the day, I pointed out that there was an opera singer in the theatre that night and we should put our names down to book our seats. He was not an opera fan, however agreed to accompany me. Agreeing, if he was not enjoying it he would leave to find the casino. I was happy with that.

The art trail did not disappoint. I loved the creative art here, I gathered the brewery tour was the same as Larry walked into the cabin a little tipsy. He put his arms around me; 'Wish we had done this a long time ago. I miss my Cassie.' My mother's advice had always been to never argue with someone who's been drinking. With this in mind I disentangled myself. What he meant was, *I miss the simple life of no arguments, just obedience.* 'Come on,' I said, 'we're going to miss the opera.' Larry lay down on the bed. 'You go without me. I'll catch up.'

The opera was fabulous. We all encored until the soloist performed one more song, then I joined my group of dinner friends for a light supper. By the time I got back to our cabin, Larry was fast asleep. Merely grumbling as I took off his shoes and pulled a blanket over him. I switched off the lights in the cabin, the gentle rocking of the boat soon had me falling into a deep sleep. My last thought was of Geraldton the following day.

By the time I woke, the boat was being moored to the wharf in Geraldton, on a bright beautiful sunny morning. Larry was still deeply sleeping. I decided to join a women's walking group before breakfast; they were fast paced. I did a half-hour with them then begged off, joining the line for the breakfast. I spied Larry in the line, he looked tired. Over breakfast, I asked, 'You look peaky, everything alright?' His answer took me by surprise, 'I just feel like we are wasting time, I can't wait to get back to work.'

'Larry, you wanted this. It was your idea, to have some fun together, relax a little. What's concerning you?' I knew any discussion on why he felt like this was pointless. Back at the cabin, I decided on a walk to the Geraldton monument hill. I had heard about the fallen solders statue. It was a long walk, but I made it; below me lay the city with the ocean as far as the eye could see. I stood beside the statue of a woman looking out to sea waiting for her menfolk to return after World War II. I felt my tears release. Here was a woman wanting her man back, to be by her side, yet Larry and I were still battling to stay together.

It was at this very spot I saw what the problem was with such clarity, it was me. With all my learnings over the years, the wisdom I had learnt, the life changing education I had received, I had expected Larry to keep up with me. That old adage *you can't change anyone they have to want to change themselves*, the myriads of seagulls circling overhead agree with their constant squawking. Larry had plodded along, knowing I would pacify instead of argue, yet something in me had shifted. I admired me. My journey, it was true, it had not been a pleasant one, however maybe that was my lessons in life *learn it the hard way*. I just knew the more I had negative reactions, the more he enjoyed it. He had never really seen me or recognised my growth, my deep spirituality, my self-belief, all of this I had had to find and decided was for me. To Larry I was simply Cassie his wife, the end.

Maybe it was better for us both if we left the ship. He could go back to his job where men were men. I would find a two bedroom villa somewhere in Rockingham until I was certain of where I actually wanted to live. I made my way back to the ship, found our cabin, placed my case on the bed, I began to pack. Larry had left a message on the back of a postcard. 'I'm in the bar.' I knew what that meant. Do I go or stay in the Cabin, my feet felt like they were encased in mud knowing Larry could be drunk, it could go either way when I appeared. He would be abusive or happy, I was never sure which.

He was there on his own talking to the bartender. Both looked my way as I entered, seeing the uncertainty on my face. 'Hello, love,' said Larry, 'this is Jerry. We've been chatting about drilling, the good money a person can make in the mines. I've given him Mick's number.' I looked around. There was no sign of excessive alcohol being consumed but one half empty schooner that Larry had been drinking. Larry excused himself.

Are all barmen like hairdressers, secret psychologists? Jerry soon had me talking about being on the road, being a driller's wife, travelling in convoy: Did I enjoy it? Did I meet many people? I, in turn, asked why

Jigsaw

he was working on a cruise ship. Was he married? Why the interest in mining? By the time my husband reappeared, we had learnt a lot about each other. Perhaps I had missed my calling, as we talked I heard a troubled heart. Whatever it was, I knew I had met a man who genuinely cared about other people.

Back at the cabin, I was questioned about my case being packed. I was honest, saying if he'd had enough of cruising, we should head back home. 'Are you mad, woman? I'm having a ball. I'm a bit anxious about work, have I ever been any different?' I unpacked while he ordered a pizza for the movie night under the stars. He had found the ship's newsletter, announcing the next city we were berthing in, his pen circling things he wanted to see. Tomorrow Karratha was next on the itinerary. A shopping tour was on offer, we decided to stay on board. I booked a seat in the art class, Larry going for another talk on sunken tall ships in the area. Tonight it was hot pizza, under the stars, wrapped up in a warm blanket on deck chairs. I remember the movie had Tom Cruise in it, I could feel myself falling asleep.

CHAPTER 46

Spending the day on board while the majority of the crew and passengers were exploring, was what we both needed. We slept late, I had a massage, then attended the art class, Larry spending the afternoon in the library using their computers. There was a formal dinner that night so we both dressed up; my black cocktail dress bringing back memories of Mel, a smile of fondness flickering across my face. We were seated at the captain's table. It was all very formal, but I enjoyed it. The following day we berthed in Darwin. We opted for a ride with hogs tours on a Harley Davies quad bike. He was a true blue Ozzie, we loved 'his patch' as he called it. We toured all the little places the tour buses couldn't get to. It was party night back at the ship, though Larry I were too tired to dance, we enjoyed the atmosphere, the food and music.

We were off to Lombok. I could hear the chains being drawn as cast off was called. The ships horn blasted as I fell asleep to the ship ploughing into deeper waters. The two days on board were full of mini shows from many artists plus the crew. Every time a bell went off, we raced to the foyer to grab a seat anywhere we could to see singers, ballroom dancers,

Jigsaw

jugglers, country dancing displays, piano recitals, food carving or animal balloon making. The food on board was delicious, I especially loved the tiny cafes hidden away, where a quiet coffee could be had while the ship parted the curling waves. I was also writing like never before. Any blocks had gone. When I wrote the ending, I felt the same feeling as I did as an empty nester, I'd lost my baby.

Lombok did not disappoint, along with some of the crew, we hired a pony and trap ride. We were taken deep into the forest to view what these lovely people handmade from the clay pits. Some of the sculptures were breathtaking. Cruising back to Cairns through the Gulf of Carpentaria the sea became slightly choppy and I was sure Larry would once again be seasick, but he handled it beautifully. We played a little game of poker at the casino. I caught up on my emails or sitting in the sun making the final corrections to my manuscript, taking a big breath as I pressed send. When I told Larry, he said with pride, 'My wife, the author!'

We had three more days to enjoy the cruise. Although I knew it must end, I didn't want it to; I enjoyed life onboard. Our next stop was Cairns. Another tour on a bus didn't tempt us and we walked through the streets admiring the lovely old buildings, many built in the early 1900s. That night we dined in the dining room, thoroughly entertained by our dinner companions, all of them in long-term marriages. They had no trouble in telling it like it was 'bloody hard work' said one of the senior women as she patted her husband's hand. 'Should have run a mile, he's nothing but trouble,' said another wife as she kissed her husband's cheek. Both men were a lot older than Larry, both had silly smirks on their faces. They were happy couples, I wondered if we would last so long as to look upon each other with a deep friendship or endearment. It certainly did not feel like it would with all the trials and tribulations we'd recently experienced, yet somehow we were both still in each other's lives.

I wanted to know the magic formula. The more outspoken of the two women answered, 'As I said, Cassie, it's bloody hard work, but in the end that's a woman's power isn't it? It's not a competition Cassie, its sharing the equality in our lives. We bring our sons up to be men, then we kindly show our men we are their equals. Yes it's hard work, but hard work always pays off in the end.' Those words made a big impact on my spirit that night.

The ship ploughed into the Coral sea once more, our destination Ellis Beach. I loved this tiny township. There was a festival on the beach. It was the stalls dotted along the beach that attracted me. This was the last stop before Brisbane then back to Sydney. We both enjoyed a chocolate lava hot shot drink and I bought all sorts of trinkets to send back to family in New Zealand. My niece, Cilleen's daughter, had been sending me emails wanting to catch up. I had not yet replied, still very aware of the impatience I was shown on my last visit. However, we had three beautiful great nieces and nephews in the family, there was no reason not to send them a little something. Then there was our daughter and grandson. Larry becoming a little disgruntled as I added colourful t-shirts alongside beaded wristbands to the growing pile of knick-knacks.

Deciding on an ice-cream as we walked back to the ship, I was looking forward to the night's theatre show; two young Asian violinists who promised to 'blow your socks off.' Larry was looking forward to chatting to the men from the previous night's dinner. We sat under a large palm tree enjoying the cool ocean breeze, when I spied at least four long black bags, being brought to shore. I looked away. Larry's arm went around my shoulder, 'All part of life, Cassie,' he whispered. It was still hard to realise that one minute they were enjoying themselves on a cruise, the next moment, your loved ones were grieving.

The Captain with a few of the crew stood to one side, their caps now in their hands, their heads bowed. We also stood with our heads bowed as two hearses drove the bodies away. The excitement we had felt about our night's entertainment sat like ash in our mouths. Once we returned to the ship, I went to the cabin falling asleep, sadness settling in my heart. Larry headed off to the bar to meet up with his now good buddy, the barman, Jerry. He woke me by shaking me. 'Cassie, guess what? Jerry spoke to Mick. He has an online interview tomorrow with the firm. We've been talking for ages. Cassie, if he gets the offsider's job, would you mind if I requested Jerry to come work with me? He's good bloke.'

Maybe now was the time to bring up the subject of what I would be expecting from Larry if I went along as his wife on the convoy. As I sat up, my stomach rolled over. Only just making it to the bathroom, the blinding headache that followed was the worst I had ever experienced. Painkillers were no use, I curled back into bed searching for the oblivion of sleep. I woke early the following morning to the sound of male voices calling out to tie the stern line; we were in Brisbane. My body felt disgusting, a hot shower then back to bed to sleep. Larry woke with a smile, looking forward to the Zoom call between Mick and Jerry. He had also opted for the brewery tour, this time to see how it all actually worked. He returned after his buffet breakfast with a hot cup of tea, two large bottles of water and half a dozen sweet biscuits. With a quick kiss on the cheek, wishing me a restful morning, he was off for the day. It was 1pm when I woke. I felt so much better, a little vertigo, which was nothing unusual for me after a migraine.

I had another very hot shower to relax the neck muscles, dressed in casual gear, ringing the beauty parlour to see if I could book in for a head/shoulder massage, knowing it would help. I had to wait for an hour but once under the expert hands of the masseuse, the remaining headache slipped away. She did comment on checking out my posture with a physiotherapist once I was home. Not a bad idea. When you're driving in convoy you don't stop for hours, too much sitting can't be good for anyone's health.

Larry found me sunning myself on the upper deck. He had been sampling the beer at the brewery, he was in a happy mood, full of news about his tour. When I asked about Jerry, Larry's smile was a giveaway. 'Think you can deal with him as an offsider? Mick rang me thanking me for putting Jerry their way. I asked if he could be on our team and it seems we have a new offsider when we get back to Sydney.' It all sounded fabulous, until I said, 'I've not seen the contract yet, Larry.' How can one person turn so quickly from overjoyed to super stroppy in two seconds? He almost spat out the words, 'Cassie, you promised, you friggin' promised me we would do this together. I found us a decent offsider and now you're not sure? When will you stop playing games? You're either with me on this or not. Make up your friggin' mind!' His hand circled my upper arm as he spoke giving my arm a shake 'My job cannot depend on whether you're happy or not. I'm over jumping through hoops for you.'

He stormed off leaving me in tears. One of the passengers had witnessed his outburst and she came over to me asking if I was okay. 'Do you need assistance? Perhaps I should call someone?' I shook my head making my way back to the cabin. Larry was already there, jumping up as I came in, full of apologies. 'Cassie, please don't bait me like this, you're either on board or not. It's not just us that's at stake, it's the contracts plus Jerry. If you say no, where do you go? I love this life. I thought you did as well.' Now was the time to let Larry know what I expected. Jerry was great and I hoped it worked out for the firm, but I still wanted to see the contract before I went anywhere. 'Your behaviour, Larry, has to change. I mean it. I just don't see myself as a woman who lets her husband stomp all over her because she has not made him happy. I'm not the Cassie you married or the scared rabbit that came to Perth. I will not accept bullying in any way or in any form in my life."

Larry pulled the contract out of the side pocket of his suitcase throwing it on the bed 'There … read for yourself, you have everything you asked for.' He was right. I was now on the insurance papers to drive a mobile home in the company's name. I was to choose the mobile home, a budget had been put in place, though not mentioned was my cooking for the offsider. I pointed this out to Larry. 'Cassie, I can't rewrite this contract. You don't understand. There's huge money involved here, not just one lousy meal on a tin plate. Can you not get your head around it, Love? I'm talking thousands of dollars per hole drilled, per contract, per day, I get paid a fare whack of it, which I might add you don't mind spending.' He pointed to the pile of souvenirs I had collected. 'Tell you what, how about you provide us with a packed lunch plus a cook dinner for us, I'll pay to have your book published? What is it? Four thousand? Will that cover it? Pop your name on the contract, put a smile on your face, let's celebrate. We have another adventure ahead of us,' he chuckled, 'no doubt you will write about that as well.'

I stood my ground. 'First, your solemn promise; no more bullying or outbursts, It's not about money, I mean it Larry. The first sign of bad behaviour from you or your offsider and I'm walking away.' He offered me his hand. That was a first, normally it was sealed with a kiss. Hopefully this time, he knew I was serious. The contract papers crackled in my hand as I signed on the dotted line. Larry beamed as he hauled me to my feet. 'Welcome to the drilling team!' From Larry, that was a complement. We moored at the Sydney Princess wharves. Leaving this home away from home was sad. There was no band or smiling crew, just a hurry up get off, we have new smiles to welcome. Our first stop over was Newcastle, but before that we had to organise the motorhome. Jerry stood beside us, his sailor's bag over his shoulder, the widest smile. He was ready to go. Larry shook his hand then slapped him on the shoulder like a long lost son. I made sure our luggage was accounted for, when Jerry offered me his hand, 'What do I call you? Boss's wife? Mrs?' I shook his hand, 'Cassie will do.' Our life on the road was about to restart in a

Kez Wickham St George

big way. Grey nomads we were not, we were a team, working together, this time, it felt right.

CHAPTER 47

Sydney is this ever-busy city, the only way for us to find the motorhome hire depot was to take a taxi. Once we arrived, we had a choice; ensuite or not, two or four berth? I now knew enough about motorhomes to check it out properly; electrical leads, water hoses, toilet cassettes, shower curtains, bedding, cupboard space, wardrobe space. The table in this one folded down to a single bed. I carefully examined the double mattress; it was brand new. Another tick on the clipboard I had been given, noting a miniscule fraying on the carpet by the side of the bed, a small chip on a kitchen utensil drawer. I had asked for a full-size three-way fridge, this had to be installed before we left. As this was to be my lifestyle for the next year or more, I was determined it was up to me to ask for what I wanted. There had been a large parcel delivered to the motorhome depot in Larry's name and I knew by the packaging that it was a swag for Jerry. We opted to grocery shop before we drove the motorhome away. Larry had given me a budget – that was a first.

We took another taxi to a supermarket, then once we had filled two trollies up with food, found a taxi back to the depot. Jerry was happy to help unpack the food. Larry was on the phone, making sure we were expected. The contract stated the drilling would start in two days. He then confirmed Jerry had his license, as he would be driving the motorhome as well. I felt such an immense relief when he produced his car license, his HT license plus a recent St John's emergency card. He had all the certificates needed so far, all except a driller's permit, but that would be taken care of in Newcastle, along with his training to drive a drill rig. It was so good that Jerry would be driving, the responsibility was not just with me, we now all shared the same responsibility to get the job done.

Once the fridge I had requested was in place, we drove out. It was time to see what Newcastle had to offer. Shopping for the water drill rig would have to wait until we arrived in Newcastle, Larry asking me to write a list of what they needed. That included water cannisters for drinking water, two (Eskies) chilly bins to keep their daily food fresh, a medical kit plus a medical contact (hospital emergency), due to our fear of snakes. The list grew long, the noise of the road was making me sleepy. Larry pulled over, 'Jump in the back, Cassie, it's about time Jerry earnt his money.' I was happy to find a comfy seat, a book to read, my laptop beside me. Larry began educating Jerry on driving the bus on the Pacific Highway in peak time traffic; not a job for the fainthearted. It's not just a silly saying that Australia runs on the back of its trucks, it truly does. They are fast and furious, with no time for anyone who is not used to this sort of traffic.

We were due at the farm by late afternoon, only just in time, the sun setting over this farms grapevines. Larry rang the house; we were welcomed with open arms. Four young toddlers stood on the veranda, each one wide-eyed as the motorhome drove up the driveway. 'Hey, guys, I'm Amber, this is Todd, welcome to Henspeck.' Then she saw me climb out of the motorhome. 'No way! Another woman! You're more than welcome now.' The two drillers were shown a spot by an old well that was to be re-drilled, water for stock and household. Todd also showed them where

Jigsaw

to park the motorhome, Amber ushering me inside. 'Welcome to the farm. It's so nice to have another woman around, are you hungry?' she asked while picking an armload of toys from the chair she was offering me. 'I've made some veggie soup with fresh bread. Hang on, I'll just grab those four little monsters and herd them off to bed.' Once this was done amongst shrieks of laughter with the question of, 'Who's that lady, Ma? Is that our Grandma?' The house quietened down, Amber brushing whisps of blond hair off her face as she sat next to me. 'God, they're a handful.' 'Twins?' I asked.

'Nope, two are mine, two are Todd's. Todd's wife left with my old man. He couldn't run the farm by himself plus care for his two littlies, I was not doing too well financially. A friend jokingly said we should get together, so we did. I'm the housekeeper, chief cook, bottle-washer here. If I had a crystal ball I think I would have run a mile,' she nudged me, 'nah, not really, we make a good team. So, what do you do? why are you travelling with two drillers,' she asked, 'I must say one of them is a spunk.' I smiled, knowing she was referring to Jerry not Larry.

I helped her serve up five bowls of hearty veggie soup. Washing then drying of dishes was allocated to the men, while we two women sat on the front of the veranda. 'Now tell me all about yourself,' Amber enquired. 'There is not much to tell really, Amber. I'm here doing what you do, looking after the men who run the drill. The older one is my husband, Larry, Jerry is our offsider. I cook, clean make sure they're healthy, able to complete their drilling contracts.' Amber gave me a sideways look, 'so Jerry's not your son?' I smiled. I had seen the look of interest from them both. 'No, Amber, my son is in his late forties, happily married, they live in Melbourne.' Two large cups of tea were delivered to us by Todd, 'I'm off to bed ladies, sweet dreams.' The cups were huge I knew I wouldn't finish mine otherwise I would not sleep. Taking a few polite sips, I also wished them a good night heading off to the motorhome. Jerry was in his swag, the torch going out as I walked by, 'Night, Jerry, sleep tight.' 'Same to you, Cassie, see you in the morning.' Larry was in the shower. I climbed straight into bed, my eyes closing in sleep immediately.

When I woke, I could hear the drill, Larry called out directions as Jerry manipulated the machinery to where the hole was to be dug. Then Larry took over. I had never seen him work a drill rig. I loved the way he seemed to tease the little levers, change gears and lower the drill with precision accuracy. He switched off the machinery, jumped out the cab greeting me with, 'Morning, love, I'm bloody starving, what's for brekkie?' Larry looked so relaxed. It felt like we all knew the roles we had to play, as each one finished their job, the other took over, now it was my turn. 'Scrambled eggs with baked beans with toasted English muffins coming right up, boss.'

Larry announced they were was off to town to buy what they needed, permits, the correct drilling papers etc. I opted for some writing time, excited I was soon to be a published author, the next book already in mind. The boys were biking into the shire. When Amber rushed out of the farm house calling my name. 'Oh good. Be a doll, babysit these four will you? I have to get stuff in town.' The option to refuse was not there. She jumped on her farm bike taking off in a rush. Todd, I could see, was working the fields. I was not used to children at all, these little ones were in all stages of getting dressed. I almost laughed when the eldest of the four pulled washing out of the basket, handing a piece of clothing to each child. They were not used to an adult offering help, my helping hand being pushed away more than once. I made a game of it. After an hour, I sort of had them looking like children rather than characters from a Dr Seuss book. We read to each other, we played hide and seek, at lunch time, I warmed and served up a stew I found in the fridge. The children gulped it down, asking for more.

Todd wandered in for a coffee and something to eat. He didn't bother with a plate, he ate out of the pot, dipping large hunks of bread in it, letting rip with a huge belch when he'd finished. The four young ones thinking it was hilarious. Imitating Dad was now on the games list. His first words to me were, 'Sorry about Amber. She's a silly girl, always thinks city life is the better one to have. Kids are much better off out here. You don't want a job do you?' I shook my head making mental notes. It was none of my business. Todd went back to work, 'If she's not back by four, there's a haunch of lamb in the cooler. We need to cook it up before it goes off.' The four kids were ready for a nap, leading me to the room they all shared. I was a bit taken aback to see what a shambles it was. One double bed, a set of bunks, both had seen better days, clothes strewn everywhere, empty baby bottles lay in beds or on the floor. I tucked each child in, after we had washed faces and hands. Another story was told, the eldest of the children, Millie, told me they all had a bottle of milk in the afternoon. I gave each bottle a hot wash, filled them up with warm milk, in no time each little face was relaxed in sleep. Butter would not melt as the saying goes.

By four o'clock, Amber was not home, I did not know Amber's number, I was getting a little pissed off with her attitude. Basting the enormous haunch of lamb as it roasted, I thought about the mouths I now had to feed. There was an enormous garden out the back, overrun with weeds, however I found a pumpkin, a handful of broad beans and a large healthy silver beet plant. I had seen plenty of potatoes in the pantry. At five o'clock Amber was still a no-show. Todd was still out farming, while the four kids who were now bathed watched *SpongeBob* on the telly. I had forgotten just how busy a Mum of four can be.

The two drillers had returned, both saying they could smell the roast from where the drill rig was parked. Larry took one look at me, I must have looked like I'd been pulled through a gorse bush backwards, as he asked, 'You okay, Cassie? What's with the cooking, the kids?' I explained

Amber had taken off early, almost tailgating them as they drove down the driveway. I served the roast with a rich brown gravy, everyone scraping their plates clean then asking for seconds. All noise stopped as we heard the farm bike race up the driveway. Amber stumbled through the door, realising there were many eyes watching her, she slurred, 'Oh fuck. Sorry.' She was so drunk she could hardly stand. Todd lifted her to her feet and said, 'Come on, ducks, let's get you sorted.' I put the kids to bed that night, while my two drillers cleaned up the dishes. Before I left for my own bed, I cut off a large hunk of the roast, perfect for sandwiches for the boys tomorrow. Amber was not in sight when I went over to the farmhouse in the morning. The bike was gone, the kids all sitting in the lounge watching telly. There is not a lot anyone can do when it's not your business. The family had a problem but I was not the one to fix anything. What I could do, was to show these kids some fun, the games I once played with my own family and our grandchildren. We played cut-outs, face painting, cowboys and Indians, hide and seek in the veggie garden. Four little faces exhausted by lunchtime, settling down to a peanut butter sandwich with a chocolate milk before their afternoon nap. Larry rang to say the truck for the drill rig would be arriving to pick up the drill in two days, 'Let's hope we strike water soon. How are you coping?' I told him Amber had gone missing again, but the kids had been fabulous. It seems my two crew and this family would be eating dinner together once more.

Todd didn't seem too concerned when he walked in to get himself some lunch. 'She's a city girl who's had her heart broken. She'll come right.' I knew then that he loved her, nothing Amber did would interfere with that. A large potato top mince pie was on the menu for dinner. Soon two huge pie tins were in the oven baking by the time the kids got up from their nap. The same as the previous night, we were all around the table eating at six o'clock when Amber repeated her drunken entry. Todd put her to bed once more, however I just couldn't let go. The kids needed

Jigsaw

a Mum or at least someone to take care of them, memories took me back to my childhood except it was my dad who was the drunk. 'Todd, in my opinion this really isn't good, for your family or Amber – she should be in treatment. At the very least, you need a housekeeper to take care of the kids.' This kind, amicable farmer looked away before saying; 'Lady, if you don't want to be here, then don't come over. No one invited you.' He then stood, took a beer out of the fridge and sat down in the lounge watching telly. Larry saying, 'Learnt your lesson yet? They're not our family, Cassie. It's a work contract, just stay in the motorhome, ignore what's going on.'

I waited for Jerry to add to Larry's comment as Eddy would have done, I was surprised by his comment. 'I disagree with you all. This should be reported to social welfare tomorrow. The blond's a lush, the Dad looks like doesn't give a damn as long as he's fed. My background Larry is exactly what you see before you; drunk Mum, shit Dad. No one was bothered and there was no one like Cassie to help. I'd report them, let the authorities deal with it.' Jerry excused himself, I agreed with them both this was not my job, however it was my responsibility. Amber needed help. I was in bed asleep before Larry switched off the lights.

Friday morning, a beautiful morning full of sunshine and promise. I cleaned the motorhome, cooked lunch for the two men, did some writing, answered emails, trying valiantly to ignore the screams and yells of children in the farm house. It all got to much, walking over to the house, the front door wide open, chunks of bread were spread everywhere, it looked like a muddy animal had entered the home. The smell of gas, wafting into my nostrils, the hair went up on my arms. My heart leaping to see the four year old boy standing on a kitchen chair, stirring a large plastic bowl of Milo and milk on the gas stove. He knew to turn the gas on but had no idea how to light it, he was imitating me when I had made them a hot milk drink, I scooped him off the chair, shutting off the gas.

Milk was all over the floor, as was Weetbix. The kids had mushed right though the house, what a mess.

In that moment, I was so tempted to ring the authorities. My finger ready to press the buttons, when I thought that there surely had to be a better way. I dialled the CWA and introduced myself. I told them of my predicament. Within the hour they arrived en masse, three seniors with two young mums with kids of their own. They took charge of the young ones, I felt such relief, I left it in the hands of the community. They knew of Amber and Todd and the family situation. What they did not know was no one was coping. I spent the afternoon chatting to many women in this community, all caring and sharing. 'None of this would have happened, if they had known.' They thanked me for my kindness and diligence. They took over; this was their concern as a community, I had done what I could. The farmhouse remained in darkness, no lights shone from the windows, no kiddies ran around, a lonely miasma settled over it under a hazy half-moon. The following day, we moved on.

CHAPTER 48

We were up and about early, the truck to transport the drill was due at ten o'clock. Right on the hour, we heard it. How excited we were to be on our way once more. The water bore was working, both the drillers attaching all sorts of rods with brackets, so water could now be pumped into the house tank plus the fields. Our next drilling site would be on the outskirts of Kempsey, for a week. Once more, heading for a farm. I had done some research on this shire there were many artists' studios to visit. The one problem with a motorhome is it can be too big park for shopping or park in many places not designed for large vehicles. Still if that was all I had to worry about I was one of the fortunate ones.

We found the farm, the GPS pointing the way, leaving the drill truck in the fields, driving the motorhome to the caravan park we'd booked into. The ablution blocks were spacious, beautifully cleaned. We all went our different ways to have a hot shower. I loved the hot steaming jets of water on my back, sliding down my neck, I would be looking for a massage therapist very soon. Making a breakfast of bacon/egg toasties, the men quickly eating whatever I served. They were quickly off in the truck to the drill site.

It was an unspoken agreement that I now did the washing and cleaning for all three of us. The three washing machines in the camp laundry were full with our gear as I pushed the coins in. Onto the washing lines, once again I took up all four lines with our loads of washing. I needed to do some grocery shopping for fresh food, but I dreaded driving the big motorhome into town.

Unfortunately, there was no other way, as I packed up my washing powder, pegs and washing basket. A senior man, introducing himself as Thomas, commented that he and his wife were once drillers who travelled the country. She had passed away so he'd sold up everything moving to Kempsey, living here for many years as a permanent camper. I was interested in his story, however I had to get to the shops. Making my excuses, I left the laundry. Making my way back to the motorhome, when Thomas stopped me, 'Not taking that thing into town, are you? I'm going in myself, you can ride with me? Saves you hauling that monster around.' 'Yes please, thank you, I would love a ride.'

Thomas picked me up at my door, in a black shiny Oldsmobile. I had not seen an original one for many years, with gleaming chrome white wall tyres. He opened the door for me, the smell of leather bringing back memories of my Dad's car. The interior was so clean it looked new, the front seat the original bench style. I loved the simplicity of it all, column change gear stick, the old radio, gold with tiny engraved cream knobs to change the channel, the original slim wood steering wheel, the dashboard made of highly varnished wood with the simplest of dials and it purred like an enormous cat as we slowly drove along the main road.

Thomas dropped me off at the grocery store, saying he would meet me in an hour. It took me back to when my folks would agree to meet somewhere; no alarms, no mobile phones. We had a watch on our wrists, it was called time management. In those days we showed respect by being on time. Shopping done, Thomas packed all I'd purchased into the boot of his car then offered me morning tea at the only café that was open in town. Thomas was a gentleman, easing the chair from the table, offering me the seat. It was a lovely morning. I learnt he was ninety-two years old, still cooking/cleaning for himself. He had never left the district, Sydney or Brisbane holding no interest for him. 'It's all too fast for me now, Lynnie.' I corrected him, 'It's Cassie.' He nodded, saying, 'I know, dear, I know your name.' As we drove home I was called 'Lynnie' again. I stopped correcting him, he could daydream, he'd earnt it. Both drillers arrived home dusty, the red/brown grime sitting in the lines of their faces. While they showered, I began cooking dinner. I had bought fresh fish, new potatoes with fresh green beans. While everything cooked, they discussed their day, the drilling had gone well, the farmer was very happy. We talked about my day. I told them about Thomas with his Oldsmobile, Jerry saying, 'You reckon it's an original?' Larry gave a soft whistle, adding, 'If it was, it would be worth a small fortune.'

After dinner, the men washing the dishes, I opened up the laptop to see if any friends in Perth had emailed me. Scrolling down past to the ones I would answer, I saw an email from the eBook publishers in the UK. My hear skipped a beat, the news *they had published me. Wait, stop, what?* I would be receiving monthly payments. "Congratulations, Cassie, you're in our stable of fiction authors, when can we expect the next one?"

In the past, I would have immediately informed Larry, tonight I savoured it until Jerry called out, 'Goodnight, Cassie, lovely meal, thank you.' I returned Jerry's goodnight, then turned to Larry, 'Nice meal, Larry?' He stretched, groaning as he did so, a moments silence before replying, 'Yes, love, it was. I'm buggered.' He climbed into bed, asleep as soon as his head touched the pillow. I hugged myself, tears stinging my eyes, whispering to myself, 'Congratulations, Cassie, you're a published author.' Suddenly I felt a kind of loneliness I'd not felt before. Although I respected the two men were drillers both working hard, there had been no interest in my day until I mentioned the Oldsmobile.

Undressing in the darkened motorhome, pulling on my nightgown, I willed myself not to be childish. My being published mattered to no one but me. Another book had been requested and that was exciting, I knew what was expected of me as part of the drilling team; I kept things ticking over so they could work. Still, a little hurt bubbled in my chest was it really too hard for them to say, 'What are your plans for tomorrow?' Well, tomorrow I was going to invite Thomas over for a cup of tea in the motorhome. I just may be able to interview him about his life as a base for my next book. The morning arrived much too soon. I was tired, grumpy, waking with a migraine, a sore lower back. It was time I had that massage, Larry suggested I stay in bed. I was glad to do so. Vertigo had set in, as I stood up, I had to hold on, as the bed tilted sideways. I rang the camp office asking if they had information on local health or massage therapists. They did, an Asian family, who offered acupuncture plus massage, hopefully it was what I needed.

Who better to ask for a ride into the town than Thomas? I felt myself walking slightly askew towards his little cabin. He was about to drive away. I called out his name, he looked over the top of his glasses then began to scold me, "I was about to search for you Lynnie, where have you been all night?" I stopped in my tracks, feeling as confused as he looked. 'Thomas, I'm not Lynnie. I'm Cassie, remember? From the motorhome. You gave me a ride into town yesterday.' He was about to say something when his eyes cleared. 'Of course, you're Cassie. How can I help you?' I asked if he was going into town. He shook his head, 'Not today, maybe tomorrow. All depends on when Lynnie comes home.' So, we were back to Lynnie again. I made my way back to the motorhome. The pain had moved from my left temple to my neck. If I couldn't find a massage soon, I knew I was in for a week of painfilled days until it receded.

Boiling the jug to make fill two hot water bottles to pack around the

Jigsaw

sore muscles in my neck swallowing some painkillers, then drew every curtain possible to kill the light. I was nearly asleep when the knocking or thumping on the door began. 'Lynnie? I know you're in there. Come out, sweetheart, I'm not cross with you.' I knew if I answered the door, I would have to have a conversation with Thomas. My body was not up to it, not today. Eventually I heard him shuffle away, waking once more when the two drillers arrived back for lunch. I had not prepared them any food. Larry immediately knew something was wrong as the motorhome was in darkness. 'You rest up, love. I'll sort something to eat.' I was happy to.

He refilled the two hot water bottles for me, placing one on my lower back, the other under my neck. Once they went back to work, it was peaceful, I slept. Waking at 6pm, when the men came home for their showers plus a meal. Larry insisting he make it, making me a very welcome cup of tea, which I downed in two seconds asking for another. Larry cooked baked beans with fried eggs, the smell of frying made my stomach flip over, I staggered outside for fresh air.

The sky was a bruised grey as dusk settled over the camp, the moon a sliver of ghostly silver. The air was refreshing and the wind a little brisk; you could tell autumn was on its way. I had curled up in one of the deck chairs, listening to the men chatting quietly, which I found relaxing. I felt the slight wind ruffle my hair, almost like a hand lightly touching me, the hair on my arms stood up, the trees were not swaying yet I could feel a breeze. Larry had seen me shiver, fetching me a blanket. He was in the motorhome making me a cuppa, when I felt overwhelmed with homesickness for New Zealand. Part of me succumbing to this feeling, which was now very rare, allowed for the tears to flow freely, the other part was sorting out the emotions that went with this feeling. I knew it was linked with spirit; there was no fear just a melancholy feeling, knowing that someone I knew had passed. I had experienced this before.

Who it was, I had no idea.

The lights were out in the motorhome by 8pm. All of us were tired tomorrow we were leaving, a day early, since their drilling job was complete. At 1am I was woken, not by sound, but a knowing there was someone in the motorhome with us. A grey shadow stood in the kitchen, looking at me. Immediately, my throat seized with fear. I sat upright not knowing what to do. I heard the words 'forgive me' float around me. Two hours later my phone beeped into life, the old saying true; no one rings this early unless there's a death. My son spoke, his voice heavy with grief, 'Mum, my Dad has passed away.' I knew his grief well, I wanted to hold him close as I did when he was a child. I had never taught them to hate their father or his family, I had taught them to understand that their father and I had not loved each other. They knew I had first married to escape a life at home where I was destined to be chained by religion. From frying pan into the fire? My life with him had been one of fear and disappointment, It was so many years ago, the emotional wounds long since healed. I was just grateful I had taught my children to make sensible choices to be responsible for their actions.

I listened to his ragged sobs, as he tried to understand the enormity of what had happened. I had learnt very early in my life that grief is not the enemy, it's a natural emotion for every human. It's when you see your own immortality that when it hits home. I said I would ring him in the morning, as I once more settled down to sleep, I now knew who and why I had been visited that night.

CHAPTER 49

The morning was filled with fog. It hung off the eves of the many caravans, mesmerising me as I walked through it to the showers. Larry noticed I still looked unwell, suggesting we just hang out for the day, leaving a day later, as originally planned. He had a large amount of paper to fill out, Jerry was happy to kick back and put his feet up reading a book. I still had a nagging headache. the shower blissfully hot on my neck and shoulders. I felt well enough to make banana pancakes for breakfast, pouring honey over them while they were still warm. Jerry making 'yumm' noises as he wolfed his down, Larry's eyes glued to his laptop as he ate. It was the small things I noticed; Jerry was thirty if a day older, a lovely lad full of energy, always ready to get going. My Larry looked tired, a little frayed around the edges as he aged. By this time, we were both in our mid-sixties. My thoughts of retirement would not be well received, but I knew we couldn't do this forever. Maybe it was time to broach the subject of retirement, and the scariest of all topics, making a will.

It was over breakfast when I told them that my book was published and now available for sale. Larry was beaming excited for me, while Jerry said, 'Fair dinkum, Cassie? Babe, that's awesome.' He turned bright red when he realised what he'd said. He spluttered to a stop, looking at Larry then at me; calling the drill boss's wife 'babe' might not be appreciated. Larry just looked stunned. He had never heard another man compliment me. Poor Jerry. He didn't know what to do until he saw us both beside ourselves with laughter. Jerry exhaled. 'I was expecting to be slapped or sacked.' This young man was a delight

Now that a day off was decided, Jerry set off on a walk into Kempsey, while Larry set off to the drill to check on nuts, bolts, tinker with drill pieces, generally clean it down. This was Jerry's job but Larry had told him to bugger off, enjoy his time off. Me? I was under orders to rest, read, as no matter what, the following day we were to move on to an overnight stop at Coffs Harbour, a four-hour drive. Our next drilling job was situated in the country just outside of Grafton. I was happy to do as Larry suggested. I tidied the motorhome and made sure clean clothes were ready. In an hour, I had everything done, the tapping on the door, as I was about to climb onto the bed was annoying. I could see it was Thomas. He was whispering, 'Lynnie, come out, dear, I'm not angry.' His voice was wobbly with emotion. I felt it was unfair of me to leave him, thinking I was Lynnie, I had no idea who she was. I suspected there was a little dementia with Thomas. Feeling a little uncertain when I took the latch off, greeting him with, 'Hello, Thomas, how can I help you today?" I got the shock of my life when he grabbed my arm, wrenched me outside shaking me. The strength for this old man was amazing. He began yelling. 'You're not Lynnie. Where is she? What have you done to her?' His voice raised again, 'Lynnie, I'm here, dear, don't be frightened I'm not angry with you.' He shook me again. 'What have you done with her?'

The two camp cleaners, who were cleaning the laundry, rushed over, pulling him away from me, his grip so tight, that one of the cleaners had to unclamp his fingers, that were dug deeply into my forearm. Thomas's face a mixture of hate and spite, as he spat out, 'You've taken my Lynnie.' One of the cleaners was busy on his phone with one hand, his other arm around my waist supporting me. The second cleaner was fending Thomas off from attacking me again. This gentle, kind man had turned into someone possessed. It was awful to watch. The camp manager had called an ambulance. I heard the sirens, watched a plume of brown dust as they sped towards the camp. They checked me out, offering a strong painkiller if I needed it.

I did not say no. Between my neck, head and my bruised arm, I was now in a fair bit of pain. They strapped Thomas to a gurney, sedating him. I will never forget the emotions I felt. I was taken back to when I was a child being beaten, bullied by the females in my family and the chronic helplessness I had felt. His crazed blue eyes never left mine, accusing me of hiding his Lynnie, until he succumbed to the drugs, his aged eyelids drooping in sleep. The police were also alerted that I had been attacked. Did I want to lay charges? I had deep bruising with lacerations where his fingernails had torn the skin on my right forearm. I had nothing to say; any words I had, would not come out. The manager had rung Larry, who was now beside me, 'Cassie, the police want to know,' he faltered, 'you know ... did he try to touch you?' he said quietly, his arms around me, holding me so tightly I could barely breathe. I was shocked, pulling myself from Larry's embrace, saying quietly, 'It was a mistake. He thought I was someone else.'

The police were really kind. I sat in one of our deck chairs outside the motorhome, Larry making our 'go-to' for shock; a hot tea. The pain killer the medics had given me was working and I was feeling pain free and slightly floaty. One female officer knelt beside me, the other stood in front of me his notepad ready, 'Can I call you Cassie?' she asked, I nodded. 'Okay, Cassie, let me explain ...'

It turned out that Thomas was once a convicted murderer /rapist. His wife had died after he had savagely beaten her. He'd been on his best behaviour ever since he was released from a ten year sentence, however his medical reports from prison stated he was unstable at times. He had been put on medication to help the delusions. I could lay charges. It would go to court, hopefully he would be put into care in an age care facility.

I also had questions, 'His wife's name was Lynnie?' The officer nodded. 'Does Thomas have family?' 'Not that we know of,' was the reply. My last question: 'If I don't lay charges, what will happen to him?' 'Well, he will be assessed by a psychologist perhaps allowed to live in the community again. We can't truthfully answer that until he's assessed.' I already knew my answer, 'I'll press charges then.' My reasoning was Thomas should be looked after, so no other person would be hurt by his delusions. The decision I had made, meant I could not leave the district until a hearing date was set. Larry was adamant, 'You can't, Cassie. We're due in Grafton. What about the contract?' I could not leave never knowing if Thomas had hurt another.

'I'll find accommodation here until I find out what's happening, then I'll find a way to join you.' Larry began to argue, his face changing from concern to anger in a matter of seconds, the two officers backing away to give us privacy. 'Larry. Stop,' I said sternly. 'This is important to me. I'm not leaving till Thomas is taken care of.' I respected the fact Larry was angry at me for making a decision without seeking his opinion first, however. It made me all the more determined to do what I saw was right. Placing Thomas into care out of harm's way I felt was the best option.

I packed a small case of clothing, my laptop, the officers offering me a ride back to Kempsey. They rang ahead, booking me in at the hotel. Both drillers were both looking unhappy, as their chief cook and bottle washer had deserted the ship. For how long? As long as it took. If they wanted to tell Mick, then so be it. I would join them soon. It was not

Jigsaw

a holiday nor was I leaving. I was doing what I thought was the right thing. Jerry gave me a hug while Larry turned away muttering, 'Ring when you're on your way.'

Everything in the small bedroom in the hotel was white, including the doona, with no pictures on the walls, white lace curtains at the window facing the street. The double bed seemed huge compared to the motorhome. I put my case on the luggage rack, kicked off my shoes and lay across the bed, stretching starfish style. I felt a sense of freedom wash over me. There was no one around looking for food, no mounds of washing waiting for me, no snoring or farting. It was peaceful. I snoozed for a good hour waking hungry, my body sore, the headache still a niggle behind the eyes. Taking two painkillers, my bottle of water was now tepid. Time to find the masseuse I had been informed of at the camp. It was not hard; a flyer of the massage clinic was in the hotel folder. I rang expecting to be offered a booking, I was told I could attend his clinic immediately, the address was across the street.

Ming's muscle therapy was written in gold, in English also in Cantonese across the door. His hands found every knot in my back then my legs, gently teasing them out, slightly shaking the muscle so it would respond. My neck was another story; my shoulders would not relax, Ming offered acupuncture, which I readily accepted. As the needles hit the mark the headache began to ease. His wife was called in to look at the scratches on my forearm, I could hear her in the other room making up a poultice. As Ming took the needles out, she stepped in binding my arm, which immediately soothed. It looked inflamed possibly becoming infected. Her soft warm hand gently touching my face once I was lying face up, 'Lady, your liver not happy – too many drugs.' 'My name is Cassie,' I said, 'yours is?' 'You can call me Pearl, I will make you good tonic, yes?' Her English was a little broken, as was Ming's, though it certainly appeared they knew their trade. I left the clinic with my bottle of tonic, feeling almost good; my body had calmed down, the headache had gone. Ming ushered me out of the door, shoving a pamphlet in my hand, 'We have good bath treatment here as well, you should try it, take care of all aches.' I booked for the following day at midday, no harm in looking after oneself when you can.

    I had a feeling the tonic would taste foul, I was not wrong , finding the room's tea and coffee facilities. A hot cup of tea was soon sitting in my hand, the pillows plumped up behind me on the bed, I began to feel calmer than I had in some while. I knew it wasn't just what had happened recently with Thomas; life on the road was demanding and I hadn't considered how it would affect my health. My phone had five messages; one from our daughter in New Zealand, four from Larry, each one demanding I reply. I would call my daughter back the following day, as it would be late at night in New Zealand. Larry's messages were full of questions. He was more concerned about the contract than anything else. Suddenly I was so tired of the questions, being told what to do and how to do it. As far as I was concerned, I would be happy to stay in this all-white room for a week. Maybe this drilling job was too much for him, that was for him to decide, I knew travel, making money was high on both our bucket lists. I knew deep inside through all the ups downs in our lives, Larry was a good man, he could be a pain in the arse, but then so could we all. I had no desire for dinner, brushing my teeth, falling asleep, waking to my mobile phone ringing. It was the local police; the hearing date had been organised for two days' time. 'A lawyer will be in contact.' They made sure I was comfortable, asking if I needed any medical attention. No, I was fine!

CHAPTER 50

My breakfast was nice; golden scrambled eggs on a crusty crumpet with a choice of tea or a hot chocolate – heaven. I booked in for a roast dinner that night, asking the waitress about the art studios I had read about. She gave me all sorts of pamphlets to read, knowing I had no transport, she kindly offered me her two-wheeler bike on one condition – to be back by three o'clock when she finished her shift. I had no idea why I accepted, I had not ridden a two-wheeler since I was in my teens. At ten o'clock I was wobbling down the main road to visit an artist's haven. Once I had my balance, believe me it took a while, I began to enjoy it. The day was overcast as I peddled down the flat country road; if only my family could see me now. This was what I needed, some play time, a free day of fun. Stopping in small layby encrusted with autumn leaves, I rang Ming to re-book my holistic bath for four o'clock. I was likely to need it. Biking was fun, I honestly felt like I was twenty again, my body happily responding to freedom the soft hazy sun and fresh air. The art was amazing, two galleries next to each other, a husband-and-wife team, one artist in clay or glass, the other mosaics or canvas. We began to chat, they discovered I too was an artist. I missed that feeling of guiding the paint to perform under the stroke of a brush.

Too soon, it was time to bike back to the hotel and handover the bike, before heading across to see Pearl. I had been expecting a call from a lawyer, but so far, nothing. The half-hour or more it took to ride back to the hotel, I sang at the top of my voice. No one heard, no one cared. It was only me in some sort of time warp, my heart full of joy. I aimed the bike at the mounds of autumn leaves as they lay on the roadside, begging me to be a child once more.

Taking my feet off the pedals, spreading my legs wide each side of the bike, the autumn orange gold from the leaves sprayed up and around me. It felt wonderful to be in the open air, no demands, no judgment. I stopped not too far out of town to pick wild roses, pushing the stems into the small wicker basket attached to the bike. Once the bike plus helmet were delivered to the waitress, I asked for a container for my flowers, an old jam jar was produced. The pale pink petals with its deep green leaves were such a beautiful contrast to the all-white room, the perfume simply country.

Ming was waiting for me in a quiet courtyard surrounded by dark brown bamboo screens. I was struck by the peacefulness of it all. A deep, round, large porcelain tub waited for me, I saw dragons etched into the rim. Steam was rising from water, where Pearl was adding what looked like dried mint to the water. She carefully unwrapped my sore arm, which I must admit had not troubled me, since she had applied the poultice. They left me alone, as I removed my clothes, happily stepping into the water, my stiff muscles remembering my bike ride. It was heaven as the water crept up to my shoulders. I laid my head back against towels placed on the edge. I have no idea how long I soaked for but Pearl woke me by ringing a small bell. 'Cassie, time for massage.' I had only had a massage yesterday, but this was different; a leg/ foot lymph gland massage.

Jigsaw

Wrapping myself in a large spa towel, pink goose bumps popping up all over as the cooler air hot my warm body. I laid face down at first, as she carefully circled my ankles, sliding up to the back of my knee, she told me in her light melodious voice, that she was using a geranium with ginger root mix. It smelt lovely. I could feel myself nodding off as she asked me to turn over. She once more encircled my ankles using a long stroke up to my kneecaps, pointing out that one was slightly swollen. It was a wonderful massage, cleaning all toxins out of my lymph nodes.

Once in my hotel room, I lay down on the bed. My mobile phone had many messages on it, the freedom and happiness of the morning was a lost memory as I once more dived into the adult world of stress and worry. First Larry, 'I'm working, ring back tonight,' was his answer to my call. I rang our daughter, *please leave a message.* The next call was to a Mr Rayford the county lawyer for the courts. He had asked to meet me that night and I invited him to join me for dinner. He accepted with, 'See you at six o'clock.' It was only an hour away. I had nothing to wear for dinner. I had packed only jeans with two tops, clean undies and my toiletries. I popped on some makeup, brushed my hair, soon seated at the dining room table just in time for Mr Rayford's arrival. He offered me his hand, 'Call me Clyde,' he said. I noticed it was a farmer's hand, the skin calloused dark brown, his nails a little stained from the soil.

He ordered a roast with a light beer and we got to know each other as we ate. He seemed like a nice person, but it was the way he said, 'Let's make sure he ends up where he belongs.' It gave me the shivers. Was there a reason for such dislike? I threw a few questions around not too sure on what he wanted me to say. 'Don't you worry about it, Cassie, just tell the judge how he attacked you.'

I was okay with that apart from one thing, Thomas was mentally ill. Could he not just say that, have it over with? Apparently not. Clyde was after blood. Thomas, no matter his ninety-year-old circumstances, was the target. Then I got it. Clyde wanted to look good in this community. I finished my meal, placed my knife and fork on the plate, then the white cotton serviette beside it. I looked Clyde in the eye saying, 'Thomas has a mental illness, no matter what it is classed as. I will not stand up to vilify him in public. He needs to be cared for, no matter his history, he's paid for that. Now, if we've finished, Mr Rayford, I'll say goodnight.'

This had to be handled with care. Once back in my room, I rang a lawyer friend in Auckland, New Zealand. His advice was to approach the judge, ask to have a private hearing. 'Say what you've just told me. I'll see what I can do from here.' It was what I needed to hear, it was good to have support. Sleep took a while to reach me that night but when it did, I slept deeply. Enjoying a breakfast of porridge with honeyed yoghurt, the waitress informing me I had a call at the reception desk, it was my lawyer friend, 'You not answering your mobile, thought I would give this number a try, everything okay? Here is what I have arranged. You're to appear at the courthouse at midday. The judge will take your statement. Once signed and witnessed you are free to go. Looks like they already know about Thomas. He will be looked after, Cassie.'

Waiting until midday was agony, my mind/heart wanting what I thought was right for Thomas and the community. Midday arrived, I met with the judge in his rooms, he asked me pertinent questions about Thomas, why had I befriended him? Did I know of his past? His secretary wrote down my answers. I signed the papers, as did the court clerk, I was free to go. On the way back to my room, I enquired about transport to Grafton. Luckily a bus was leaving at two o'clock. 'Shall we book you a seat?' 'Yes please.' It was time to join the two drillers. As I packed my small bag, I rang Larry once more. He was still upset but relieved that I would be arriving late afternoon. 'I'll pick you up at the bus depot. Ring me closer to your arrival time.' Once I was seated on the minibus, I rang our daughter, learning about the violent earthquakes in Christchurch,

Jigsaw

that destroyed the city plus many lives.

I could hear the terror in her voice as she told me that our grandson had been left all alone at the primary school he was attending. She had found him terrified, crouched under the main staircase. 'He was so scared, Mum, I really don't know what to do?' Hopefully, the main quake is over but with many small aftershock sink holes were appearing throughout the city, homes and buildings destroyed, much like my poor girl's spirit. I never flinched when she said 'Mum, my boy really needs some help. Can I send him over for two weeks just to calm him down?' I did not flinch when I answered, 'Just tell me dates and times, hun, I'll be there to pick him up.' There was nothing more I could do but listen to her as she let go of her fear, asking me to look after him. 'He's had one hell of a shock Mum, he won't come out from under his bed.' I had no idea how I was going to finish off the next four weeks with the drillers then be there for our grandson. I just knew I would move heaven and hell to hold him close, to let him know he was loved and safe with us.

Larry was not too happy once I was sitting in the cab of the motorhome breaking the news to him. I was heading back to Perth as soon as the contract was filled. Our grandson is going to live with us for a while, until he feels safe about returning to Christchurch. I would be heading back to Perth as soon as the contract was filled.

When Larry was not happy, everyone knew about it. To top off my news, Jerry our offsider had been talking to Mick, the CEO of the drilling company. They'd had some glowing reports about both drillers, they were considering training Jerry to run his own drill. Larry was certainly not happy about it. I could see Jerry getting a little annoyed, 'Mate, I don't have a choice. I can stay with you, or I can take this opportunity. What would you do in my place?'

I cooked dinner, making a mental note that we needed more fresh vegetables and fruit. The bread was stale, the groceries were running low. Serving homemade hamburgers with chips, I could hear them both enjoying my cooking after fending for themselves. I joined them for dinner. If I could get a word in with Larry while Jerry was present, perhaps he would be calmer about what was happening.

I explained to Jerry what had happened in the Kempsey courthouse, the news about New Zealand. All he could say was, 'Shit! Is the little fella okay?' I assured him that I was sure everything was going to be alright, eventually. 'I may have to race back to Perth to find a house to rent very quickly.' He understood, 'You do what you have to. I'm sure we can manage.' Larry glowered saying nothing. 'I'll speak to Mick first thing in the morning, tell him what's happening once I speak to our daughter. I don't like leaving you both without a cook, but family first, right?'

As I washed and dried the dishes, Larry took the tea towel from me. 'Have you thought this through? It could mean I'm taken off here, I'll end up back in the Pilbara, doing four-week stints. I thought you were happy with the nomad life.' I let go of a big breath. Why could he not see that this was important for our family, not a fun holiday, more like a mental health break for our grandson. 'Let's find out when she can fly him to Perth. Once we know times and dates, we can make plans, okay?' Larry nodded. I could see the stress written all over his face. 'Honey, it's not forever. It might be for two weeks or a month. You may possibly even be finished with all the contracts by then. Let's wait to see what tomorrow brings.' Fingers-crossed it would work out. Sending out a prayer that I would not desert the ship 'so to speak' before our time was up. There was a small pile of washing waiting for the laundry. The kitchen bench was a mess, covered in plates. I knew that Larry was okay at cooking a simple meal plus cleaning up after himself when he felt like it. This was his way of saying he was not happy.

CHAPTER 51

Why is it when you need a good sleep, you toss all night? Larry was the same, both of us worried for different reasons. At 3am I got up, boiled the jug making us both a cup of tea. It would be 7am in New Zealand. I rang our daughter putting my phone on speaker, her voice trembling with tears, 'Hey, sweetheart, I have Dad on the phone with me,' warning her before she said anything untoward about him. They did not have the best relationship, both angry about past grievances. Their night had not been good. Every time the ground shook with aftershocks, our grandson would wake, screaming. We switched to FaceTime; her face was grey, huge black smudges around her eyes. Larry took one look at his eldest daughter saying what I was hoping to hear; 'Why don't you both come over? We can shout you both, just get out of that place. Get on the next available plane.' There was relief in our girl's face, 'Are you sure? Thanks, Dad, I'm really grateful.' From that very moment Larry's fatherhood kicked in. He pulled me into his arms. 'I think our eldest needs a break, don't you?' I was overjoyed to share this with him; a problem shared is a problem halved, so they say. Instead of me calling Mick to explain why I may have to leave, Larry took over. Mick agreed that if I had to leave suddenly, they would understand. Larry assuring him that he would finish the contracts with Jerry driving the rig back to Perth.

Then the universe stepped in nudging us. When Jerry almost carrying Larry back to camp, staggered to a stop outside the motorhome. The drill having caught Larry on the descent twisting his arm and shoulder badly. I gave him painkillers, rubbed his shoulder with liniment, insisting he go to bed. He was in a lot of pain all night. More painkillers in the morning as he was determined to finish the job, I drove into Grafton buying groceries. Investing in a sling, asking the local chemist for advice.

'We have a local hospital here perhaps he should get an X-ray,' I agreed, so when they arrived home that night, I insisted on a visit to the hospital. I was amazed at the speed we were seen. The X-ray showed very little, as the shoulder was swollen and bruised, a steroid injection was given to help. Their advice was come back in two days, they would do a scan. The injection helped so much, that by the time we got back to camp, Larry was almost jovial. On a phone call to our daughter, she told us she was having trouble selling her belongings. Her landlord had been understanding but still wanted this week's rent. Her car was up for sale when Larry asked what it was all worth. 'A grand? Give it away if you have to. You can start up new over here.' She was appreciative but still had to organise passports. 'Once they are here, I will notify you then you can book the flights.' We were all on tenterhooks. Larry's injury was no better by the time we left Grafton, once the drilling had finished Jerry and Larry were at loggerheads.

Jerry advising Larry's injury needed reporting to head office for insurances, while Larry dismissed it, wanting no one to know. Me, insisting on the scan before we left Grafton, did not make my husband's day any better. Larry and hospitals did not go together, shouting him a Chinese meal across

Jigsaw

the road while we waited for the scans to come through. When we returned to retrieve them, the receptionist said, 'Here is your copy, Larry. Oh! I've also sent them to your employer! They'll send them onto the insurance company.' Larry was livid, 'You what? Who told you to do that?' We both knew the firm would have talked to Jerry to see what exactly was going on. I drove back to the campground, Larry knowing the firm had Jerry up for his own drill, he began muttering what he would do to his offsider.

'That little creep, I knew he was too good to be true. All his offers on learning the ropes, he's nothing but a dirty sneak.' I tried to calm him down but it was pointless. As we pulled up at the camp, Larry bolted out of the cab door, 'Sore shoulder or not, I'm going to thump that little shit.' Jerry greeted us with a wide smile, wiping his hands on a rag, but then saw the look in Larry's eyes. 'Whoa, old man, who the hell do you think you're pushing?' Both of them were set to have one hell of a fight, I knew Larry was no match for the younger man. There was only one thing to do. I blasted the airhorn on the motorhome. Other campers strolling out to see what the problem was. The two men stopped in their tracks. I drove the motorhome into its parking space; time for some common sense. As the three of us talked, it became very clear that Jerry thought the world of Larry. 'I did not say a word. They rang wanting to talk to you about another contract. I told them you were at the hospital, the rest you know.' It was time for apologies, Larry calling it quits for the day.

I wanted to have a good look at the scan results, exactly what the outcome was. The report was inconclusive 'further tests should be done.' It said Larry had tendonitis in his right shoulder. It had been treated with steroids, another to be had in two weeks. More tests were advised, to be done in a month's time. The worrying part was his age, they were looking for complications for the future. For now, it was massage, painkillers, rest up when it inflamed again. Larry's decision was to carry on. I can train Jerry up on drilling, it will be fine. Famous last words.

Kez Wickham St George

We left under grey, cloud-burdened skies, heading to Lismore. It was late at night when we arrived, with two days at the farm, then onto Ipswich, where a four-day contract was expected. It had begun to rain, torrential rain, I was uncomfortable driving. Larry took over, making sure Jerry was handling the rain, driving the drill truck behind us. Arriving at the farm we discovered they had ordered a well to be dug, months ago. However, at the rate the rain was coming down they wouldn't need one. Still we were there, the job was to go ahead. For days it poured with rain, I had never seen rain drops so big or so much water from the sky. We were surrounded by toads as big as dinner plates, the noise they made so loud we had to yell at each other to be heard. For the first time, I saw snakes thick, long, very deadly under the motorhome, hiding under the pull-out annex. Globe spiders sheltered, as big as your hand. Plus every other insect seeking shelter was either inside or under the annex of the motorhome.

Just the once, the farmer's wife waved to me, as she rode like the devil down to the farm gate letterbox, grabbed her mail, then took off once more. The weak headlights I saw disappearing into the gloomy rain-filled day, made me feel very much alone. I spent my time writing and making little treats for the two men who tracked deep red mud home every night. It stuck to their boots, under their fingernails. Jerry asked me if he could use our shower, both men caked in red mud, which if not cleaned off immediately, would stain the white shower box. To add to these few miserable days, there was no phone service, the passing storm blocking any signal until it passed. Our daughter's situation was worrying us both.

When the time came to pack up and leave, the rain had not eased. The three of us were delighted to know our next stop was at a motel in Ipswich. The council had hired the firm to drill two large deep drains. I was so looking forward to a little more room to stretch out. The phone reception had been awful out on the farm. Larry braked outside our motel room, but his news was not good. 'Only one room booked, sorry, Cassie.'

'No one has informed the office there was a female travelling with us.' My heart sank, I opted to sleep in the motorhome. Jerry was not having it, 'No you won't. I'll take the bed in the motorhome. You and the boss can have the room.' I gave a big sigh of relief then discovered my other wish was granted. Opening the bathroom door, I nearly squealed with delight. Yes, I had a 'shub' – a tub under a shower; big enough to sit in with my knees up. Bliss! The two men had maps out, finding what road went where and arranging meetings with the council. 'Looks like you won't see us except for dinner, it's a big job. We may have to take the week. How are the kids doing?' I had not rung them yet. As they left to sort out paperwork, I rang 'the kids.' My son was worried as he hadn't heard from me for a while, I then rang our family in Christchurch, who were still waiting for passports. Her council had deemed the house she was in 'un-liveable' and they had sourced a motel for her plus a support school for our grandson. She had told them of her intention to leave New Zealand moving to Australia, the council promising to track their passports for them. They were now out of danger, but still very frightened.

Ipswich council was amazing, insisting on feeding the two drillers, while they were on the job. I didn't mind at all. The cleaning lady at the motel was Maori. Once she recognised my accent, we became instant friends. I can't say I was bored, I had stories to write, a motorhome to clean, the red dirt from the last farm we drilled at having left pink stains everywhere. Jante, my new friend was the one to enlighten me about cleaning pink stains off white plastic, as no matter what I did or what method I used the pink stain clung to the plastic like it belonged there. I knew once we returned it to the Brisbane motorhome depot they would charge the company for a commercial clean, if deemed appropriate, it would be taken out of our wages.

Jante was an absolute godsend. She sang in Maori as she mixed her lethal batch of cleaning products into one big sticky pile. Wearing industrial strength rubber gloves, and eye protection, with a mask, I layered the bathroom with the concocted brew, while Jante tackled the kitchen bench plus the nightstand beside Larry's side of the bed; 'It's either going to clean this muck off or its going to melt the bugger.' For some reason that tickled my fancy, I backed out of the shower cubicle chuckling to myself. The chuckle becoming contagious, her laughter more like a musical giggle. I made us a cup of tea in the motel room, Jante scooted back to her workshop, producing a packet of Tim Tams, Australia's favourite chocolate biscuit. 'Let's wait for half an hour before we rinse that brew off,' was her suggestion. It sounded good to me. As we chatted about families, we discovered just what a small world we lived in. We had very distant relations on my father's side; It was a weird feeling to hear names I knew, rolling off her tongue.

It was time to clean the paste off. My first swipe of the paper towel showed a clean white patch, hope blooming in my chest. From Jante, I could hear her crows of success. 'Okay, what was the mix you used?' When she told me, I was wide eyed. I was not good in chemistry, but I had a feeling you would not want it on bare skin. Jante swore it was mainly Ajax, baking powder with white vinegar. I gave the bathroom another hot soapy rinse, just in case. Larry was impressed on how white it was, I forbade any one to use it, including Jerry until we got to our next drilling spot. In the meantime, Jante offered to show me the town. She picked me up the next day. I was now called Aunty, a sign of respect for any elder from the South Pacific islands or New Zealand. Our first stop, her home in the suburbs, her profession as a cleaner clearly showed, everything was organised.

Then a ride around the township pointing out tourist interests, followed by lunch at one of the local pubs where Jante showed me off to

Jigsaw

her mates as her Aunty, the 'famous' author. Then back to her home to meet her family.

I was about to ring Larry to say I wouldn't be home till late, when she said to invite them for some Kai (dinner). It was a long night as we unwound the relationship ties and who was in whose blood lines. It was midnight before we returned to the motel, when I woke the two men had gone to work. The joy of meeting so many people who were semi related to me was still buzzing inside my chest. Today was for me to explore, as Jante was working. I walked to the bus stop, enjoying the brisk air, with a list of art galleries I wanted to see.

A miniature version of the big cities 'hop on hop off' bus turned the corner, my tummy did the usual 'I'm on an adventure' flip. We stopped off at the antique centre and l walked around the huge building thinking of how every piece had come from another country, every article was beautifully displayed. I hopped on another bus, this one going to the main art gallery. The art on display was amazing, from the deepest of colours in one modern art piece to the brightest hue in another. I dreamt of one day exhibiting in a place just like this, perhaps in Perth when I returned. Two hours had flown by, when I spied another bus visiting the olive grove that also grew lime trees. This was fun, the tasting bar had me intrigued. Who knew olives could be made into a purée with a tang of lime? It was delicious, knowing Larry would enjoy this treat I purchased two jars. It was three o'clock by then and time to think about going back to the motel. I had seen an advert offering archery or paintball on the bus. It wasn't my thing, but I felt both men had been working all hours to complete this drilling contract, perhaps it would be perfect to give them both a little down time.

CHAPTER 52

Purchasing a large mushroom quiche with a packet of a fresh salad mix from the corner deli, I cooked a sweet potato mash, plus green peas to accompany the meal. As I began dinner, I realised it had been two nights since I'd taken the time to prepare a nice meal for the men, the council had provided that for them. Fingers crossed they would be home tonight to enjoy the meal with me. When I heard them arrive, my heart warmed. I served them a large helping of each, our little crew of three were happy to be together, relaxing, talking about our days. I was telling them about the archery plus paintball advert, both agreeing it was time they had some down time. It was agreed that he would ring the next day to book them in for an hour or two. Just before going to bed my phone rang.

Our eldest daughter had received her passports; 'I'm arriving in two weeks, folks, hope you're ready for us both' Our grandson was in the background singing, 'I'm going to live with Nana and Grandad.' I looked at Larry. He was still in a lot of pain with his shoulder, the painkillers just not enough to help any more. His good arm snaked around my waist,

Jigsaw

'It's okay, love, I know where your heart is. We'll make plans to fly you out from Brisbane as soon as we can.'

I was torn in two. Larry's face was pale for some reason, I knew without a doubt my place was here at this moment in time. I had a niggly feeling in my gut, it wasn't just about Larry. Something was going on, but I had no idea what it was! 'Let's see what Goondiwindi looks like first, shall we?' He nodded, as he rolled over searching for sleep. I could see real pain on his deeply lined face. I wondered if we should just call it quits? Go home see what the hospital says in Rockingham. Sleep evaded me, getting up to make myself a hot drink. A cup of cocoa in hand, I sat in the dark sipping, my mind trying to find out a way to finish the job together, then go home. I had enjoyed myself in so many ways, met wonderful people, had wonderful experiences. Larry not so much; his life was all about drilling the next hole. I did notice that the next three townships were one-day contracts until we reached Tamworth, which was a three-day contract. First Glen Innes then Coff's Harbour for one day at each. When I say a day, it was usually a dawn start and often a very late finish. At times drilling small wells could be difficult in some areas, even if a place was a farmer's delight, ten feet down they would often strike solid rock, then it was literally blood, sweat and tears.

When you see the miners come off their shifts, some of them look beaten. It's not an easy job for anyone. In a weird way, I was here as the support person. I was the one who cheered them on, made sure all they had to do was get up, eat good food, hang in there to get the work done. I listened to their concerns, then encourage them to do it all again. I also got to tour, go to places Larry would never visit. I had met so many people, had small adventures, learnt so much, spent plenty of time writing, living life. I wanted to saviour every last minute. I felt It was all coming to a close, very soon. *In that early morning, this book was born.* When Larry woke at the chink of dawn, light coming through the window, I was still typing, reading from my notebook and drinking my fourth cup of tea. I also had a solution. As he was training Jerry to be a driller, I suggested we should have a heart-to-heart conversation with him, making sure he understood the contracts, finances, he could take on more of the management, often if Larry was busy he would leave a list saying, 'Order this please, Darl, we need it in two days.' If Jerry was willing, it would leave Larry some time off to relax a little, hopefully we would make it to the end. Larry was agreeable to that idea. We thought we had it all planned out, when fate stepped in kicking us both so hard it was a struggle to breath.

Larry had wandered out to the motorhome, banging on the sides to wake up Jerry, There had been no answer, which annoyed Larry banging on the door again. 'Come on, mate, time to wake up. They'll be here to pick us up soon.' Still no answer. Larry seated himself at the table, grumbling, 'I wonder if he's sneaked off, got pissed and flaked out somewhere in town.' I rang Jerry's phone. It dialled out to his message bank, his voice asking to be left a message. This was not like Jerry. He was usually the one to get up early calling out, 'Come on, old man time, to get to work,' which I might add did not impress Larry at all. Larry had enough, wrenching the door open. It was darkness inside. Larry using his phone torch. He started yelling, 'Come on, Jerry, wake up,' then, quietly, 'shit, Jerry, come on, don't play silly buggers.' Then silence. Larry's eyes were huge as he stumbled out of the motorhome. 'My God, Cassie, the boy's gone,' he whispered. My mind went numb, *gone where?* 'What do you mean?' I stammered. 'He's dead, Cassie.' Larry's body was shaking as I pulled a rug around his shoulders, questions incomprehensively tumbling out. The police were called first, then Mick.

As we waited, I rang Jante. I gently closed Jerry's eyes, his face grey and cold. I smoothed back his black curly hair, tucking the sheet up to his chin. When she found me I was still holding his hand. She took mine away before tucking his cold hand under the sheet. Thankfully Jante and I had the same belief; that no one should die alone. It was up to us to set his spirit free. The curtains were pulled back to greet the bright dawn, we opened up all the windows, the door was flung open, fresh air rushed in. She sang a soft song of grief, we watched as a piece of paper softly fell from the bed to the floor. As we waited for the authorities, I began to read it; it didn't read like a suicide note to me. We were asked to leave while the police took photos, bagged the evidence, including the note. They were unsure if it was suicide or a natural death. They, in turn, rang the hospital. An ambulance quietly arrived, taking Jerry's body away.

Larry had rung Mick and they were busy contacting Jerry's emergency numbers. The motel owners could not do enough, neither could my friend. She hugged me as I sobbed out my sadness, 'Whatever they find, he's at peace, Cassie.' Larry sat slumped in a chair, the police investigating first Larry, then myself, on Jerry's recent actions. Only hours ago, he was calling Jerry, now they were describing him as the deceased, it did not feel right. We were asked to stay where we were until the morgue had rung with their findings. The phone in Larry's hand ran red hot. Mick was concerned for Larry's mental wellbeing plus the contracts yet to be finished. A decision had been made to send another team out to take over, so we could return back to Perth to have some counselling, plus some down time. The motorhome would be returned to the hire company; they were sending someone to collect it. It was late afternoon we had been waiting for Mick to call back, when the phone rang. Larry put it on speaker. 'Hello, Larry, is Cassie there?' I called out that I was. 'I have just spoken to the morgue. They found a serious heart defect in the mitral valve. Jerry suffered a fatal heart attack … Now I know this is hard for the two of you, he was a good friend to you both, but we need to put things into perspective so, Cassie, are you able to pack up Jerry's belongings? Then to Larry, please have all the drilling reports up to date for a handover in two days' time. Do you have any questions?'

I asked about his family. 'There's no one, Cassie. We did ask for next of kin when we signed him up for the job. He has nothing here. His last job was on the ship, we will contact them to see if they can help. In the meantime, bring his gear back with you. We'll store it here till we know more. Anything else?' I had a question, 'Without next of kin to contact handle the body, would there be a cremation handled by the local authorities? Who would be there to say goodbye?' There was a second of silence, 'Do you want to be there, Cassie?' I knew with all my heart that's where we should be on the day. 'Yes, Mick. We owe Jerry that much.'

There were all sorts of legalities to sign, Mick was consulted. This was the firms business and we both knew Mick knew his stuff. All he said was. 'I've been informed the cremation is tomorrow at ten o'clock, here's the address. You two are booked on a red eye out of Brisbane tomorrow night. Your e-tickets will be waiting for you, try to get good night's rest. Thank you both for attending the cremation, I'll be in touch very soon.' We both grieved for this young man, who had bought a smile to our faces, there was no sleep.

Tears fell frequently from us as we talked about the days when it all got too much for Larry, and Jerry would do something silly, bringing a smile to the boss's face. He complimented me all the time on my cooking skills, when I gave him his clean washing, he would bury his nose in the laundry murmuring, 'Mm, smells just like home.' Why had I not stopped to ask 'Where's home, Jerry?' Why had we not thought to ask him about his family or their whereabouts? Did he have a partner, wife or children? We knew so little. We knew nothing other than we'd met him on a cruise ship working as a barmen. I did remember broaching the subject of his family once, Jerry had tapped the side of his nose then smiled. To me that was saying not for discussion.

CHAPTER 53

Everything moved forward in a bit of blur. I packed up our gear from inside the motorhome and Jante suggested we give any blankets, doonas etc. to the Salvation Army. God bless them, once they knew our situation, a team arrived, stripping the van of all bedding, including pillows, then they emptied the pantry plus fridge. These lovely people had made us hot mushroom soup. We tried to sip it, any hunger we had, long since gone. They cleaned everything, including the bathroom, fridge/kitchenette, as well as the windows inside and out. Our job was to attend the funeral, then catch our flight home.

Larry and I went into rote, our brains numb. He had hardly spoken since he'd found Jerry's body. I knew his own mortality had kicked in. None of us know when that day will arrive, and a scripture my folks often quoted popped into my head; 'Death will arrive like a thief in the night.'

We took a taxi to the crematorium. The silence of the chapel as we walked in was, as they say, deafening, our friends lonely coffin sitting on a dais. The chaplin entered from a side door, shaking our hands, 'My name is Robin, are you the deceased's family?' We informed him of the circumstances. We knew of no one related; we were his work colleagues. He offered to say the Lord's prayer, Larry looked at me, I nodded. With only the three of us to farewell Jerry, the coffin was lowered. It trundled towards a small hatch in the wall. The Lord's prayer was on my lips as the coffin passed through the hatch, silently closing, the two small doors softly swishing together announcing the end.

Larry whispered, 'Bye mate.' He had a defeated look in his eyes. I grabbed his hand, as the tears that glimmered in his eyes now slowly traced down his cheeks. We had farewelled one of the 'good ones' as Larry put it. A cup of lukewarm tea with a biscuit was offered by the staff. We accepted; anything to break the silence of death. I had left our bags at the motel office, once there I quickly found Jante. She took one look at my face, opening her arms. 'Why not stay here for a while, you're more than welcome to stay with me.' To be honest all I wanted to do was wrap myself up in a blanket to sleep. It was a sad 'no.' I had Larry plus my family to care for, 'It's time we went back to Perth. Please stay in touch.'

As we left to catch our plane to Perth, a police car drove up, they were returning Jerry's sailor bag. 'Sorry for your loss, ma'am.' The young officer looked embarrassed, 'Would you return it to the management in Perth?' Larry carefully laid the bag on top of our own luggage, both of us acknowledging this was all that remained of our friend's life, a lone canvas bag with a few pieces of clothing. It felt like Jerry's existence never was. We had done our best to pay our respects for his friendship. Jerry never seemed to be a lonely man. He was always ready with a smile or a kind word. I was reminded of a quote – 'A smile can hide many unhappy thoughts.' I wished I had gotten a little closer to him. It knew it was through my fear of my past experiences of men, I had put up tall fences.

The airport was so full of noise, life, people busy going places, families greeting each other, families farewelling each other. To me it was like a lungful of fresh air, though Larry remained cocooned in his grief. I slept most of the way to Perth, woken only to eat or drink. I did try to watch a movie, but my eyelids were determined to close. Larry had the window seat, refusing food. I left him to sort out his own emotions, it was hard enough sorting my own.

Before we had put our luggage through the ticketing desk, I had opened Jerry's bag, hoping I would find that piece of paper he had left behind. Perhaps written on that, would be a clue to where he belonged. My fingertips touching the soft plastic envelope it had been inserted into. I did it without Larry seeing me as I knew what he would say, 'Leave things alone.' I had put it in the folder I was taking on board. At any other time I would be writing by now, but while Larry slept, I read Jerry's last words.

It was titled *Beautiful People Don't Just Happen.* It described how the beautiful ones in our lives have known strife and struggle. How these people seemed to have an appreciation for life with music, art, and conversation. How their understanding of life filled them with compassion and empathy. I had not known what a sensitive soul Jerry had been. I could feel the tears fill my eyes, making a dash for the bathroom. I held his written words close to my heart, allowing the tears to flow. If I had known his thoughts, imagine the conversations we could have had. Washing my face, I made my way to the hostess area, asking for 'a really hot cup of tea.' One look at my face alerted her, she lightly touched my hand, 'Everything okay?' I stood in the tiny galley, staring out the window, watching the clouds dot the blue sky, a paper cup of tea was placed in my hands. I raised my cup to the sky, *goodbye my friend, safe travels wherever that may be.*

'Ladies and gentlemen, please fasten your seatbelts. In fifteen minutes, we will be arriving in Perth, the city of lights. Welcome to Western Australia.' All I could think of was, 'Thank God I'm home safe and sound.' Larry woke up trying to stretch his still painful arm. He looked at me saying, 'Home.' That one simple word, I knew then our working days were numbered. It was time to find a home for our family, look after our grandson and sort out Larry's health issues. I was ready to send in my second book to be edited. There was so much healing to be done. Trauma of any sort needs releasing before it sticks to your insides, causing havoc to heart and mind.

Once landed, our bags collected, we sourced a small hire car, soon on the main highway to Rockingham. Surprisingly, many things were different, the main roads had changed. An hour later, the 'Welcome to Rockingham' sign arrived. Larry's hand reached out for mine, 'Here we are once again, back where we started.' It was the first time in the past seven days that I had seen my husband give a glimpse of a smile.

A local motel was found and booked for a week, my friends doing their utmost to find us a home. It took two weeks to find a rental home big enough for us all, as our family arrived two weeks after we moved in. In that month, I don't think my feet touched the ground. Furniture, bedding, living room, fridge, washing machine … the list went on. Larry's shoulder had been operated on, the surgeon commenting that the inside of his upper arm muscles 'were a mess.' Thanks to Jerry's nagging insistence, the firm had reported the accident. We were now covered by the insurance.

Then the day arrived when our family walked off the plane into our open arms.

The airport at night is always exciting to me, even more so when waiting for your family to walk through those 'exit customs' gates. One small, blond, blue-eyed young man wrapped his arms around me. 'Nana, I've come to live with you.' His mum was looking weary. 'Hey, Mum. I guess I can say I'm home.' I held them tight, our grandson looked at his grandfather, questioning, 'Do I hug you?' Larry held out his one good arm, 'Come here, mate, it's good to see you.' Our daughter was already sensing something was amiss, looking at us both she asked, 'We are welcome?' 'Oh, honey,' I cried, 'you are so welcome. We had a bit of sad news concerning a friend recently. You are a breath of fresh air. Welcome to Australia. Let's go home.'

The months sped by. Our daughter, after a month of searching, found employment, buying herself a car then finding a small villa of her own to rent. Our grandson was loving school, his mind set on becoming a pilot. Larry finally healed. It took a good three months with physiotherapy, however he had not talked about Jerry since we'd arrived home. I had rejoiced being back with the art society. Book number two had been edited, although I was struggling through the blue and red lines, the comments which made little sense. I was determined to enjoy the experience, educate myself, learn and grow. Once I had finished my side of editing, I would ask a friend to proof read it, before I emailed it to the publisher. We had wonderful neighbours, my old mates Heather and Fern were, once again, visiting regularly. That was until Fern met our daughter, it was instant dislike between them. Fern saying while she lives with you I will not visit again. I was shocked, my family came first. I was asked to take part in an art exhibition, but then decided to have one of my very own. A mad flurry of abstract art took place, the exhibition a huge success, selling out over the night. Soon came the invites to run/join mosaic classes, journalling classes, creative writing classes; it filled my days. Weekends were with family and friends, I now realised just how much I had missed them all.

Larry was not so happy. After his surgery recovery, he was back in the Pilbara on the water drill. Mick had sold the firm, any empathy that Mick or his associates had shown to their staff, was swallowed up into the Maws of a huge mining firm. Larry was now a number, we both missed the old way of mining, a more friendly way. When they suggested he leave, they took the cowards way out of it. They rang me with a complaint about his opinionated behaviour. 'It had to stop, or …' My answer in return was to, 'talk to Larry. If he doesn't know his behaviour is upsetting, then it's up to you to provide counselling for him.' On his next trip home, I could see he'd had enough. He told me of an incident that had been hidden from the mining fraternity. He had advised the team he was working with not to mine in a certain place, as it looked unstable, pointing out he would be remiss and be held accountable if he didn't point this out to the company.

They had told him, 'That's rubbish, you drill there or go home.' He did as he was ordered, it nearly took his life. A massive boulder was let lose by the drilling, as it dropped onto the drill Larry was working on. Fortunately he had heard the crack of the rock as it broke away and he jumped from the cab and ran. All of this had been videoed by his offsider, Larry showed me the footage. I felt nauseated, as he would not have survived if he had not been extra vigilant. He'd been home two nights, when he was called by the company, asking him to send them the video. He did, but two hours later he was asked to remove it from his phone. When Larry refused, within a matter of hours, he was offered a very large compensation package. His resignation was also asked for. Together we decided it would be better for us to accept. Larry's mining days were over.

What would we do now? Pack up? Go back to New Zealand or stay put to see what would happen? It's funny how life works. It still amazes me how everything is all planned out, you just have to follow the prompts and opportunities. I began to notice a pattern I hadn't recognised before. Once an opportunity was accepted, there was a space, a pregnant pause, maybe a small struggle to overcome, but then another opportunity would emerge. I began to read *The Secret* by Rhonda Byrne, and I soaked up every word. Creating a vision board for myself, rejoicing in the space between pause then opportunity. Writing down a small list of my deepest desires; health foremost for myself and family, travel, a reputable

Jigsaw

Australian publisher, with their help, being recognised as a bestselling author. Spending a half-hour every day before I journalled I felt a deep gratefulness for my life so far, but still acknowledging the ups and downs of all I'd been through. I was so grateful for meeting Jerry, as without him joining our crew, our drilling adventure would likely have come to a close much sooner. I had seen and done so much in the last year, a feeling of peace settled in my heart.

CHAPTER 54

We had been in our home for a year, when we had news that Larry's family had moved to England, his sister seeking treatment for a serious brain tumour. Jerry's ashes had found their way to our home via the new drilling company, delivered by a courier van on a beautiful summer's day. When I look back, it seemed odd that the delivery person whistled as he walked up our driveway delivering the ashes of the deceased. I signed and accepted the small brown parcel, placing it on the coffee table staring at it for such a long time. So in the end this is what we all amount to, a small box of dust. Our grandson had grown from cute and cheeky, to an explosive angry teenager. Once more, he lived with us on the weekends, giving his mum the freedom to build some sort of social life for herself.

An offer to be published internationally arrived in my emails. I read it with such excitement. Sending off my manuscript, very surprised when the publisher phoned me asking to meet. We met in the city of Subiaco where he told me he would take me places, my book would be read by thousands, I was one of the best authors he had read in a while. Wow …

my ego blossomed. A book contract was offered for $5,000, I signed on the dotted line, knowing I would have to borrow from our super to for pay it, my intuition kicked in with a feeling that something wasn't right. I ignored that feeling, soon learning my lesson. Investing in another who has an enormous ego, zero experience in publishing, was my mistake. My book went nowhere, my friends bought it, their personal critiques were harsh, I remember feeling the greyness of bitter disappointment curl around me. I felt humiliated, hurt, swearing to the heavens I would not write again. I also knew when you are represented by another who has no interest in making sure you are nurtured or cared for as one of their authors, the fault does not lie with you. Maybe the time was not right. Bugger it, he was not going to ruin my dream, I would keep writing.

Larry began to train in real estate, while my art world flourished. I had requests for my art from South Africa and London. Family came to visit from New Zealand for four weeks over the Christmas holidays. We did not know her or her family all that well, Larry constantly yelling at the two girls every day to 'clean up your bloody mess,' that was left behind in the kitchen or lounge. We were both more than happy, to wave them off at the airport, exhausted from the experience.

The phone call we received from Larry's sister informing us she had 'perhaps four weeks to live,' certainly helped make the decision to pay a visit to England to say our goodbyes. I was not that close to her, however Larry was, so we made plans to travel to the UK with a couple of nights in Singapore then Dubai. My brother-in-law offered us accommodation at his home in the outskirts of London. The simple act of buying new luggage sealed our hesitant decision, the excitement building, every day packing a top or skirt, knowing we would be touring in Dubai.

If I thought life fairly settled, I was very wrong. An email from a relative of Jerry's waited in my inbox, asking us to meet. Finding out that Jerry had family was a shock. I rang the number. They were a senior couple, who had hired a private detective to find him. They knew we had his ashes. Apparently posting ashes overseas was a not approved of with the postal service, 'Would you consider travelling to New Zealand?' They were happy to provide our fares we were not to worry about the expense. I was gobsmacked.

I had never picked up that Jerry was a New Zealander. To me he had looked European, Greek, maybe Italian. Excitement fizzed through my veins. When I told Larry, his face made me smile. He had never been comfortable with Jerry's death, even less so having the ashes inside the house. When they had been delivered, he had wrapped them in a woollen blanket, placing them in a small carton, cello-taped it tightly then popped them on a shelf in the shed.

It was time to leave for the UK, a taxi was ordered for 3am. Once seated on the plane it all became very real, I was a nomad once more. Ahh Singapore; a land of exotic wonder. We toured like we were teenagers, everything was exciting, temples and markets whereever you looked, I fell in love with the orchid gardens, the art. Dubai was amazing, everything I hoped it would be, the markets, the people, dining in the desert, belly dancing, the crisp whiteness of the men's costumes, the women's sensuous dark eyes peeping from under-embellished glittering veils. Shopping in the souks of spices and jewellery, its history of such wealth, I wanted to do and see much more.

London, I adored, knowing I was standing on Tower Bridge, touching the very stones where our history began. Or an hour out of the city, walking across a small bridge made by roman solders in AD 43. Everywhere I looked, touched or stood was steeped in rich history. When my husband surprised me with a holiday, I found myself in Paris for five days. Oh my dear Lord, every day and every night we ate, drank and soaked Paris in; The Moulin Rouge, The Louvre, La Fayette Gallery, flower markets, the Eiffel Tower, The Palais Garnier (opera house). The LaMelo hotel where

Jigsaw

we stayed, was a dream come true, from the hotels rattling eighteenth century elevator to the art décor in the reception area. I adored Paris with every fibre of my being, it was here that the young Larry I knew and married returned. He also loved Paris, wandering along the Seine one warm morning, greeting artists and artisans, eating fresh croissants, he took the biggest breath, 'Cassie, I could happily live here.' Finally that gleam of interest in another world showed.

It soon became obvious to us both that the only reason the invite had been extended to me was to care for their now mentally frail mother while the brothers visited their sister. This brought back memories, what was it they had disliked in me? Was it because I had seen the hypocrisy so I stood up to them? Was it because as an emotionally young fragile thirty-year-old they had sensed my vulnerability. Yet, after all the dislike thrown at me in the past, here I was, cleaning up after their mother, so they could be a family. It struck me how ironic the names they once called me were now flung at the woman who was once the matriarch of the family. Then day came when I was invited to see my sister-in-law, as I entered the hospital room there was a weird tension in the air. I went to hug her, she did not respond. She quietly thanked me for allowing her brother to visit her, turning her face to the wall she closed her eyes. I was dismissed. Wow, till her deathbed she carried some sort of stupid dislike. How very sad, I had hoped for old fences to be mended. I was wrong. She passed the day we left to fly home.

Once again, sorrow slithered between Larry and me. He pulled the grey blanket of grief over his head. It was pointless even trying to speak to him. I actually felt a little guilty. I was on such a high, full of the places we has been and seen, wondering if we would ever return. Any conversation about London, Paris or Dubai, he ignored. I began to blog my adventures, at least this was one way to share two of my passions – travel and writing. I was finding it hard to sit still.

Kez Wickham St George

At last, once home I settled down, making contact with Jerry's family. Again they offered us the opportunity of a no expense trip to Wellington. When I rang our travel agent to book flights, they had a few different ideas. One of them was for or a little over $6,000, we could fly to Singapore, have four days in a boutique hotel, then a special deal from Princess Cruises to cruise around Asia for two weeks on board, then arriving in Wellington. I wanted to shout, 'Yes please,' but first I had to talk to my husband. Larry was still grieving. I approached the conversation with trepidation, not knowing the outcome. He was still locked in his own world, he snapped out his answer, 'Whatever, you do whatever makes you happy.' I so wanted to repeat his words to me when my Mum died, when I was lost in grief, 'Get over it, we have a life to live, she's dead.' Instead I rang the travel agent.

The travel agent worked it all out for us and we left within a month. Flying to Singapore, onto the cruise ship in Singapore, we would cruise to Thailand, Vietnam, Cambodia, then disembark in Wellington. It was perfect, flying home to Perth four weeks later. I rang Jerry's family with our ETA, explaining the detouring via cruise ship, they insisted on paying $3,000 towards expenses, I declined suggesting flights from Wellington to Perth would be enough, they insisted, 'We are grateful you are bringing our Jerry home.' Our daughter began grumbling, 'I came here to have family, but you're never home.' Our grandson kept asking us if he could carry our bags.

Two weeks before we flew to Singapore, a member of the local art group informed me she belonged to the local government global friendship committee. There was a vacancy on the committee and asked if I would be interested. The following week I was asked to send in my bio and reasons why I wanted to join this committee. I did as requested and was accepted; as their arts ambassador, we would meet every three months. We had four days before we took off, Larry looking so much better, he had begun to shout when we conversed. Our daughter and I both suggesting gently that there was no need to shout his reply. He looked hurt we had critiqued, it had become very obvious there was a problem. The day before we sailed off, Larry was fitted with temporary hearing aids.

Singapore was still superb, now a little wiser about seeing the sights, we hired one of the local tuk-tuks who showed us, not only guided tours, but destinations unknown to the tourists. Countryside temples, orchid gardens, with amazing sculptures. We were invited to view a private Zen garden, also the zoo and the Raffles hotel where we enjoyed the famous 'Singapore Sling'. We loved eating at the outdoor vendors. The night before we left for the cruise ship, we did a night tour at the amazing Gardens By The Bay; it truly took my breath away, I promised myself that one day, I would return. The cruise ship shone brightly in the late afternoon sun; my pulse raced with excitement. Our cabin was perfect, Larry surprising me when he placed the little box of ashes on the vanity top. He gave it a little pat. 'This is for you, mate.' Then I understood why Larry was okay to cruise once more. It was his farewell tribute to a lovely young man. The deep booming of the ship's horns as we left its moorings, as before, got to me, seeping into my gut and filling me with excitement.

Once settled on board we booked our Thailand tour. Larry preferred the temple tour, while I went to a high tea and dance ceremony, it was beautiful. We met for dinner. I was really enjoying this way of touring, each doing our own thing. Our dinner companions were two senior women who were deeply in love with each other. Now, I and the rest of the world knew my husband's views on gay couples, his opinion not a pleasant one.

However to my surprise, he really warmed to them, inviting them to sit with us at the theatre that night. Later in our cabin, all he could talk about was these two lovely ladies, how fascinating they were and how they were well-travelled and educated. I was waiting for the but … but nothing. Somewhere between Cambodia and Vietnam, these three ended buddying up going on tours together. Me? I toured on my own, soaking up every sight every sound. We met in our cabin to change for dinner, joining Denise and June for dinner. I adored life at sea, you did not lift a finger, nothing was too much bother for the staff. It wasn't long before we were due to moor in Wellington, New Zealand. We packed away our clothing. Our meal that night on our own, we sat under the stars tucked up in deckchairs watching the night sky. Larry held my hand. 'Thank you, Cassie.' I asked, 'For what?' 'The kick up the bum I needed. I was so much in my own head I forgot to ask how you were feeling.' I did not know what to say when he continued, 'I apologise for the way you were treated by my family, they were really unfair.' I nodded. I felt like I'd been waiting forever for him to admit this. 'Hun, you never said a word in my defence, all you had to say was, 'That's my wife you're speaking to.' However you were all part of the catalyst that made me realise abuse, lies, backstabbing and bullying is not okay. I've written about it, spoken about it and will continue to do so till my last breath.' Wellington, my birth city, lived up to my expectations. It was cold, wet and windy. Some folks love it, I was not one of them. We wished our two lady companions a safe journey. They were staying onboard to cruise around the South Pacific islands. We had two days in Wellington.

In my emails, were e-tickets from Wellington to Melbourne, then onto Perth. Larry rang Jerry's family, we were to meet up the next day at the Titahi Bay senior's village where they lived. A hotel had been booked for us overnight and a cab had been booked to drive us to meet them. The morning arrived, we had just finished breakfast when we were called by reception. Our cab had arrived. Larry had packed the small box of ashes in my carry-on bag. It was time to meet Jerry's family. Titahi Bay senior's home was an hour's drive away. The scenery had changed since I'd last

Jigsaw

been there. What was once country, was no longer. Every spot available had a house of sorts on it. I had spent my childhood in some of these country places. They looked very different now.

We swung into the senior's village finding cottage number 40. The door was flung open, we were welcomed with open arms. Three people stood in the room, two seniors and a woman in her fifties, who was introduced as their daughter. I placed the ashes in their hands, both seniors trembling with grief. We were offered refreshments, they could not do enough for us. *Were we happy with our hotel? Was the ride out here comfortable?* We talked about our cruise, our lives in Perth. They showed interest in Larry's stories about Jerry. Something wasn't right, I could feel it. We spent an hour or two with them, when both seniors began looking weary, it was time to leave. The daughter showed us out. She had been very silent during our visit, her eyes constantly straying to the box of ashes on the sideboard. She had been the one to light two small tea candles on each side of the box. I noticed as we talked about Jerry that her hands were clenched together. The cab drove up, its headlights shining through the curtains. Larry was already seated in the cab, when it sunk in, turning, knowing as all mothers do. 'He was your son?' She nodded, her pretty face now scrunched up in grief. Her tears released as I held her briefly, quietly telling her, 'He was a wonderful man. I am so grateful he came into our lives.'

CHAPTER 55

I was so very happy to wake up in my own bed, in my own home. Larry had left early, he wanted to catch up on his real estate exam finals. My day would consist of washing, ironing, filling the pantry, catching up with my family and friends. My phone plus emails both had a myriad of messages; they could all wait for another day. My cup of tea was barely touched when the doorbell went, my neighbour making sure it was us. Her foot raised to enter, eyeing the cup of tea as she made the enquiries, 'How did the holiday go?' I thanked her for her diligence, claiming chronic tiredness. I closed the door. I needed some time alone until normality settled into my days, to become part of the community once more.

My birthday arrived. Larry, busy with his training, had come home to a steak casserole with mashed potatoes with green beans, plus a rhubarb slice with custard desert. We talked about our day, he was looking forward to gaining employment once training was over, I had spent the day shopping, gardening or writing. Every year, I don't know why, I would wait for him to surprise me with flowers or a small gift. Every year he

Jigsaw

forgot. When our daughter rang and sang Happy Birthday to me, he heard her. 'Oops sorry, love, did I forget again?' Was all he said.

Another year passed by. In that year so much happened; I could have cried with relief when I finally found a publisher. She was local, after a cup of tea together at a local café, she agreed to read my manuscript. If I was compatible with her outlook in life, she would be in contact. I was on tender hooks as this publisher was going places, I wanted to be on the journey with her.

The nomad spirit was still with me when the friendship committee had decided to pay a visit to their sister, city Ako in Japan, I was asked to join them. If I agreed, we would leave in December three months away. Our grandson began his days at a very popular college, our daughter had rocketed to the top in her employment, now in training to tutor in her profession. Larry decided the corporate world of real estate was not for him, he did not enjoy sales, nor did he enjoy office work. Instead, he found employment with a road management firm, between that and a few minor health problems between the two of us, life was busy. The publisher contacted me to say my written work was a fit with her ethics. I was so excited when she said, 'I always knew we would work together. I've been watching your progress.' She had my manuscript sent off to an editor. I worked diligently with the editor as it became a polished version of my story, then passed onto a proof-reader where, once more it was polished to the point of publishing. It took many months, with the publisher suggesting it was the beginning of a trilogy. I accepted and signed with joy, a contract for three books. Of course, there were finances to arrange, it all simply fell into place.

One humdinger of a book launch was planned. Over one hundred people were invited, sixty attending. Before I stepped out the door, my publisher rang, 'Cassie, are you excited?' Was I? I could hardly speak. I wasn't sure if I heard her correctly when she said, 'More good news.

You've become a bestseller before the book is launched.' My goals were manifesting quicker than I had ever thought possible. When the excitement was over as I was getting ready for bed, I placed another red tick on the vision board beside *bestselling author*.

I began to write in earnest, words spilling onto the screen. At night when my writing muse woke me, it flowed onto paper. November arrived, everyone counting down to the Christmas holidays, Larry wanted to stay at home. His excuse was, 'I don't want to holiday in a place full of screaming ankle biters.' Our daughter had made plans to travel to Margert River, requesting that we have our grandson for the week she was away. Christmas shopping, tree decorations, food plus gifts were high on the to do list, as the invite to Japan had arrived with a fixed date. I was one of six people who had been invited to go. We left in the first week of December, it was suggested I go as the arts ambassador for Rockingham, I felt honoured.

Japan was very beautiful. Every day, sumptuous meals were served with such precision. I had never seen a meal made into such art before. We visited art galleries, wineries, small factories, community run sports facilities plus attending many council meetings. I was made to feel welcome at every doorstep; these people were a delight to be with. Meeting and making friends with Jinn, a well-known Japanese artist/poet. The Ako council providing us with a translator, Michiko, she and I soon becoming close friends. I suggested a collaboration with a book of poetry and short stories between our two countries. Michiko agreed to be the editor/translator, my job was to write to encourage the art lovers in Rockingham to join us in the book with art/poetry or short stories. I was so excited about the possibilities of forming a corridor between our two countries. To say goodbye to Michiko was one of the hardest things I had to do. Her sweet nature, winning my friendship immediately. I knew I had found a writing sister who saw me in the same light. We remained in

Jigsaw

contact, touching base every week. I would send her the art or poetry, I also wrote three short stories for the book. This book was published by the Rockingham council, they then held a celebration of the two cities coming together in the arts. I added another tick to my vision board. This was way beyond what I had ever dreamed of. I was now published in Japan as a co-author and co-complier. What an honour! One I knew I would treasure for ever.

Larry picked me up at the airport on my return. He looked lonely as he stood there waiting for me. 'Have a good time? What was Japan like?' So many questions came tumbling out then, 'I missed you.' This was very unusual but confirmed by our daughter the next day. 'Mum, he was bloody miserable the whole time you were away. I guess the old man still loves you.' In no time at all our grandson arrived originally for a week, he had other ideas, which he broached with us, he would camp out in our backyard and agree to a curfew. If we agreed, how do you say no to a young man who is seriously trying to figure life out? He and his granddad sourced a small tent and air bed, he was ours for eight weeks. Although he was hard work at fourteen, he was loveable, every night he would curl up in the bean bag I had made him for Christmas. To my surprise, he loved documentaries. Larry and I did as well, so we watched David Attenborough, stories on how Christmas was created. We ate ice cream, went on beach walks and swims, bonding more than ever before, we discussed life, the possibilities that are around us. My advice was, 'You just have to ask, wrap it up in a dream, then wait.' Larry's advice was, 'Education and hard work.' Christmas came to an end, life once more settled into a normal routine.

Book two of the trilogy was well on its way. I was invited as a guest speaker for a homeless charity, the topic motivation. This one was on a boat on Perth harbour, which was magnificent at night. It was a black tie opening night, both of us looking very chic, the MC, a woman they called Velveteen.

Kez Wickham St George

She was a well-known entrepreneur, statuesque in build, with a voice that could melt wax. For some reason, she thought Larry was the man of her dreams. As she introduced each speaker, her eyes would wander to him, flicker her eyelashes then would seductively smile. I took my turn on the small stage, introduced myself. I began speaking about living a life with purpose. I was about to step down, but in a tight skirt and the swaying of the boat, I stumbled, pushing Larry into her open arms. Velveteen in turn crammed my husband's face between her heaving breasts, 'Like what you see?' she laughed. My husband's face flamed; it was covered in her body oil. He stood out on the deck until we docked and literally leapt off the boat. 'See you at the car,' he snarled as he stalked off. I felt for him. What a stupid stunt to pull in public. I rang the coordinators the next day with a complaint. They asked why. 'Best to ask your MC.'

We were into March the following year already, and book two of the trilogy was with the editor when the publisher announced she was having a writer's retreat in Ireland. *Would I care to join in as one of her authors?* OMG, would I! There was no convincing Larry he immediately agreed to accompany me to the UK and visit his elder brother, who now lived in Scotland. The travel agent greeted us by name, offering refreshments. I could see Larry's face paling with the thought of all that money flying out of his pocket as I added to my wish list; a visit to our family in Dubai, then onto London. From there I would travel to Ireland, Larry to continue to Scotland. *Then home?* No, I chose to visit Spain; Barcelona then Majorca. I had always dreamt of visiting the famous buildings of Gaudi. Arriving in Dubai, we stayed with my nephew, it was lovely to be welcomed by his family, wined, dined, taken out, introduced to many as his family, as we toured and shopped.

Then onto London, where we were invited to stay with family, a niece from Larry's side. I was unwell for two days, catching a virus on the plane. I was tucked up and told to rest, which I did. Feeling better after two days

Jigsaw

in bed, we once more walked the tower of London Bridge, I was still in awe of this city's history, we toured on a hop on/off bus around Piccadilly Circus and Times Square, stopping of for afternoon tea at Kings Cross station, catching a train to once more wander through Waterloo and Paddington stations. The baroque art style from early 1900s, the architecture in these stations, stunning. We both wanted to see the canal barge boats. They were amazing, their decks festooned in veggie/floral gardens, amazing spots of colour everywhere. I loved the gentle white swans that flanked the canal right in front of our niece's home. The last night we were there, our niece cooked us a lovely meal, and admitted to me, 'I have no idea what the family's problem is with you! You are both always welcome as far as I'm concerned.' If any disappointment in this family remained, it was gone in a second as she hugged me close, 'I'm proud that you're my aunty.'

Larry and I parted at the airport, I was off to Ireland. I wondered if my Irish DNA would rise up, speak loudly. I was met by my publisher with other authors. What a welcome, I loved it. The castle, the hosts, the Earl and his wife were perfect. The butler, well, he was one amazing man who made sure every single person in every room was catered for. Sadly, the virus I had caught on the plane began to effect my health. I was fatigued most days, trying so hard to keep up with everyone else. My chest was on fire once we were in bed, my coughing often woke the other authors. I swallowed painkillers every night and morning.

When it was my turn to stand and give my speech on the authors' day, I was only able to get out two sentences, my throat closing up. On the gala night, when we dined with the Earl, he asked if I would take his arm to be walked to my seat. A bagpiper piped as the Earl escorted me to my chair, I felt very honoured. This was a dream coming true. As we began our dinner, the Earl turned to me. I could feel a cough in my throat. I tried to swallow, but my answer to his question, was a harsh hacking bellow in the poor man's face. I left the room, the butler finding me sitting on a cold wooden staircase. He offered to find me a super-hot lemon drink, I nodded. It was delivered on a silver tray with one small peppermint sitting pertly beside the glass. I will be forever grateful. I rejoined the group as they sat around the fire chatting sipping sherry, The conversation animated, as the Earl described a motorbike jaunt he had taken in his younger days, still highly embarrassed I was just grateful to sit quietly and listen. On the day before I left, I walked the castle grounds. I heard a fox bark, saw wild deer disappear into the deep green lush woods, both reminding me of my beautiful New Zealand. Here was the answer to my question, did my DNA remember part of my ancestry was Irish? Some of the authors claimed they moved, felt right at home; mine was more subtle. A quiet nod to my ancestors, a knowing that my spirit belonged to my homeland. It was not homesickness, just a warming in my heart. I knew my roots and to me, that's all that mattered.

Then the icing on the cake. I met Larry at the airport to fly to Barcelona, with a goodbye to Ireland and London. *Would I revisit? Who knew.* The moment I stepped into La Sagrada Familia, dreamed of and built by Gaudi, I was in heaven. The sculpture, the artwork, the history; we both had headphones as we walked through this amazing work of worship, art, every step bringing joyful wonderment to my heart. I was finding it hard to leave. We hired a tuk-tuk, the driver took to us like a duck in water, driving us to the spots that tourists never see. We stood at the edge of a religious street parade; every instrument available was being played yet we understood the beat, the statues wreathed in golden floral tributes. We indulged in a night time shopping spree, stopping off at a used clothing boutique, purchasing two beautiful silk shirts, all for a pittance. We walked the seashore, buying tacos, eating ice cream, rode on a double decker bus around the city, visiting castles then another bus into the country, coming to a small village. Every shop filled with artisan

Jigsaw

handiwork. We spent four days exploring this beautiful city, our next stop Majorca. But before I left, I paid a visit to the four-hundred-year-old olive tree in the middle of a small village, at dusk it already had a dense ring of people around it. Apparently if you touch the tree your wish would come true. Problem was so many tourists had touched it, the poor plant was in sad condition. The powers that be had fenced it so no one could reach in and touch a leaf.

It was here that Larry and I danced in the streets; nothing like a street party with a magical beat in the music. We ate locally wherever we were visiting. I bought small trinkets for my family back home. The Basilica de Santa was an enormous castle; it was closed to the public, only open to those who could afford to pay the enormous price of a private tour. The Castell de Bellver, we could not enter as repairs were being done. We opted for a double decker tourist bus, it did not disappoint. We saw so much, beautiful water ways, beaches, who could miss the millionaire's boating – or should I say boasting – playground.

The sky was a topaz blue, the sun warm on our skin. We attended a Spanish night club, the flamingo danced by women and men, both so passionate. Dinner every night was under a night sky. As we paid our account at the desk, I asked the receptionist about the snow on the ranges we could see from our hotel room. 'The Pyrenees,' he said. Excitement gripped my gut, Larry and I looked at each other, both wanting to continue on this adventure. Then common sense took over. We were booked to leave that afternoon, into Singapore for two hours then a flight to Perth.

CHAPTER 56

Knowing the adventure was over, I craved for more travel; it fed my writing, it made me happy. A close friend suggested a cruise to the South Island of New Zealand, I said yes and booked. Instead, my world came tumbling down, or should I say, Larry's world came tumbling down. While at work one day, he had a stroke, no one bothered to ring to tell me. He was in the hospital being diagnosed when he rang. I was at home, the second book was edited and proofread, ready for me to read, approved then finalise with the publisher. I had noticed the lateness of the hour, he would normally have phoned about four o'clock saying, *'Put the jug on I'm on my way home.'* At six o'clock I had rung our daughter, 'Have you seen or heard from your Dad tonight?' She knew I was concerned, she offered to call the police to see if they knew anything. I rang his work number for the fourth time; still no answer. Messages flew between our daughter and myself. I rang friends who were on route to our home, they had not seen him either. I was becoming very concerned. When he did ring, he sounded drunk. 'Cassie, I'm in hospital. They think I've had a stroke.' My heart was racing. I asked, 'What hospital?' but there was no reply. I phoned his number a nurse answered. 'He's in St John of God Hospital, are you his next of kin? Please wait, I'll find his doctor to talk to you.' It took forever. Finally, I spoke to a woman who said, 'Hello, Cassie? I'm Larry's doctor. At the moment he's having tests to determine what happened. It would be better if you remained at home. Visit in the morning when we have a clearer picture of what's going on.'

I felt helpless. In tears, I rang our daughter informing her of her Dad's whereabouts. 'I'm coming over to pick you up, Mum. Stay the night with us, we can go sort it out in the morning, okay?' We arrived at the hospital the next day, just as they were trying to sit him up. His face was slack on one side, he tried to look at me but he slipped sideways, the male nurse only just catching him. Then he threw up, the nurse pushing a sick bag under his chin. His left arm was numb, I knew in my core that his recovery was going to be hard for this highly independent man.

A week was spent in hospital, then he was transferred to a stroke ward. That's where I learnt true gratefulness, to be thankful for everything I had. In his ward, was a young mum who had had a debilitating stroke while in childbirth. Her husband held their baby close to her, the poor woman completely immobilised. Another teenager next to Larry, could not speak or walk.

Larry slurred, lurched sideways, one side of his face was almost frozen. When alone, I allowed myself to grieve for the man I once knew. In two months he had improved and was now home. It took a year of physiotherapy and counselling for him to come ninety-five percent right. Medication, care and the professionalism of the staff was amazing for him. There were times when his moods swings were fierce bouts of rage, every day he could go from happy to angry in a flash. His harsh rude accusations about our family, including me, became too much. I asked for medical intervention and a councillor for myself, to help me understand his condition. I was reminded of my days of abuse when I was so young, married to a habitual bully. Those memories began to make me fear this man I called my husband.

The counsellor asked me to see my doctor. It seems I had locked any abuse away into my subconscious. Now with Larry's anger aimed at me twenty-four seven, it bought back those memories, hence constant bad dreams. I was offered medication. I declined. I believed that once Larry came right, normality would walk back into our lives. Hopefully I would be proved right.

I launched my second book with a very small private book launch, Larry having a mini stroke the day before. My heart was heavy. There were no accolades, the sales not good, while I looked after one very angry man. The stroke had affected his larynx, the snoring so loud it's a wonder the neighbours didn't complain. If I moved while I was asleep or took up too much bedspace, I would wake to being kicked and shoved back to what he said was *my side of the bed*. I chose separate bedrooms until he had calmed down. I was on constant alert, knowing I was being watched so there would be something to argue about. I was assigned a councillor; her advice, 'Leave him. Teach him a lesson. He might be unwell, but he has to learn to respect you, at least.' I asked, is this what all wives of angry stroke victims do, walk away? She cancelled my counselling. Emotionally, I wanted to run as far away as possible, believe me, but logically it felt wrong. There had to be another way. I was not ready to throw my life away, not yet.

Art is such a great commodity for healing. I began to involve Larry. He was wonderful at making frames for my art exhibitions. I encouraged him to join me in making a costume for the Mandurah wearable arts festival. He loved being creative. He soon began to realise that his stress was calmed by gardening. He now had his very own big veggie garden, he was loving it. His medical team were wonderful, the psychologist saying he had made a very quick recovery. To assist his memory, it was suggested he now do the cooking for the two of us. Apparently cooking consists of memory and equations and maths, another thing I didn't know. After eighteen months, he was given permission to return to work. The separate bedrooms proved a blessing. I no longer worried if I woke to write in the small hours of the morning, or that I would disturb him to heal properly when he needed rest.

As Larry progressed, life became better every day. I had been invited to run a three-day creative workshop at the Cairns library. Perfect. I emailed back accepting the opportunity. Flights and hotels were booked by the library. It was exciting, exactly what we both needed, a break from everyday life. The three days I was in class teaching, Larry went touring. Once I had finished teaching, we would find somewhere for dinner and walk along the beach. On one of these balmy nights, Larry's phone rings, it was from our youngest daughter who we had not seen or spoken to for four or more years.

Through the family grapevine, she had learnt of our whereabouts. She now lived in Cairns with her husband and child. She invited her dad *to meet up and have meal with them.* His grin was from ear to ear he almost shouted, 'Where and when?' She named the place, then added, 'Don't bring her.' There was silence, the hurt showing on his face. I said, 'You go. Meet our granddaughter and takes lots of pictures for me. I still have a morning at the library.' As I showered, I let the tears fall. I had spent years ensuring, this tiny scrap of humanity, would grow to be a healthy adult. In that moment, I was wondering why.

With all workshops finished, I was determined I was going to see Cairns, come hell or high water, so, I hired a car. Larry deciding he would tour with me. We had a ball together: from cable cars, river tours, to train rides. Walking through ancient mouldering forests hand in hand, he told me he had spent some time with our youngest daughter and our grandchild. When Larry asked me to join them, I took the bull by the horns, I agreed; perhaps a confrontation would work. I was wrong. The baby only just placed in my eager arms by her father, when she was snatched out of my arms, our daughter's voice screeching, 'She's not for you, don't touch her.' I left the café immediately, vowing if we ever met again, she would be apologising to me.

Once home, Larry felt well enough to begin short caravan trips again; I insisting on short trips so Larry did not exhaust himself. On one of our trips I had felt unwell, more lethargy than an illness. I put it down to the weather, as it had rained nonstop. The good thing about being cooped up in a van was that book number three began to emerge. Once home, I decided to have an afternoon nap as a headache had been behind my eyes all weekend. Larry let me sleep. Waking at five o'clock, I knew something wasn't right. I tried to stand, but my legs wouldn't hold me. My hands shook. My body was in so much pain. Calling out for help, Larry carried me to the bathroom, then bundled me up into the car, the hospital only ten minutes from home. A wheelchair was found as I found walking impossible. The emergency department was full. Every movement I made, pain jack-knifed through my body. Thank heavens I had a doctor who cared. He medicated me with pain relief ordering a myriad of tests, then ordered me back to bed. I slept for hours, waking, taking pain relief then falling back to sleep.

Our doctor rang the next afternoon, asking Larry to bring me in to the surgery. The first tests had arrived back. I was diagnosed with adult leukemia; the shock in the small room between all three of us making us mute. I thought my doctor was going to cry as he held my hand, 'Cassie, there are no "whys", it happens to the best of us. We will get you through this. You are one very sick woman. I want you into hospital for more tests immediately.' The next week, I had every known blood test available. My white blood cells were massively inflamed. Between sleeping, I read books or documents about the disease. It seemed with adult leukemia, there

Jigsaw

was a shortened lifespan. I was scared but curious. It certainly makes one think deeply about the whys of life

When the doctor rang with the news that after the tests, it was conclusive that I did not have adult leukemia, MS or Lupus. I felt my body sag with relief, finally being diagnosed with chronic polymyalgia. *The cause?* It was suggested that the cause was PTSS (post-traumatic stress syndrome). It seems the stress of life had caught up with me. Holistic treatment was so expensive, I chose the medical route, something I'd never done before. This time my old standby of exercise, potions, portents or herbs was not going to work. This time my body was in serious trouble and I had to reach out for help. What happened next hurt me deeply. Heather, my trusted friend, turned her back on me, choosing to be seen with another of my acquaintances, announcing on Facebook, 'The true blue besties forever.' Larry's arms went around me when I burst into tears. *What had I done to deserve this?* It was his wisdom that made sense. 'I've always thought they were a nasty twosome. It surprised me when you fell in with them. You wait and see. What's your favourite saying? Karma will catch up.'

Larry was the perfect nurse. I only had to look sideways, he would be at my side. My body began to do all sorts of weird things, when I tried to walk, I tottered sideways. My balance was shot. My once straight hair grew like never before, it began to curl, from a salt and pepper colour it changed to a shinning silver. My bladder was on constant alarm, sudden staggering dashes to the bathroom became normal. I would often fall asleep in the middle of a conversation. We tried going to the movies but I slept all the way through. My nails, which had always been weak, now became like iron. My temperature went haywire. Headaches plagued me every day; not the vicious migraines I had once suffered with, this was very different. On reporting to the specialist quite casually about my eyesight, I was rushed off to an emergency consultation. It seems along with polymyalgia often comes white cell arteritis, which can cause blindness. I proved to be negative, we were both so relieved. Those I had called friends dropped away, like I was something nasty served up on a plate. One stalwart mate, hung in there. She was once a nurse, she understood that my body was being attacked, it was doing its best to cope. Finally, the rheumatoid clinic asked me to attend, Larry pushing me into the consultant's rooms in a wheelchair. The specialist saying, 'I want to see you out of that by the end of the month.' He changed the medication, prescribing bumper amounts of steroids, plus medications called methotrexate and celebrex. I religiously swallowed medications, so I could walk without shaking or staggering in pain. It took me back to my mother's illnesses in the early 1950s. They were an opioid and addictive. Today it was steroids, also addictive however my body was grateful from the relief of chronic pain

CHAPTER 58

I had no option but to leave the three community groups I was working with. If I couldn't stand upright, my main mode of transport now a wheelchair, I knew I would not be able to participate as a leader. Although it was unspoken, I knew I would not be welcome. Once among these groups I had a position of authority or one of major support. A friendship committee, more or less said 'thanks very much, next.' Another group sent an invite to attend their next high tea to say goodbye. Cissy the entrepreneur from Rockingham was also attending, she made it obvious she was more than happy to see me unwell. The third group emailed me; *sorry you're unwell, please feel free to re-join when you're better*. I was taken back by all three groups, each one I had spent so much of my time helping with promotions, encouraging others to join, always there to support in any way. Larry picking up on how I was feeling offered his wisdom, 'Cassie, you should know by now people are fickle, they have no idea who you are, not really.' That one sentence made me laugh as I had wondered that about him not so long ago.

Part of my treatment was no stress. The medical staff warning me stress was not part of a healthy lifestyle. I was to remain calm and positive at all costs. I felt I should be writing a book on the subject. Just once, Heather came to visit. I was barely learning to stand without the wobbles. I found her presence offensive, asking her to leave, my door was no longer open to bullies or dishonesty. On the other side of the coin, I had two ladies knock on my door, both unannounced, offering spiritual healing in the way of crystals, oils, plus massage. They had arrived in different cars, not knowing each other. By the time they left, we had begun a strong friendship.

There was one incident that bothered me. I had been asked to attend a well-known networking group in the city in Perth. It was a ticketed event, by invite only. I was on the point of refusing when Larry suggested I go; *you have nothing to lose*. He pushed the wheelchair into the auditorium. Some people knew me, but most did not. Those that did were surprised to see me in a wheelchair.

A light supper was offered to all, as I was low down, everyone began eating and drinking above my head. Wine was served on trays held above my head, droplets of fluid falling onto my top. Food crumbs from those conversing around me were in my hair on my skirt. No one bothered to enquire if I wanted a drink or a plate of food. No, they stood above me, talking, laughing, drinking, eating, ignoring me. I felt humiliated. As I was on carpet, I couldn't push the wheelchair on my own. I finally pulled on the jacket of a well-known entrepreneur asking, 'Could you please push me to the door?' He looked stunned, so I asked again. His wife finally said, 'Oh for God's sake, she's not contagious,' she stopped and looked at me before adding, 'are you?' To think I had admired her. In fact, I had admired them all, craving their deluxe lifestyles, ignoring what I had in my own life. I was pushed to the door then left there. Larry had waited outside, thank god. If I did not already know what it was like to be ignored, treated as if I didn't exist, I did now. Tears simmered till I was tucked up in the car. I was embarrassed that I had once sought any sort of relationships with these people. I felt shame I had once desired to be like any of them.

It was very clear I was being shown something here, after six months, I was weaned of the majority of medications, slowly. On bad days, I would rest, read. Massage became even more important. On good days I began to write book number three of the trilogy. Larry had gone back to work part-time. The road to recovery was a long one. It was one step forward where medications were decreased, then two steps backwards, as the lack of medications caused pain, I persisted.

I could feel the improvement in my body every week. I began to complete some very light gardening chores, Larry keeping an eagle eye on me. We had decided as soon as his retirement payments kicked in, he would retire. It seemed to bring him peace to know we did not have to watch every penny. We were not where we had planned to be financially, health care is not cheap, but life was more important now. Both learning very fast, that friendship comes in all shapes and sizes. One year had passed, book three was looking good. There was something about this book that kept me from sending it to the publisher. I had no idea what it was. I attended a Christmas social with another well-known group. Here I met many new faces all seeking recognition in their varied fields. It came as a shock to realise I was now the older woman in the room. It felt uncomfortable to wear that particular hat but there was no denying it. With what I had been through over the years, this recent bout of ill health had begun to show.

The question I asked myself as I looked in the mirror was, were they the lines of wisdom, or was it age creeping in? Was I looking at myself through the eyes of others who believed in ageism, or was I ruining my own outlook in life by thinking along those lines? One day, I found myself reading a post I could have sworn was meant for me:

Kez Wickham St George

'As we grow older, real beauty travels from the face to the heart. Appeal turns to charm, hurt to wisdom, great moments to shared memories. The true beauty of life is not how happy you are now, but how happy others are because of you.'

I volunteered my time. I had the time so why not? I also answered a call for a popular USA TV/radio show who wanted a co-host. I put my hand up and once a week we would interview with an author or artist. It was on volunteer basis, I loved it. My passion for radio ignited, I volunteered to a local radio station, I was presenting book reviews on radio. I loved it. I was asked to mentor another writer, it snowballed I had more than I could handle, happily sending them off to publishers when their manuscripts were looking good. In one year, I had eight authors published, promoting them on the many platforms that I was offered.

Larry and I discussed a holiday in Tasmania over the next Christmas break, to catch up with an old friend who lived there. I was 95% well, this island was amazing, a truly beautiful place that is so much like New Zealand, we both felt right at home. We toured for four weeks, seeing something of interest every day. We took a day river cruise on a paddle steamer, we picnicked in the bush, rode cable car rides, stopped at quaint cafes off the beaten track and at bush pubs to listen to music played by the old timers. Everything was magical, filled with wonderful and new experiences. The wood carving art was amazing, everywhere you looked you would spy a carving of sorts, on the sides of roads or tucked away in the bush. We found the cutest little café at a beach called Penguin Bay.

It was trying valiantly to exhibit the local art, but what a mish mash. I couldn't help myself, offering some advice, they tried a different way, selling two small art pieces immediately. I left my business card with them, just in case I was invited to exhibit one of my own art pieces there. They rang the day before we left Tasmania, offering me the part-time job of exhibition caretaker. Larry pulled the car over. 'They what?' I repeated

Jigsaw

myself, 'They want me to work with them.' I could see his mind ticking over; fresh start, new people. This was my dream job, with the added bonus of a little extra cash flow. A perfect opportunity was right in front of us. All I had to do was ring back and say four words, 'When do I start?'

CHAPTER 59

What stopped us? Well, we had family and friends in Perth we loved to socialise with, and we had a grandson that we felt still needed some guidance. Between the two of us, we had planted a magical garden. We had placed birdbaths, that I had mosaiced, under trees that were now full of leafy shade. The birds would greet us, sometimes landing close. They had grown to trust us, as they returned year after year to raise their babies. Larry had built me a lovely gazebo out of second hand materials and I'd found an old three-seater swing which Larry had repaired and I had re-cushioned. It was here I had felt the healing in my body, as it knitted itself back together.

Fresh fruit and vegetables grew in every nook of the garden. Hung on the fences were some of my huge art pieces which Larry had framed. Between us, we had given plus received many celebrations in this back yard we called 'ours.' During the past ten years, we had dug, planted, weeded, moved and mulched our once sand-covered back yard, into our grassy, tree-filled haven. Boring to some, heaven to us. We had never had a visitor who hadn't given us some sort of compliment about our achievements. To begin again seemed pointless when we had created what we wanted. The house itself was small, but with no young family, just the occasional weekend visit from our grandson, it was all we needed. We had built our home.

Larry had also become a bit of a local handyman in the area, always on call to fix taps, washers or mow a lawn. He had made good mates as well, so it was not just me giving up my life, it was us, giving up a life we had built together. I rang the café, my ego saying *just do it*, my heart whispering you know where you belong. Once home, an emotional roller coaster began. I was still conflicted; I wanted to keep my third book to myself a little longer. I rang my publisher asking for assistance; *what do I do?* Thank the Lord for this level-headed woman. Send it to me, let's see what I can do with it. However, four or five times I went to press send to end the trilogy, each time I withdrew my hand my gut saying, 'not yet'.

One morning as I stood under the hot stream of water in the shower, a memory flashed before me of many years ago before I'd left New Zealand. One crisp, chilly morning, I had been meditating, many scarfs shawls wrapped around me as I sat drinking in the clear air of the ocean. I was recovering from a migraine, feeling drained of energy, my heart beating in time with the waves washing onto the shore. In that moment, I'd had a vision, a dream, intuitive forecast, whatever you want to call it. I was standing on a stage, speaking to a large group. They were applauding, a large stack of my books growing smaller as they were being purchased. The vision had been so detailed I felt like I had stepped into another realm. I had simply shaken it off at the time, thinking that it was silly. Now, as the hot water ran down my spine, the memory returned, the light bulb moment was clear. I knew what I had to do before the book went to the publisher.

My hand was shook as I re-read the prologue of book three. This was perfect movie material. I rang a young lady I had recently met at a networking event in Perth. She was a short film producer as we spoke of my idea, she was keen to meet. We arranged a time for the following week. It was a whole week of playing the *shall I? shan't I?* game. Then came imposter syndrome, *what makes you think you are good enough to make your story into a short film?* Maybe I should cancel, or should I wait until she'd read it. Perhaps she would say 'no' anyway. The day arrived when I'd planned to meet with Sally, I cleaned my home from top to bottom. Larry, who was now fully retired, offered to make some scones. He could see I was super nervous. When she arrived, I could not have wished for a more gracious, caring person to sit at my table. I told her my idea.

She asked to read the prologue. I felt like I wanted to sit under the kitchen table, as I used to as a child. She read, silently, while I waited then gently smiling at me, she said, 'Cassie, we can definitely give this a try. May I take this home with me to see what I can do?' I agreed. So, it was a 'maybe'. After she left, the enormity of what I'd just done, swept over me.

Who did I think I was asking this successful film producer to even consider my work? I pressed the send button, delivering my final book of the trilogy to my publishing team. Three days later, I received a message. 'Hey Cassie. I think we can make us a movie.' It took my breath away. Larry pulled out a chair in the shed, making me sit down as I made him read that one sentence. 'I'm so proud of you,' he smiled, 'look what you're achieving.' I held my breath, *what was this going to cost? Would I have the finances?* I no sooner put the word around to the authors I had mentored, when I had offers coming in. They wanted to host the movie. Everything flowed along; no struggling, no emergencies. When I informed my publisher, there was a stunned silence. At first I thought I should have pre-warned her, but I repeated, 'The prologue to book three is going to be a short movie, entered into film festivals around Australia.' Again silence, then, 'I knew there was something about you, Cassie.'

When I was invited to attend the casting, it was such a surreal moment.

Jigsaw

I doubt anyone would understand unless they were in my shoes. The actors were chosen, filming began. I booked the launch of book three of the trilogy for the 27th November. I invited the press, local radio station, friends, acquaintances, the mayor and councillors. A book launch is always a celebration, however this one was a dream come true. A week before the launch the movie producer rang, 'I think we have a movie, Cassie.' We had talked often, had many meetings, by then, updates were regular. I could feel my dream manifesting in a big way. The book launch was fabulous, books selling, myself and my publisher thrilled.

Soon tickets to attend the premiere of the movie went up for sale. How exciting to see your movie on screen? Larry and I walked hand in hand on the red carpet. Our love for each other had now quietly deepened, a special kinship, a deep mutual respect for one another had formed between us.

As the theatre lights dimmed to darkness, the film played, the actors on screen began speaking the words I had written, the scenery was just as I'd described it. I felt so blessed, proud for my work to be showcased in this way. As the film came to an end, the audience wanted to know more. I stood centre stage as the audience applauded, just as I had seen in my vision so many years before. My hand shaken by many people that night, everyone asking, 'Cassie, photos with me, please?' There were books to sign, influential people to chat with. Once home, Larry's voice was sifting in through my thoughts of just what had happened. 'I'm so proud of you,' he said as he put his arms around me. 'So, what's next?' he asked. Good heavens give me time to take a breath, the enormity of what had occurred hit me. My photo was in the papers, the trilogy selling well. *What happens next? I had no idea.* Following the launch, I had invites to speak at book clubs, schools and libraries often taking us onto the back roads of this country. Invites to attend dinners raced into my inbox. Magazines offered front page features, asking me to write book

Kez Wickham St George

review columns for them. But still, there was something bigger calling. My poetry book was released, I agreed to attend two local writer's retreat as a speaker. However, deep in my very core I heard my DNA calling; my ancestors wanting their stories written. I have Irish, English, Jewish, and Maori blood that has called to me since I was child. So where and how do I start with the lives of my nomadic family? Which side calls to me the loudest for their story to be told? Where do I begin? Maybe in Aotearoa (New Zealand), where both sets of great-grandparents sailed to, the journey they undertook not of weeks but of months at sea in a ship its white sails billowing, its bow plunging into the deep blue waters.

CHAPTER 60

Cassie had requested I finish the research of our family. Some of their stories sat in a tatty manila folder in front of me. She had often referred to her stories as a tapestry, each piece connecting us to one another. From what I had seen in this book was one of knowing your own truths. To me, Cassie's journey had been inward, her own emotional growth important to her, to live her life with empathy, self-love bound together with wisdom, she had listened to her heart. Freely admitting her mistakes, then being emotionally castrated by those that she believed in. Always believing and encouraging others to tell their own story. I knew to honour her; I should accept this challenge.' As I opened the thick brown folder, a jumble of penned notes, newspaper clippings, aged sepia photos were mixed in with letters, envelopes from around the world with faded postage stamps, some dog eared, some pristine. Notes bundled together with fraying elastic bands, all spreading across my desk, excitement building in my chest as I began to piece my family together. It was when I read her last words, I finally understood my aunt had been born with a powerful mission to right the wrongs of our ancestry. Her last words were.

For a very long time our Ancestral wisdom has been lost, buried in a midden of untruths, myths and insults. Every attempt over many decades has been made to cut the Crone wisdom from our roots, yet it exists in every breath we take. The wisdom of our past is the alchemy to the present. The rich Mythical ecology of all sacred females, a resurrection of the powerful magic that flows from us the wise women, our ancestors within in the Tapestry of life.

The End

ABOUT THE AUTHOR

We are all unique walking stories just waiting to be told.

Kez Wickham St George is the driver of her own creativity, and her passion is to inspire and nurture others to tell their stories. Her values are simple; when you touch a heart with your story you can change another's life.

Travelling extensively, including the length and breadth of Australia, she has collecting stories and experiences. Now with ten novels published, the first three; *Adventures in the Outback,* published internationally, three paranormal books published nationally. Also, two children's books that now reside in many different countries and with the two royal families of UK and Denmark. Beginning of 2019 her first book of poetry, *Entwined* was published, forming a corridor between the City of Rockingham and Ako Japan, its sister city, bringing the poets and artists of these two cities together. In 2020, Kez co-authored a reciprocal book from Ako Japan *Entwined two.* Late 2019 an invitation to be a guest speaker at a writer's retreat at Crom Castle Dublin Ireland, this placed Kez on a global stage as a speaker and international Author.

In 2020 and 2021 her recently published trilogy *Metal Mermaid, Cuppa Tree* and *Scribe* became a number one bestseller and best read five-star in her category of adventure/caravanning.

Kez is also a popular speaker, however, mentoring and consulting to assist others to tell their stories has become a large part of her life, running creative writing workshops, with a little bit of art included for those that have a story to tell. Encouraging people to do what they love has resulted in eight of her writing protégés to becoming published authors in the past two years.

Kez believes that writing has many roads, she now writes for magazines, and reviews many books on two radio stations, including her own Facebook review. Being a prolific author has many opportunities, from the book *Scribe* a short movie is being filmed, which will visit all the film festivals around Australia. Next year is looking like a busy year for Kez as she introduces another anthology and will dip her toes into research as she finds out why her maternal grandparents left Kent, England, in 1900 to sail off to immigrate to New Zealand. Life is full of magic. But most of all Kez believes, *'You become what you believe.'*

BOOKS BY
KEZ WICKHAM ST GEORGE

The Campfire Trilogy
published by MMH Press

I did not want the story to stop. These three books are the beginning of Tara's journey into the world of shades, where those that have passed over have not left their stories behind them. An exciting trilogy that takes you on adventures through Australia and New Zealand. They will wake your senses to the adventure of storytelling, which the author, Kez, does with inspired passion. Kez is what I would say is a reader's entertainer, once you open that first page, you dare not put it down, as you don't want the excitement or adventure to stop.
M Hodges – Hokitika, NZ

Kez is a master storyteller, her candid tales of adventure and travels encountering many different characters, including those of the underworld, left me wanting to know more. I found in this book, the third campfire trilogy's Scribe, *wanting to look over my shoulder at any shadows passing by. This author brings her lead character to us the truth and honesty about how relationships can be stretched to breaking point. I also enjoyed the humour Kez brings with her stories, encouraging you to see the funny side of life. When we suddenly take a twist into the paranormal, an encounter with a new acquaintance Tanby, it has Tara rattled emotionally, along with a near-death experience so close to joining those of the underworld, as Tara is unexpectedly summoned to scribe for those who have left this mortal coil. I loved the tricky double ending. I found this book to be a real page-turner – once you start, you don't want to put it down.* Scribe *is a mix of adventure, fun, humour, thrills and spills, and I, for one, can't wait for the anthology* The Book of Shadows *to be published in 2022.*
S Beardsley – Perth, WA

Essence
published by MMH Press

Anthology – The Colours of Me
Co-authored by Kez Wickham St George & Michelle Weitering
published by MMH Press

So many authors joined us in this beautiful book of heartwarming personal stories of their lives. Each story adding to the beauty of living a life with compassion, forgiveness and empathy. To assist in funding our chosen charity Careers Australia please visit **www.mmhpress.com** to purchase.

Join Kez on her next adventure, book two of the *Storyteller* series as she weaves a *Tapestry* of stories from the many women who were her ancestors.